SOLDIER NO MORE

An Undercover Journalist in Zimbabwe 2000 – 2010

by

David Lemon

Grosvenor House
Publishing Limited

All rights reserved
Copyright © David Lemon, 2011

David Lemon is hereby identified as author of this
work in accordance with Section 77 of the Copyright, Designs
and Patents Act 1988

The book cover picture is copyright to David Lemon

This book is published by
Grosvenor House Publishing Ltd
28-30 High Street, Guildford, Surrey, GU1 3HY.
www.grosvenorhousepublishing.co.uk

This book is sold subject to the conditions that it shall not, by way of
trade or otherwise, be lent, resold, hired out or otherwise circulated
without the author's or publisher's prior consent in any form of binding or
cover other than that in which it is published and
without a similar condition including this condition being imposed
on the subsequent purchaser.

A CIP record for this book
is available from the British Library

ISBN 978-1-907652-99-8

Other Books by David Lemon

Ivory Madness	:	College Press, Harare 1983
Africa's Inland Sea	:	Modus Press 1987
Kariba Adventure	:	College Press 1988
Rhino	:	Puffin Books 1989
Man Eater	:	Viking Books 1990
Hobo Rows Kariba	:	African Publishing Group 1997
Killer Cat	:	College Press 1998
Never Quite a Soldier	:	Albida Books 2000
Never Quite a Soldier	:	(South African Edition) Galago Books 2006
Blood Sweat and Lions	:	Grosvenor House Publishing 2008
Two Wheels and a Tokoloshe	:	Grosvenor House Publishing 2008
Hobo	:	Grosvenor House Publishing 2009

DAVID LEMON

What They Said About:
Never Quite A Soldier

An amazing firsthand account of the Rhodesian Bush War
- Galago Books, Johannesburg.

A Classic
– Thirty Degrees South publishers, London.

A chilling book that tells how a country fell apart.
– Pretoria News.

Lemon tells a highly readable story
– Armed Forces Journal, Johannesburg.

I am the richer for having read it.
– John Davison, South Africa.

I have never read such a personal, human related story.
– Gareth Loxton, Afghanistan.

This book is one of the best I have read regarding the Rhodesian conflict.
– Stephen Dunkley, Collector of Military Books.

An exceptionally fine work – and there aren't too many of them around.
– Dave Willis, Former Rhodesian Special Branch officer.

Author's Note

Once again I have written a purely personal account of a nasty little slice of African history. My views are stated honestly and if I have offended anyone with my opinions, I do apologise, but I am Zimbabwean and probably not as dispassionate as a reporter ought to be.

A number of people put their lives, liberty and livelihoods on the line in order to help me with my stories. I have mentioned a few of them in the text by their real names, but in most cases I have changed their identities to protect them from a paranoid authority. They know who they are however and know also that they have my gratitude for the risks they took. For those others who opened their hearts and lives to me and who I have not been able to include in the book, I am sorry but I am very grateful to you for showing me exactly what is happening in my own country.

My thanks are also due to a number of lovely people who helped in the production of **Soldier No More**. Nic Lywood did the cover painting from two of my *Murambatsvina* photographs and Jilly Wright was once again a tower of inspiration with her advice on the manuscript. Sheila Young helped with photocopying and an unexpected printing crisis, while my daughter in law, Gillian drew the map. The staff at Grosvenor House were always there for me when I needed them and poor Lace had to put up with my self-absorbed reclusiveness and tears of memory for months. Only another scribbler's spouse will appreciate what that entailed. Others helped in so many ways and to you all, I extend my sincere and heartfelt gratitude.

For the record, the events as outlined in the book are not necessarily in chronological order, but I have described them exactly as they took place, using notes made at the time and my articles for the Sunday Express as reference points.

Dedication

This one just has to be for my small friend of so many years

Mary Jane.

She knows who she is.

Prologue

The rear compartment of the van looked dark and uninviting. I was so nervous that my chest was hurting and for a moment, I hesitated. The vehicle looked new and carried government number plates, but once I was inside I would be effectively trapped should anything go wrong. This was my last chance to pull out and we both knew it. My companion held the rear doors open and looked somewhat quizzically at me. His brows lifted in brief enquiry, the expression in those deep brown eyes softened for a moment and I could see what he was thinking, although there was no condemnation in his expression. He probably stood to lose more than me in any case and to abandon my plans at that moment, would have freed us both from a great deal of tension. We stood completely motionless for perhaps two seconds, then the spell was broken and I stepped forward to climb into that dim and uncomfortable interior.

Once again I was well and truly putting my head on the block. Only two other people knew what I was planning to do and neither of them would blame me if I pulled out before beginning, but I would have to live with myself afterward and that would be difficult. I have always had a deep-seated fear of personal failure and it has landed me in a lot of trouble from time to time.

Now it looked like doing so again.

Without saying a word, the big man closed the doors behind me and the reality of my situation suddenly terrified me. My heart seemed to hammer against my ribs, my mouth was dry and my stomach felt as though I had swallowed a rugby ball. The metallic taste of fear filled the back of my throat and I wanted to be sick.

It was very dark outside and I found it difficult to make myself comfortable in the back of the van. I had nothing to sit on but the bare metal floor and the chill crept up through my backside, even before we started to move. I had been given a blanket to hide under if necessary, but it was old and smelled pretty foul. In fact, the whole interior of the van stank of fermenting mealie meal and my nausea increased. The blanket was not likely to be of much help and if we were stopped and challenged, even a cursory glance into the vehicle would find me. How I wished we had thought to put something bulky in the van so that I could have crawled behind it, but it was too late for that.

I just had to trust to luck and hope that I wasn't caught. If I was, the consequences would be horrendous. If I was lucky, I would be shot out of hand, but if not, I faced hours, perhaps days of interrogation and torture, with a very long stint in the notorious Chikurubi Prison to follow. That was not a pleasant prospect and I wondered what I was risking so much for. This surely wasn't what modern journalism was all about. I should be sitting in a comfortable, open plan office, writing my stories from telephone contacts, not languishing in the enclosed rear section of a filthily uncomfortable van, with my heart threatening to burst through my chest and my mind churning the possible consequences of what now seemed an insanely suicidal venture.

I wasn't even a proper journalist damnit!

There was a muted call from the front of the van, but I didn't hear what my companion said. His meaning was soon clear though and I felt the vehicle slow down, going through the gears in the African way as we approached some sort of obstacle. Huddling beneath my blanket, I prayed that no search of the van would be forthcoming.

I was totally helpless and couldn't help wondering if I was being set up. Would the soldier do as he had promised or would he merely drive me straight to the guardroom or whatever they had in this place and hand me over to his colleagues for interrogation? Not for the first time that evening, I cursed myself for a fool.

I could hear voices from the front and wondered what they were discussing. They were speaking in Chishona that was too fast for me to follow, but I heard a number of laughs and repeated references to 'Dynamos,' so I knew they were talking football. There was no tension in their tones and slowly the frenetic hammering of my heart began to ease. I concentrated on breathing as evenly as possible and allowing my muscles to relax. Perhaps we were going to get away with it. This was no time for complacency however and I made myself stay very alert and ready to react should the rear door of the van be opened. Quite what I intended to do, I had no idea. At my advanced age, I couldn't hope to put up much of a fight, but knew that I would have to try something. The thought of being scooped up and taken away like a rabbit to the slaughter was not a pleasant one and I determined to sell my life dearly.

"Ah, you just take it easy Boss," I heard someone shout in cheerful English. "You can buy me beers when we have R and R hey."

There was an answering chuckle from the driver and we were moving again. Ever so gradually, I felt the tension easing from my body, although my heart continued to beat a frenetic tattoo against my ribs and my mouth was desperately dry. I definitely wasn't cut out for a career criminal and made a conscious effort to concentrate on what I was doing.

We stopped again and after a momentary pause, the engine noise died away and I heard the scraping sound of a handbrake being engaged. The van lurched as a body shifted and then I heard the thump of a door closing. Suddenly all my senses seemed crystal clear and I knew everything was going to be alright. In a perverted sort of way, I suppose I must have been enjoying the tension.

The rear door swung open and there was my companion silhouetted against the night sky. I wondered where we were, as everything seemed very dark.

"Come," he whispered urgently. "There is nobody about and we don't have much time. The alarms and searchlights will go on again in forty minutes, so we must be out by then. I told that idiot at the main gate that I have come on a surprise check of security while the systems are down, but he will probably warn the others that I am about."

Seconds later, I was out in the cold night air, breathing deeply as my eyes struggled to adjust to a different sort of darkness. There was a scent of frangipani and new mown grass in the air and I looked anxiously around me.

"We are close to the main workshops," my companion told me in muted tones. "I will be expected to park the vehicle down here in order to surprise everyone. Most of the guards should be on their break now but there will still be patrols, so we must go quickly and silently. You stay close behind me and let's see how we go."

The stars were bright overhead and the air had a chill to it, but I concentrated on following my companion as closely as I dared. Dank fronds of creeper and heavy ferns brushed at my cheeks but I ignored them. Like me, the soldier was dressed in very dark clothing, but he wore a black baseball cap, bearing some sort of official insignia while I had a woollen balaclava wrapped around the top of my head.

Time seemed to pass with infinite slowness and I was acutely conscious of everything around me as we walked. An owl hooted in nearby trees and I saw the big shoulders tense in front of me. Hearing an owl during daylight is regarded as an evil omen in Shona culture and I couldn't help wondering if that applied to nocturnal owls as well.

We skirted a gravel drive leading up to the front of the house and I could not suppress a gasp as the mansion appeared through the darkness. The massive building towered above us with conical, pagoda-like protuberances at either end. The gleam of white paintwork in the starlight gave it a silvery sheen, but it was big – very big indeed. Columns, balustrades and huge pillars were everywhere and although much of the place was in darkness, a few dim lights glowed from behind those mighty walls. This was more like a hotel than a house and from the outside at least, more ornate than the palaces of Windsor or Buckingham. I stopped to gawk but my companion had other ideas.

"Come on; we must hurry," he rasped through the darkness. "Keep that hat down over your face. Your white skin shows up badly in this light."

Criticism was apparent in his tone and I cursed myself for not blacking up before coming out. It was an elemental precaution in such circumstances, but it was a very long time since I had been to war and I had forgotten the basics. Rolling the balaclava down across my face, I hurried after my companion.

Moments later, we climbed seven wide steps to a columned veranda that seemed as spacious as an empty football pitch and crept past a carved, wooden door that must have been four metres tall. My companion seemed to know exactly where he was going and taking a bunch of keys from his pocket, he sifted through them with infinite care, obviously determined not to let them rattle. Ten metres beyond that impressive main portal, he stopped before a smaller door, this one set well into the wall itself and almost invisible unless one knew it was there. Sliding his key into the lock, he turned it quickly and motioned for me to pass him.

It was cold and dark inside, but once again it was difficult to suppress an audible gasp of wonder. Despite the lack of light, I could see that I was at one end of an enormous entrance hall, with pillars and life size statues all around me. They looked like vaporous ghosts in the gloom and I felt a prickle of dread that was quickly dispersed by my companion.

"Up the stairs," he murmured and there was tension in his voice. "If we move away from the front of the building, we can put a few lights on and you will get your pictures. I will leave you alone while I carry out a check on the lower floor. I must let myself be seen or the gate guard's story will arouse suspicion and that could be dangerous for us both."

I knew what he meant. He had as much, if not more to lose than I did and not even the strongest man can stand up indefinitely under torture. If either of us was caught, the other would also be in deadly danger.

The house had that indefinable atmosphere about it that all unoccupied buildings seem to take on and there was scaffolding on one side of an ornate, curving staircase. Dust sheets covered some of the furniture, but we climbed swiftly and seconds later, my feet had sunk to the ankles in deep pile and I was gazing with awe into the most magnificent room I had seen in my life. I don't know whether it was the main bedroom, but it was large enough to contain the average English council house and still have room for a triple garage and a swimming pool. A massive four-poster bed occupied the centre of the room, a toweringly mirrored dressing table took up almost an entire wall and luxurious armchairs were arranged in one corner. There were at least three alcoves that I took to be dressing rooms and thick drapes hung down on either side of French windows which led onto a small, railed balcony. Almost absently, I wondered what the view was like.

The impression of unbelievably ornate luxury was heightened when my companion flicked a switch and discreetly placed wall lights lit up that enormous room, giving it an aura of pampered luxury.

"I will leave you to it," he whispered. "Try and use side lights if you can. All of them have dimmer switches, so turn those down before switching anything on and stay away from the windows. I will have most of the guards with me in the control room, but a few will still be patrolling the gardens and if you are spotted, God alone knows what will happen. You have," he checked his watch, "less than twenty-five minutes to do what you want and then we must go. If you hear me speaking loudly as I approach on my way back, then find somewhere to hide until I can come for you."

"But where will you be?" I asked plaintively. At that stage, I wasn't really sure where I was.

"Don't worry, I will find you. By then you will probably be lost in any case. This place is too big."

With that, he was gone and I was alone in the brand new and almost complete mansion of Robert Mugabe, the President of Zimbabwe. Adrenalin coursed through my veins, my nervousness had disappeared and suddenly I was in my element. Once again, I was living life on the edge.

Wasting no more time on gawking, I hurried to get the job completed.

PART ONE

(The Background)

Chapter One

(Reasons Why)

Of course it started well before that night.

I was never quite a soldier, but when the liberation war in Rhodesia ended and my country became Zimbabwe, I was at a loss. Life, which as a fighting copper had been lived on a high edge of fear, excitement and occasional boredom, settled down to the humdrum existence that most people endure and I did not know how to cope. My restless spirit needed excitement and in the increasingly plastic world of the late twentieth century, that was a commodity in very short supply.

Some of my friends and acquaintances went in search of other wars. In August 1982, I watched a horrific item on the evening news. White soldiers from South Africa had been killed by the Zimbabwe National Army in the Sengwe communal lands in the South East corner of Zimbabwe. Although it was not readily identifiable, I knew in my heart that the bloodstained corpse with the winged dagger tattooed on its wrist was Dave Berry. He and I had played cricket together and were friends, but Dave was a soldier to the core and had found himself another war. He would not have wanted to die any other way.

Kevin Woods was a predecessor of mine as operational commander of Charlie Troop in the police Support Unit. He took to clandestine ops and became a double agent for South Africa, paying for it initially by being sentenced to death and then spending seventeen years in Chikurubi prison after an operation went wrong. Many others went on to success or otherwise in various armies or security firms but a soldier no more, I settled down to life as a Zimbabwean writer and grew increasingly discontented with my lot.

I wrote novels and my tale about corruption in high places, Ivory Madness was reasonably successful, although I was miffed when – for political reasons – my main villain was changed from being the Minister for the Interior into a mere Cabinet Secretary.

'We don't want to get anyone upset," my publisher warned, but I was not happy about that even though the book continues to sell nearly three decades later.

I wrote articles for the Herald newspaper and enjoyed it when my name was recognised by readers, but even there I fell foul of the new regime in Zimbabwe. Following an incident in Marondera, I wrote a piece, entitled 'True Freedom is Freedom of Expression,' but the editor obviously passed it on to the authorities as subversive material. I was visited by a former colleague, then fairly senior in the Central Intelligence Organisation – the feared secret police of Mugabe's Zimbabwe.

"Wind your neck in Mr Lemon," he advised. "I don't want to lock you up."

Yet again I was angry as well as frustrated. An old lady had been incarcerated in police cells for making an unguarded remark about the waste of fuel used by the presidential motorcade and I had expressed my disgust at her treatment. I was an up and coming journalist so that was my job, but not for the first time in my life, I was being naïve. This was Africa and criticism of those in high places is never allowed in that continent. I duly 'wound my neck in' and concentrated on rebuilding my life.

For eighteen months, I enjoyed an idyllic existence on Lake Kariba, living in rustic conditions on the shoreline and taking tourists on cruises in Queen Two, arguably the best-loved and most reliable schooner on the lake. It was great fun but boredom soon set in. As the only person to have rowed the lake in both directions, I knew what I was talking about when it came to that wonderful stretch of water, but answering identical questions on the subject day after day soon began to tax my patience to the limit. Queenie herself helped keep me sane however.

On one particular occasion, she refused to start when it was time to come home from Sampakaruma Island. I am no mechanic at the best of times, but brandishing a large spanner and trying to still my hammering heart, I smiled confidently at my, as yet unconcerned passengers and headed below. Sixteen cylinders of mighty Rolls Royce engine confronted me and looked extremely daunting. Where should I start in my efforts to find the problem? I didn't know. Bryn Daley who owned Queen and knew her inner workings like the back of his hand was in Harare and somehow I had to get that lump of a boat – I no longer loved her – back to Kariba before it was too dark to see. The engine looked the size of a barn and all I could do was talk to her.

"Come on Queenie; don't muck me around please. Let's go home."

Tapping gently on the engine block with my spanner – I had to make the clients think I was doing something – I gave her a pat and returned to my captain's chair. Taking a deep breath, I pressed the starter button and with a reassuring cough that great big, oh-so-beautiful engine rumbled throatily into life. The passengers clapped and I tried to look as though fixing recalcitrant engines was just part of the experience. If only those people knew...!

But exciting moments on Queen were hardly enough to compensate for the general boredom of my existence. I wrote stories but they were criticised for their lack of political correctness by publishers. My account of rowing the lake was turned down by both my own publisher and by Longmans in Harare because there was no 'feminine interest.' That baffled me as I had done the row on my own and I was a mere man. How could I include any feminine participation apart from naming those very few ladies I had met along the way?

'Change the name of your boat,' was one suggestion.

The dinghy had always been Hobo, but Longmans wanted me to rename her Rudo (love) to make the narrative more acceptable to female readers. The official reader for College Press decided that I was a 'racist, still enjoying being a Bwana in uncivilised Africa.' I did the row for the adventure involved, not for any colonialist ideals, but as a mere scribbler I was in no position to reply. Totally demoralised, I left plans for the book in abeyance although it was eventually published some fifteen years after I had done the row and republished in 2009.

With my general state of boredom and writing frustration, I was becoming ever more fractious and difficult, so it was probably inevitable that my marriage, which had suffered so during the war years, should once again come under considerable strain. I don't suppose it came as any surprise to anyone when Missy and I were divorced in 1988 but for me it was traumatic. I had a new book, Killer Cat coming out with College Press in Harare so needing to get away from everything, I approached the boss, Ben Mugabe (he denies any connection to the Old Man) for an advance. He eventually allowed me a thousand Zimbabwe dollars which not only bought me a return air ticket to the UK, but also gave me enough money to keep myself alive in England for the requisite three months. That gives some indication of the disastrous way the Zimbabwe dollar lost its value over the years between 2000 and 2008. Just before the currency finally became completely worthless and was scrapped for the American dollar, a thousand dollars wouldn't buy a box of matches. In fact, it would not have bought a single match.

In England, I set myself up in an isolated caravan in rural Gloucestershire and settled down to write. The scheduled date of my return to Zimbabwe passed by unnoticed and I revelled in the feeling of freedom engendered by my isolation. I had no electricity in my caravan and my water came from a perennial spring – desperately cold in the winter months. Words rattled from my typewriter and I was relatively content with my lot.

Two of my stories for teenagers were accepted by Penguin in Johannesburg and I felt sure that I had 'arrived' as a writer. That merely showed how ignorant I was of the literary world.

My life was pleasant enough but it seemed devoid of excitement and I soon grew restless. Investing in a solidly built and very basic mountain bicycle, I took it out to Nairobi on Aeroflot – it was all I could afford – and from there, headed south to Cape Town, arriving nearly five months later. On the way, I suffered one bad fall, was arrested twice, beaten up by armed soldiery on another occasion, contracted amoebic dysentery in Tanzania and generally had a wonderful time. Unlike my Kariba row, I was a long way from being the first person to do the trip but it restored life into my being and made me feel that perhaps I could settle down to being a displaced Zimbabwean in England.

I was being naïve again. Africa kept calling and I missed my elephants. I have always considered myself rarely privileged to have been brought up in some of the more remote parts of Central Africa and that had given me the opportunity to walk in the bush from an early age and learn to appreciate the gentle dignity of wild elephants. They can teach human beings so much in the way of humanity and I have always loved them with a passion that borders on the fanatical.

There were no elephants in Gloucestershire. I lived in one of the prettiest corners of the country but it seemed somehow empty without those great grey giants.

Perhaps I was kidding myself. Perhaps I used the lack of elephants as an excuse. In truth it was probably the lack of excitement that was wearing me down. I had new friends in England but as far as I could see their lives were ruled by the weather, the newspapers and what was currently the fad show on television. They didn't know elephants. They knew nothing about the horrors of the bush war and its aftermath. They had not heard about *gukuruhundi* because the Mugabe regime had not allowed news of the Matabeleland massacres to escape. Thirty thousand rural Matabeles had been murdered, but when

I tried to explain, I was looked on with fond condescension as a ranting colonial. I was the token foreigner in my little village and I would never really be part of the community.

Even when I remarried in 1996, nothing really changed. We had a lovely wedding and a honeymoon in Wales before I took my new bride off to Africa for six months. We spent time in South Africa, Zimbabwe and Zambia, meeting up with family, old friends and the wild life. Two months alone with me in the lower Zambezi Valley soon cured Lace of any fears she might have had about lions and other dangerous animals but although she enjoyed herself, she never really saw Africa as part of her future. My friends were all rough Zimbabweans and the usual sally when I introduced her was to the effect of 'Why on earth did you marry HIM? Don't you know about him?'

For an English lady, struggling to cope with African custom, this sort of rough and ready humour was difficult to understand and although she returned to Zimbabwe with me for the millennium (where else could a Kariba Boy watch the new century come in but beside the Great Lake?) that was the last time she visited my country.

It was shortly after a motley array of fireworks and a huge intake of beer had signalled the arrival of the third millennium that the wheels fell off in Zimbabwe. Robert Mugabe, still regarded by the rest of the world as one of the better African leaders drew up a new constitution and submitted it to the people for approval. It would have increased government powers of property repossession and installed him as President for life, but everyone expected it to sail through virtually uncontested. After all, Mugabe had been in power for twenty years and would surely die soon. What difference would a few new rules to extend his power make?

The people had other ideas. After three days of voting, they rejected the proposed constitution and although the president appeared to take it in his stride, this result threw him into a rage. Two weeks later, the first farms were invaded by 'war veterans' – most of them too young to have been more than toddlers when the war ended – and white farmers were thrown off their farms and out of their homes.

At the time I said to Lace that this was a drastic measure on Mugabe's part. He had made mistakes in the past but the people could cope with shortages and the odd case of government-sponsored corruption. If the farm invasions were to become widespread, that would mean far more than mere mismanagement by government. Zimbabwe has always relied on agriculture to feed the masses and bring in desperately needed foreign exchange. If farmers were prevented from growing crops, it could well lead to mass starvation and eventual anarchy. It was not a nice prospect and my heart cried for my lovely country.

But for me, the holiday was almost over and soon after the invasions began, Lace and I flew back to Gloucestershire. We have a sixteenth century cottage there and between us run a gardening business, so serious though I felt the situation in Zimbabwe to be, we had to get back.

But even as spring descended upon the English countryside and the population brightened with the approach of summer sunshine, my heart and mind were in the dark recesses of my own country. Using the internet, I surfed everywhere for information on the farm invasions and entreated almost everyone I knew to email me with any story they might hear pertaining to the situation.

It was when Dave Stephens was murdered that my resolve to tell the world about the escalating and ever more brutal chaos in my country really hardened. I had met Dave in the Ruzawi River country club only a few weeks previously and he had seemed a gentle, unassuming man with the welfare of indigenous Zimbabweans very much in his mind. In the entirely white, raucous and overtly racist climate of the country club, he had stood up for his principles and been respected for it. He was popular in the community and coupled with his liberal outlook on racial politics, therein lay his undoing..

A father of three, Stephens was abducted from his Athlone Farm in Macheke and driven to Murehwa police station, where he was held up before a baying mob, made to drink diesel oil, then wantonly shot. Friends and fellow farmers who tried to rescue him were badly beaten and left for dead in the bush. One of these was Stephan Krynauw, an old friend of mine and as I read awful accounts of the incident, I knew I had to do something about it. Mugabe and his villainous henchmen could not be allowed to get away with this.

Feeling that the only way I could possibly help was by writing about the problems in the world press, I sent letters off to every major newspaper editor in the land, offering my services as a roving reporter. With seven books to my name at the time, I could surely write; I was a Zimbabwean and while not fluent, could converse comfortably in both Chishona and Sindebele, the two official indigenous languages of Zimbabwe. That meant I could get into places where other journalists would not be allowed and I could come and go in the country on 'family visits' without being challenged. I still had many contacts in the police, government and CIO who would prove useful, as well as friends around the country that would provide me with stories to be followed up. I was even prepared to pay my own fares and not claim expenses, so was surely a bargain for any editor who cared about what was happening. All I wanted was a market for my stories.

Only one person replied. I suppose the rest took me for some sort of crank, but Phil McNeill, who was then Deputy Editor of the Sunday Express did write back. Understandably he was cautious and non-committal.

'We will certainly look at your stories,' he told me. 'I don't guarantee to use every one but if you can send me stuff that is relevant and news at the time, I am quite prepared to put it in the paper.'

It was enough for me. I was in. I was a journalist and fulfilling a lifelong ambition. I was also in a position to bring the problems of Zimbabwe to public attention and perhaps I could provoke somebody into taking action against Mugabe and his murdering thugs.

I had already approached my local Member of Parliament, David Drew who represented Stroud for the Labour Party. When I gave him details of some of the atrocities taking place, he seemed sceptical.

'This is propaganda from an opinionated minority,' he wrote on fancy notepaper. 'The only hope for change in Zimbabwe is via the movement for Democratic Change and their efforts are being hampered by that minority.'

He went on to rant about the evils of 'the colonial past' and fatuously declared that 'until there is an apology for wrongs done in the past,' there was no hope for Zimbabwe and little point in he and I continuing the discussion. I was aghast. That 'opinionated minority' were under siege from government sponsored hooligans at the time. Friends of mine had lost their lives; others had lost their homes and livelihood. Anarchy was already the rule and this political nincompoop was telling me that it was all propaganda.

As for apologies, who was to make them? Is everyone responsible for the perceived misdeeds of their forefathers? Cecil Rhodes and his pioneers took over a land, already laid to waste and ravaged by the newly formed Matabele nation, themselves banished from their homeland by the Zulu king, Shaka. Certainly the system installed for governing the country was racist and wrong by modern thinking, but Rhodes was acting according to the custom of the time. Besides, the original land grab surely could not be blamed on those who tilled the land in the year 2000. Of the farming community at the time, over eighty percent of them had bought their farms since Independence in 1980 and had 'certificates of no interest' signed by various Ministers of Agriculture. They were farmers and were feeding the nation. Most of them were prosperous but they had earned that prosperity. What possible apologies did Mr Drew want them to make?

There was no answer to my question – the man was an experienced parliamentarian and could run rings around me in argument so I left him alone in disgust, but after another approach to Baroness Amos of the Foreign Office had been fobbed off in similar fashion, I was determined to rub their politically fawning noses in their words.

I was a journalist now. I had the power of the Press behind me. Feeling that I could conquer worlds, I duly booked my flight to Harare, armed myself with such journalistic accoutrements as a laptop, reporter's notepad, dictaphone and tiny camera, then set out to do my bit toward publicising the horrors taking place in my own country.

PART TWO

(Farm Invasions)

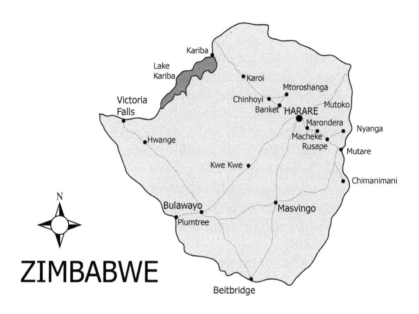

Chapter Two

(Welcome Home)

It was hardly the welcome I would have wanted and I felt a faint churning of apprehension in my stomach. I was already in trouble through no fault of my own and felt that this was hardly an auspicious beginning to my first journalistic expedition.

"What is this? Why are there no entry stamps?" The Immigration Officer flicked through the blank pages of my brand new European Commission passport and looked somewhat distastefully at me over his spectacles.

"My last one ran out."

That was true enough. My old British passport had run its course after ten years of faithful service and I now had this flimsy red excuse for a travel document. "They only last ten years, you know."

"Of course I know. Do not take me for a fool because I am Zimbabwean."

It never pays to be facetious with African officialdom and I have travelled enough through the continent to be aware of this. Inwardly cursing my own stupidity, I made my apologies.

"I am also Zimbabwean," I put in winningly. "I am home to see my family."

He was unimpressed and waved my immigration form in front of my face.

"You are British," he told me forcefully. "You are not Zimbabwean, but I need to know why you are here. Where is your old passport?"

I had been looking forward to this day for months, yet I had been back in my own country less than twenty minutes and my temper was already rising. Where was the friendly hospitality that has always been part of Zimbabwean culture? Willing myself to remain polite, I pandered to the man's whims. In view of the task on hand, I could not afford to offend him.

"I am sorry, Officer: I have not kept my old passport, but if you look me up on your computer, you will find that I return to Zimbabwe every year in order to see my family."

"The computer is not working."

However, he seemed mollified by my obsequiousness and picked up the heavy stamp on his desk. With a flourish, he slammed it down on my passport before handing the document across to me.

"You can stay for two weeks."

I was aghast. I had a return ticket that entitled me to nearly ten weeks in Zimbabwe. Quite apart from the inconvenience, I didn't relish the bureaucracy – and the extra payment - that I would need to endure if I changed the date of my return flight.

"And then what? My air booking is not for another eight weeks."

"Then you reapply – next."

The officer sniffed his disdain and I felt a surge of indignation at this petty harassment. No wonder tourists no longer visited the country. Reporting to an Immigration office every two weeks was irritating enough for me, but I could do it in Kariba where most of the border control staff knew me well. For other visitors, it could prove a major bar to enjoyment of their holiday. The elderly British lady behind me in the queue had told me that she was out on a three-week family visit. Like me, she had been looking forward to her arrival in Zimbabwe, but after two weeks, she would have to find the Immigration offices in Harare and probably stand in a queue for hours, just for the right to finish her visit. It was obvious that the two-week limit applied to holders of a European passport, but I couldn't see whether other nationalities were subject to the same restrictions. Whatever the case, it was another large nail in the coffin of tourism where Zimbabwe was concerned.

In fact, the situation was to get considerably worse, but that unpleasant little greeting to my homeland made me even more apprehensive than I had been before. I had arranged with Phil McNeill to write under the name of Bryan Graham, and as I stepped outside the airport buildings, I tried to immerse myself into a totally new personality. For the moment, David Lemon had disappeared and I had to live and think as Bryan Graham.

Later in the day, I wandered into the city centre in search of something to write about and if nothing else, it was instructive. Harare has always been known as Sunshine City, as much for the good humour of its inhabitants as for the climate, but the place had changed in an indefinable way since my previous visit. The sun still shone and people were still friendly, but behind the smiles, eyes were troubled and friendliness was tempered with wary suspicion. In the shops and supermarkets, basic foodstuffs were in short supply and the possibility of a violent run up to the presidential election was making everyone nervous.

My first stop was inevitably Meikles Hotel. What a wonderfully elegant hostelry this is - so serene, so gracious and so completely unflappable that it seems part of an altogether easier age. Meikles was as gloriously luxurious as ever, but I was immediately struck by the quiet. One receptionist was on duty and she looked bored to tears, while a few businessmen chatted quietly in the coffee lounge. Even the Hunters Bar was deserted and the barman told me that things had been bleak for months.

"One entire wing is already closed down," Simon Kasekere dried glasses with practised efficiency as we talked. "Soon Meikles will be gone and we will all lose our jobs."

It was a theme I was to encounter throughout the city. Even more than the prospect of violence, the thought of unemployment and ultimate starvation seemed to be preying on everyone's mind. After an excellent start in November, the rains had disappeared and the prospect of drought was an ever-present worry for all Zimbabweans. If a drought were to hit the country, it was only those with steady employment who stood any chance of survival. With the maize shortage already acute, everyone else would starve.

While Simon and I continued our conversation in desultory fashion, we were joined by Abel Charambani, a city lawyer who told me that he specialised in human rights. After a shaky start, during which he questioned me rather unsubtly about my antecedents, Abel accepted my story of being a Kariba businessman, in town for a short while. He went on to tell me how difficult it had become to keep his children fed.

"I have a good job and earn a regular salary," he said, "so money is not my problem. What worries me is how I am to feed my family. Zimbabwe has just about run out of maize and without a crop coming in this year, things will get worse. When we hear that mealie meal is available in a shop, we rush around, to stand in a long queue. It is worse than the fuel shortage because a man can do without a car, but we all have to eat."

And the violence? I could not resist a little gentle pumping. After all, this was what I was back in my own country for. Abel shook his head in obvious despair.

"It is not too bad during the week, but on weekends things get pretty rough. Three Saturdays ago, I was woken at seven in the morning by the Youth Brigade. They said there was a meeting being held a few blocks away and I must attend with my family. When I told them that I was not interested in politics, they kicked their way into my house, stole my food and my beer and then ran off laughing, to intimidate somebody else.

'These people are dangerous," he went on. "They care nothing for politics, but they are like animals and will do whatever is asked of them by the government. In normal times, they would be locked up as criminals, but now they are allowed to do what they want. Everyone fears them."

Over the following weeks, I was to hear many more stories about the Border Gezi Youth Brigade and at one stage, I had a run in with them myself, but it was ordinary black Zimbabweans who suffered most from their depredations. Abel went on to tell me that since his encounter with these government-sponsored thugs, he had spent every weekend in town.

"We stay at a cheap hotel and the kids can play in the parks, but I cannot keep it up even on my salary. I don't know what is to happen."

And if Mugabe were to win the next election, would the situation get worse? Having been in the country a matter of hours, I was not sure how feelings were running on this question, but Abel rolled his eyes.

"We have to cope somehow. We are Zimbabweans and have nowhere else to go. You *warungu* (white people) can live in Britain or Australia, but we are stuck here and must pray that the situation improves. Only God can help us now."

I was reminded of his words later in the day, when I met Bobby Turner and Alec Kay in the bar at Harare Sports Club. Both men were commercial farmers, but Bobby came from Macheke and Alec from Chinhoyi. Both of them had illegal settlers on their farms and like Abel Charambani, were struggling to bring up families in an atmosphere of supercharged violence. Their answers to my question were curiously similar to Abel's.

"We have no choice but to see it through," Alec told me. "I have an engineering ticket and my wife can get a job anywhere, but this is still my country and I love it here. I am going to stick things out in the hope that the world will see sense and do something about the maniac who is destroying us all."

"He has even taken our firearms away," Bobby chipped in. "Every white farmer in the land has been told to surrender his weapons to the cops, so that is the last we will see of those. Since the farm invasions started, we have been harassed and hassled. Some of us have been murdered, others beaten and humiliated yet we have kept our cool and not fought back.

Now the bastard is taking our only form of defence should things get really bad and we can only wonder what new form of intimidation he has in mind now."

It was a government decree that was to be rescinded a few days later, but when it came out, it caused despair and a feeling that it was the last straw among the farming community. Even as I pondered on Bobby's words and wondered what would happen when all the farmers were disarmed, his mobile phone rang and he moved apart from us to answer it. When he returned, his face was pale.

"Those bastard war vets have set up a block on the road leading to my house," He told us quietly. "That was my neighbour, warning me not to come home for the moment. Thank God my wife and kids are in town."

"So what will you do?" I asked, but all his only reaction was to shrug and take another gulp of his beer.

"Go home tomorrow or the next day, I suppose. Eventually they will get fed up or too drunk and move off. Then we can go home and try to farm with what we have left. I just hope they don't trash the house."

At the time, the situation was new to me and my meeting with the two farmers preyed on my mind for days. However, such are the realities of life in Zimbabwe today. My battered little nation has stood so much over the past decades, but I was to learn that they still had a great deal more to take.

Mind you, I had another shock to my system waiting for me on that first eventful day. I had arranged with an old friend to borrow a vehicle for the duration of my stay, but had neglected to tell him that I needed to be inconspicuous. I was a working journalist now and with government paranoia about the overseas Press running at an all time high, I did not want to attract attention to my activities. As far as the authorities were concerned, I was out on a family visit and would spend most of my time in a safari camp outside Kariba.

"A foreign correspondent hey," An English friend had made the quip when I told him about my deal with the newspaper, but I did not feel like any sort of correspondent. I was merely a middle-aged grandfather, excited to be back with his family and anxious to find out what was going on in the country I loved. I would certainly send copy back to Phil McNeill in London, but at that stage, I didn't much care whether he published my stories or not. In a remarkably short time, my attitude was to change and I would find myself relishing the journalist's role and actively looking for things to write about, but at first, it seemed more like a chore that I could have done without.

Late on that first afternoon, my Harare-based friend took me to a panel beater's yard in the industrial area to see my new set of wheels and I immediately wished I had been more specific.

My 'new' vehicle was an old Toyota land cruiser, recently painted from nose to tail in garish gold. She had multi-coloured flashes down the sides to give her a more rakish look and the final straw as far as I was concerned was the words 'Malawi Gold' stencilled in large black letters on the front and back of the vehicle.

Malawi Gold is a form of *dagga* or cannabis that – according to aficionados of the weed – makes for a superb smoke. I did not really want to be an advert for the stuff, but I didn't seem to have much choice, so I turned to the grinning owner of the vehicle and rather helplessly smiled my thanks. He beamed at my obvious gratitude.

"I had it done specially for you," he told me happily. "She looks good hey?"

She didn't, but only a very good friend will lend one a vehicle to do with as he wills for nearly three months, so I kept my thoughts to myself. And to be honest, the 'Ganja Bus' as we called her for obvious reasons, did me proud. Over the next few weeks, we were to cover many thousands of kilometres together and the old girl gave me very little trouble. She was very much a 'trundler' and we rarely exceeded a hundred kilometres per hour, even on the emptiest of roads. This meant that we spent many hours alone together and she listened without complaint to my burbling. On one occasion, she was to get me out of potentially serious trouble and wherever we went, we caused a stir.

When I stopped in towns or even in bits of empty countryside, a crowd would quickly gather and I would find myself answering searching questions about the Ganja Bus. Street kids in Harare would look after her without charging for the favour and I made many new friends, just through the dazzlingly unusual quality of her paintwork.

As I drove back to the Holiday Inn that first evening, I couldn't help reflecting on my first day back in my own country. It had been enjoyable, disturbing and altogether different. My one worry concerned my own ability to write well enough to do justice to the situation, prevailing in Zimbabwe. I had promised Phil McNeill that I would concentrate on human interest stories and as a novelist, I had written for newspapers before, but this was different. I had no official accreditation, didn't even belong to the National union of Journalists and would have to email my copy back to London without my messages being detected by the authorities. The Public Order and Security Bill had just been promulgated and it imposed draconian punishment on anybody speaking out against the government or its policies. I could not even use my own name and if I was caught, I could expect a lengthy spell in Chikurubi prison. That was not a prospect that appealed.

It was in a very thoughtful frame of mind that I retired to bed that night. I had the feeling that this was to be an interesting trip indeed and pushed any niggling imps of doubt to the back of my mind.

Chapter Three

(A Farmers Lot)

One of the things that had always disturbed me about the farm invasions was why none of the farmers seemed to fight back. Martin Olds was the exception and he had died in a bloody gun battle with government troops in Matabeleland. They had surrounded his homestead and Olds, defiant to the last had taken them on. He was fighting insuperable odds and the end result was inevitable but my argument was that if more farmers had done the same, the government might well have backed down in the end. Farmers would have died, but at least -like Olds – they would have gone down fighting.

My sons disabused me of my naiveté.

"They have wives and families to look after Dad," Brian told me. "It is not worth losing your life for an ideal."

"We had wives and families to look after when we fought for Rhodesia and our way of life," was my reply. "We laid our lives on the line and many good folk died, but at least we kept our pride."

"And where did that get any of us?" My younger son Graeme was more dogmatic. "Look at the situation we are in now."

"You were lucky in that you had the police and army to back you up," this was Brian again. "These chaps have nobody to turn to except their neighbours. Martin Olds' neighbours tried to assist but the police would not allow them anywhere near the property, even though they could hear the gunfire."

Nevertheless, it was one aspect of the situation that perplexed and worried me. Men of all colours and creeds in my country have never lacked courage. Man for man, we lost more people in the world wars than any other Commonwealth country and during the bush war for Zimbabwe, the entire population had shown almost unbelievable fortitude, no matter which side they were on. I needed to delve into this with the farming community who were at the sharp end of the troubles.

"Do you want to talk with a commercial farmer who is in real trouble?" The quiet question came in on my telephone. Word had quickly spread as to what I was doing and this was my first step toward being a 'proper' journalist. Having readily agreed to the meeting, I was driven out to Gateway School, an excellent educational establishment in the Western suburbs of Harare. It wasn't quite what I expected, but I was assured that I would understand when I spoke to the farmer.

His name was Terry Ford and I met him in a box-like office behind the main buildings, where he was in charge of supervising school transport. His desk was covered in loose papers, but he had the rugged physique and seamed face that denotes a lifetime on the land. After shaking my hand, he carefully shut the office door, checking that there was nobody in earshot. My contact had obviously explained what I was doing in the country and although he was wary at first, Terry readily agreed to talk with me.

"I would rather you didn't use my real name," was his only request and in my first report on his troubles, I called him Tony Gibbs. He is dead now, so I have no worries about protecting his identity and if my words can do anything at all to bring his killers to justice, I shall be extremely pleased.

Terry was a loose-limbed, shambling gentleman – in the true sense of the word. He spoke softly and even though he was working in the city, he wore the traditional Zimbabwe farmer's 'uniform' of faded shorts, a short-sleeved shirt and baggy long socks over worn *veldskoens* – the loose fitting suede shoes of Southern Africa. He had been born fifty-four years previously on Gowrie Farm in Norton, some thirty kilometres from Harare. His mother was born on the same farm and her father was born there too. With only three hundred and fifty hectares of land, Gowrie was officially too small to be subject to the government reclamation exercise, (the lower limit for designated farms being four hundred hectares) but abundant water made it a desirable property and even though it had been in the Ford family for nearly a century, it was coveted by a number of important personages.

"The president's sister, Sabina Mugabe was the first to want the place," Terry told me gloomily. "She came around nearly two years ago and told me that she was taking the farm over and I was to move out. My marriage was going through a rocky period at the time and that was the final straw for my wife. She decided that Zimbabwe was no longer a safe place for white people and flew off to New Zealand with my sons."

When I asked him how it was that Sabina Mugabe was not living on Gowrie nowadays, Terry looked thoughtful.

"It was the power of the Press that sorted things out, I suppose," he said slowly. "Somehow the newspapers came to hear of it and the resultant publicity seems to have scared the lady off. At least I have heard no more from her since."

Two years later, the farm had ceased to exist as a viable property and with it, the livelihoods of Terry Ford, his twenty workers and their families had gone. Although he was still in residence, Terry was no longer allowed to work his lands, nor did he have the inclination to do so.

"Thank God, I no longer have family here to worry about," he said with feeling.

So how did this all come about? Why had the farm been lost? Terry's story was one that is all too familiar to Zimbabwe farmers and one that I was to hear on many occasions over succeeding weeks.

"When the farm invasions got going early in 2000," he said slowly, "we had a few so-called war veterans coming on to the farm and making trouble, but they were fairly half-hearted and moved away in time. A few months ago the situation changed.

Two war vets called Wamba and Chitumbo arrived with their followers and they were nasty from the start. Both of them were armed with AK rifles and having broken the doors down in the farm cottage, they set up residence there. They would use my tractors and fertilisers whenever they felt like it, although they never seemed to plant anything. They spent hours politicising my labour force and held all night drinking sessions when a great deal of damage was caused to buildings and equipment. The police were called on a number of occasions, but even though they are only fifteen minutes drive from the farm, they never appeared.

'My main crop is seed maize," he went on and I was struck by the gentle simplicity of the man; "but I also run cattle, sheep and horses, so the farm is well utilised. This year I prepared the lands for my seed maize, but immediately after I planted, the war vets planted their own maize in the same lands. Naturally enough, when the inspectors came around, they declared my crop worthless and I could not blame them for that. Even worse than losing all that income however, was the fact that having planted their maize, these blokes ignored it until the land was completely overgrown. You could hardly see the maize plants for the weeds that had grown over them. It was heartbreaking and made even more so, when they drove my cattle into the fields one night. The *mombies* had a good feast and the war vets claimed Z 600,000 compensation from me for ruining what they said had been an excellent crop. It has cost me almost that amount in lawyers' fees so far and we are not getting anywhere.

'I even offered to share the farm with them," he shook his head in obvious frustration, "but they want the lot."

Far worse was to follow.

"Two days ago," Terry went on, "I had a visit from a retired Army colonel named Mugare, who told me that the farm was now his and I had to move out of my home. I told him that I had nowhere to go and suggested that I move into one of his Harare houses, but he assured me that the system doesn't work like that. When I pointed out that with two businesses of his own in Harare, plus another plot in Ruwa, he was hardly one of the landless peasants at whom the land redistribution programme is apparently aimed, he merely laughed and insisted that I move out as soon as possible. My two war vets are determined that he won't have 'their' farm, so I can see trouble brewing.

"Then yesterday," Zimbabwe farmers are a tough bunch, but Terry was close to tears. Although I didn't know it at the time, he had only recently won a long battle against pancreatic cancer and in the process had found solace in religion, but the situation in which he now found himself was obviously taking its toll; "my driver dropped me at the school first thing in the morning, but when he got back to the farm, the truck was hijacked by Chitumbo and driven away to heaven knows where. The driver managed to get a message back to me – for which he was later beaten half to death – and I notified the police who for once in their lives actually attended. They rang me this morning to say that there is no trace of the truck, so I am now stuck in town with no house, no farm and no vehicle. My dogs and livestock have not been fed for two days and my labour force have fled, so there is nobody to feed them anyway. I earn very little money at this job and am at my wits end, wondering what to do.

'The outside world seems to have forgotten Zimbabwe and we farmers have nobody to turn to, so the future looks bleak for folk like me. I keep praying for miracles, but it isn't working. At the moment, I am virtually destitute and do not know what to do about it."

When I asked him what passport he held, Terry laughed somewhat hollowly.

"With my background, I can only have a Zimbabwean one. I applied for help to the British Embassy in the nineteen eighties but they were not interested, so even if I want to leave this place, there is nowhere for me to go."

And what would he do if matters came to a head on the farm and he found himself under personal threat – fight them off? Terry smiled, but there was a bleak look in his eye.

"I couldn't if I wanted to. I have never had a firearm in the house and don't particularly want one now."

Those words were to assume awful significance later on, but at the time I merely wondered at any Zimbabwean farmer remaining unarmed. After all, most white Zimbabweans – myself included – have been brought up with firearms and look upon them as ordinary household items. It seemed somehow odd to think of this big farmer out there in the thick of things without anything with which to defend himself.

I left Terry Ford's cluttered office, sharing some of his frustration at the situation. I had never been to Gowrie Farm, but it seemed tragic that a viable concern that was so integral a part of the Zimbabwean economy was being allowed to waste away, just to feed one man's lust for power. In the early days of Zimbabwe, I had come to almost admire Robert Mugabe for his pragmatism and his oft-repeated talk about reconciliation between previously warring factions. He had preached peace between black and white Zimbabweans, but his high ideals of those days seemed to have vanished as he faced for the first time, a genuine challenge to his leadership and quest for power.

As for Terry Ford, I promised to visit him again, but I was not to be given the chance and he was to play a further, major part in my story. At the time though, this first interview with a farmer in trouble made me realise that the stories I was after, would not be found in places like Harare. I had to get out into the farming area and see things for myself. Two days later, I went with David Bradshaw and the Ganja Bus to spectacularly beautiful Mtoroshanga and had my first run in with the people who were wrecking farming areas and with it, their own hopes of a happy and prosperous future.

* * *

David Scott Bradshaw worked with me in those heady days when I was a policeman at war in the land, then known as Rhodesia. We fought together for an ideal and in the end, were defeated by economics and the increasingly liberal tendencies of Western nations. With British help, our homeland became Zimbabwe and many embittered white Rhodesians left the new country to rebuild their lives in other parts of the world. Braddles and I did not. We remained in our own country and although I have since made a living by basing myself in Britain, he stayed on to raise a lovely family as true Zimbabweans.

After a wild and boisterous youth, Braddles went farming in Malawi, but the call of home was too strong and he soon returned to Zimbabwe and worked himself up through the hierarchy of the Zimbabwe Tobacco Association. When I called into his Harare office, he held the title of Deputy Director of Production in the organisation and when I told him what I was doing, he was only too pleased to assist.

"I will take you to see Pat Ashton," he promised, showing me the picture of a bloodstained white man staring defiantly out from the cover of a *Zimbabwean Farmer* magazine. "His house has just been trashed and his kids frightened half to death."

So it was that we came to be driving through the spectacular hills of Mtoroshanga on our way to Landfall Farm, where Patrick Ashton had once worked the land.

Ashton proved to be a burly Englishman who exuded bonhomie. When I met him, Pat was more concerned about the workers left on his farm than the beating he had received.

"I just hope my son can get the tobacco crop in without any more trouble," He said. "I have nearly three hundred employees and if we lose the crop, they won't get paid."

Ashton was the latest in the long list of Zimbabwean commercial farmers to fall foul of the Zanu PF youth wing of President Mugabe. Landfall was a prosperous farming set up, producing tobacco, maize and mangoes, but the farm had been occupied by one hundred and fifty illegal settlers, among the most prominent of which was Sergeant Makiwa, a serving member of the Zimbabwe Republic Police. Although the settlers initially tried to prevent Pat from planting a tobacco crop, the local District Administrator intervened and eventually forty-five hectares were planted and the Ashtons were allowed to attend their mangoes."The settlers have made no attempt to plant a crop themselves," Ashton told me. "but since they arrived on the farm, one hundred and twenty four irrigation pipes have been wantonly destroyed and forty-six kilometres of drip tape (a kind of punctured hose pipe, used to irrigate mangoes) have been burned or slashed. These creatures have left farm gates open and then made outrageous demands for compensation for non-existent damage to their non-existent crops. We have taken it all and tried to smile, but last week it all came to a head."

Ashton had been working in the lands when his son, Philip had radioed to say that settlers had invaded the house and garden.

"They were holding both my sons, together with Phillip's girlfriend Sandy and even as he spoke to me, the radio and cell phone were snatched from his hands."

Remembering the moment, Pat Ashton's face contorted with emotion, but whether it was grief or anger, I was not sure. Calming himself down with a visible effort, he continued with the story.

"I rushed back to the house, but was unable to get through the gates as one of our trucks had been parked diagonally across them. This was obviously a deliberate ploy and as I pulled up, I was surrounded by a frenzied mob of settlers. Some of my own labourers were with them and all were armed with axes or sticks. They screamed abuse and began smashing the vehicle to get at me. The windows broke, showering me with glass and I realised that there was no way I was going to get into the house. I managed to turn my truck around and was lucky to escape with only a few cuts and bruises. Not knowing what to do, I rushed across to my neighbour's homestead, from where I contacted the police. They gave the usual excuse about lack of transport, but Rod Huck – the neighbour – and I went around and collected four constables, who accompanied us back to the farm.

'Once we were back on Landfall, I argued with the settlers, pleading with them to release my children, but they merely laughed and taunted us even more. The cops did nothing, merely wandering around and looking on as my kids were beaten and humiliated."

Phillip Ashton, a small, dark dynamo of a man laughed as he broke into the conversation.

"It was a bit frightening at the time," he admitted. "But we put our own humour into the situation. When these blokes wanted us to *toyi toyi* and chant Zanu PF songs, Sandy and I did a few jive steps which really threw them. We invited them to join in and one or two tried before they were told off by their leaders. They had already stripped our shirts from us in case we carried bugging equipment and it was all quite cheerful in a funny sort of way, but when they started beating my brother Adam's dog, things became a bit nasty. The dog is an old Jack Russell and Adam tried to protect it, so they beat him instead. I tried to intervene and also took a few whacks, but they didn't do any real damage. We told them that Sandy was a South African who had nothing to do with the situation and after some discussion, they left her alone, but it was pretty unpleasant for all of us."

While this was going on, two cows and four sheep were shot and butchered right outside the house. A fire was made and most of the settlers left the embattled whites alone and joined in the feast. The policemen also ate heartily and when neighbouring farmers telephoned the British Embassy in Harare (Pat Ashton has a British passport) to report the shooting, they were told that nothing could be done.

"I was bloody angry," Rod Huck told me later. "Some ass of a civil servant told me that if we had heard shots, it was probably too late for any reaction anyway. I told him that if that was the way, Britain protected her own people, it was no wonder that their country was in such a bloody mess!"

That could have been of small comfort to the Ashton family although they were eventually released unharmed, apart from having been frightened out of their wits and totally humiliated by the invaders of their home. When I asked him why he had been targeted, Patrick shook his head.

"I don't know. I have always supported the democratic process and have no links with MDC or Zanu PF. The invasion of my house was a deliberate act of terrorism and a local Zanu PF counsellor, Mr Mbamba was in the forefront of the troublemakers."

It was Phillip who provided a possible motive for the violence.

"Dad has done wonders for the local hospital," he told me. "He set up a health scheme for workers, so that everyone pays a small subsidy and gets very cheap treatment. He raised the funds for a brand new ambulance, so the people are better off here than they would be in other districts and they love him for it. He is mobbed wherever he goes and Zanu PF don't like to see a white farmer becoming too popular, so they want him out of the way."

The scenario, Philip painted seemed extremely likely, particularly as Rod Huck next door had experienced little trouble with settlers or war vets on his farm and Pete Hulme on the other side had been left unmolested. I later visited Pete and he was enthusiastic about his tobacco crop.

"Thank God these bastards have left me alone," he said happily. "I am hoping to make a killing when this lot gets to the sale floors."

"I won't leave," back on Landfall, Pat Ashton was grimly determined. "As soon as we get the homestead straight, I shall be back farming and my wife, Sally will be out here in the house as always."

Getting the homestead straight was not to be so easy. When I visited Landfall, I was appalled. It was the first time, I had seen what the so-called war veterans and illegal settlers could do to a family home and the damage was sickening. Everything that could not be carried away had been wantonly smashed, years of paperwork and letters were scattered around the lawns, there was human excrement everywhere and what had once been a fine old homestead was a battered ruin. Phillip shook his head in despair.

"I don't know how we will get it together," he said, "but Dad seems pretty determined."

I was about to photograph the destruction with my little disposable camera when our visit was interrupted by the arrival of two smartly dressed men in a green pick-up, which contained seven surly youths crammed into the open back.

"What are you doing here," this was Mr Mbamba himself and I told him that I was a family friend, seeing the damage for myself.

"This is liberated land," he shouted without allowing me to finish. "It belongs to the Zimbabwean people, not to the white farmers. You foreign people are not allowed here. Go back to Britain now."

He was working himself up into an obvious rage and the youths had moved to surround us. Instinctively, I moved closer to Braddles and although none of the youths appeared to be armed, the mounting tension was almost palpable in the midday heat. My sense of outrage was building up too, but my companion nudged me firmly in the side so we wished the newcomers a polite farewell and made our escape.

"Liberated land indeed," Phillip scoffed as we drove away. "These bastards have stolen it and as Dad bought the farm after Independence, he can hardly be accused of taking it from the people."

It seemed an intractable situation, but I couldn't help reflecting on the way back to Harare that if the remaining Zimbabwean farmers were to show the same determined spirit as Pat and Phillip Ashton, some accommodation with the settlers could surely be worked out in time – provided Morgan Tsvangirai of the Movement for Democratic Change came into power at the next election. If Mugabe and his thugs remained in charge, the position on the farms could only get worse.

* * *

I was back in Mtoroshanga a couple of days later, but this time on a very different mission. The man I had come to meet was not prepared to speak with me in any place where we might be seen or overheard.

Kennard Matizwa was a farm manager, but when we met, he looked more like an escapee from the local intensive care unit. His right eye was swollen shut, one ear was heavily bandaged and his face showed extensive bruising. He walked with a curious, shuffling gait and I guessed that his ribs were painful as well.

"You should see the rest of me," he quipped when I commented on his injuries. "I made the mistake of opening my mouth in the wrong place and received a beating for my pains."

Kennard learned his farming at Gwebi Agricultural College outside Harare and was a quietly spoken, humorous man, who obviously enjoyed his work. He was employed by a prominent white farmer and had agreed to meet me while he was doing his rounds in the tobacco lands. After a leisurely drive out from town, I parked the Ganja Bus under a shady *msasa* tree and smoked a contemplative pipe while I waited for Kennard to arrive. He eventually sputtered up on a dusty motorbike and as soon as we had shaken hands, he gestured expansively around him at the growing tobacco.

"Look at all this," his enthusiasm was almost palpable. "Money growing in the ground. We are going to have a lovely crop this year, but it is in jeopardy at the moment because of the political hassles.

'I know it isn't really mine," he went on, "but I have almost total control of the farm and the work force. The Boss does his bit, but he doesn't often query my actions and I can always go to him for advice if I am stuck for an answer. It is almost as good as having a farm of my own."

But like so many farm managers in troubled Zimbabwe, Kennard now had more than his usual share of problems.

"The squatters arrived nearly six months ago," it was the same old refrain. "They pegged out their plots, but none of them have bothered to plant anything. They call themselves war veterans, but most of them are younger than me and could hardly have been born when the liberation struggle ended.

'At first, they were just a nuisance and camped beside the security fence around the main house. I have a cottage half a kilometre away, but the noise these people made kept me awake most nights. When they first arrived, I was ordered to attend a *pungwe* (a political indoctrination session) near the barns, but I refused and was beaten so badly that I ended up in hospital. Then I threw a bunch of settlers out of my house and was beaten again. A month ago, I was tackled by a group of MDC supporters and when I told them that I did not support Zanu PF or the MDC, I received yet another beating. They are beginning to recognise me in the local hospital, but it is very tiring. So far I have been beaten maybe six times and I am no longer sure which party supporters are beating me at any one time."

He smiled again through swollen lips and I marvelled at the spirit of the man who could keep his sense of humour after so much pain and trouble.

"The squatters hate me and the farm workers are suspicious of me," he went on slowly. "Although I am black, I am not really one of them because I work closely with the Boss. If I tell one of them off, he will run to the workers committee and they report directly to Zanu PF who send their thugs down to 'discipline' me. My employer has done what he can to protect me, but he is a white man and the party line is that white men no longer have authority over anyone, even when they pay their wages."

But what of the future, I wondered. How long could men like Kennard continue to do their jobs in such circumstances? For once the smile was missing.

"I don't know," he admitted. "Life for commercial farmers is very difficult at the moment and the problems are everywhere in the country. The local committee of Zanu PF for this area have politicised the workers to a tremendous degree. A few weeks ago, virtually everyone here supported MDC, but Zanu PF have now ordered every farmer to pay his workers a substantial bonus. They have timed this move to coincide with reaping of the tobacco crop, which means that – no matter what they feel about it – the farmers have no choice but to comply. Even a day of being left unattended can ruin a crop and most farmers are already struggling for cash.

'You cannot blame the workers for taking their bonuses, but now they are thinking that perhaps Mugabe really can make life easier for them. They are merely labourers without education and few of them have the sense to look beyond their next meal anyway. I fear that unless something drastic happens in the fairly near future, most of them will vote for Zanu PF at the next election.

'I would hate to see Mugabe back in power."

Kennard's expression was almost wistful and he spoke with feeling, so as tactfully as I could, I asked who he would be voting for. That battered smile was immediately back in place.

"I keep one foot in each camp," he told me with a chuckle. "It means that whoever wins, I shall still be in favour, but it also means that both factions continue to beat me whenever they feel the need."

We parted with another firm handshake and as I watched him ride away in a cloud of red dust, I couldn't help shaking my head in wonderment. I was still unsure as to his political inclinations, but with black farmers like him learning their trade under more experienced white employers, there surely had to be a future for large-scale commercial farming in Zimbabwe.

Chapter Four

('The Good Life' in Nyanga)

Although the vast African sky showed no sign of impending rain and I knew that what was left of the national maize crop was in desperate danger if it didn't come soon, I was chuckling as I drove out of town. A good friend of mine worked as an insurance assessor in his spare time and the previous day, he too had been in Mtoroshanga. Over breakfast at his house, he told me the story.

"I was taking a short cut down a farm road that leads to Banket," he grinned around a mouthful of toast. "Coming around a bend, I was confronted with a horde of yelling farm workers, all running toward me. Some of them were hurling rocks into my path and others brandished big sticks and for a moment, my blood froze. I thought I had driven straight into a war veterans ambush and knew that if I stopped, I would be in trouble."

John had been driving a Hyundai saloon car and having no real choice in the matter, had merely pushed the accelerator to the floor and felt the car surge forward.

"The next thing I knew," John was obviously enjoying his tale and I was agog to know how he had got out of his predicament, "there was one hell of a bang on my windscreen and for a fleeting moment, I was eye to eye with a huge snake. These blokes had obviously been chasing it and in my fright, I hadn't even noticed the damned thing until I ran it over. Fortunately, it was killed by the impact and when I climbed somewhat shakily out of the car, the chaps mobbed me. They reckoned I had deliberately run the snake down. If they had known that I was too frightened to even see it, they probably would have handed me over to the local war vets, but instead I was a ruddy hero. The snake was a monster too. A black mamba, we laid it out beside the car and it was quite a bit longer."

It was a lovely little story and in the climate of modern day Zimbabwe, it was nice to have something to laugh about for a change.

As for me, I was on my way into the mountains. Although I had been offered accommodation – 'to see things for myself' – on a number of farms around Harare, I had telephoned an old friend, living in the Nyanga mountains and she had promised to introduce me to people out there who had stories to tell.

It was lovely to shake off the clutter and bustle of the city, but as I drove sedately out into the farmlands of Marondera and Macheke, I was immediately struck by the changed aspect of the countryside since I had last been there. This had always been big country and it brought back many memories, both good and bad. Passing through Theydon, my stomach contracted as I remembered tracer bullets shredding the night as I drove through a terrorist ambush all those years previously. Looking out over the Macheke plains, I remembered the old feelings of joy at being granted my own huge area, where I was Member in Charge of the local police and lord of all I surveyed – I thought so anyway. My picturesque little police station still huddled among tall trees just off the main road, and I almost went in to see how it was but decided that I would probably be disappointed, so drove rather wistfully onward. As I passed through the town, I remembered the bad times – and Macheke had certainly had those in abundance – and I remembered the good times. I remembered the larger than life personalities who farmed in the area and couldn't help smiling at the memories. This was an area where tobacco and maize were grown in vast quantity and a great deal of money had been made by ambitious and hard working farmers. It did not look as though much money would be made in future years.

Countryside that I remembered as rolling fields, where irrigation sprays whispered in the sunshine and both tobacco and maize grew in lushly tended rows as far as the eye could see, now had an unkempt and overgrown appearance. There was no livestock to be seen and the farmhouses I drove past had that lost and empty look that any dwelling takes on when loving owners move out. Paintwork was peeling and in one case, part of a roof had fallen in.

The lands were even worse. In place of the crops which had helped to feed a nation, all I saw was grass and weeds, occasionally broken up by small patches of maize, often beside a mud hut and obviously grown for the use of whoever was living in those dwellings. Even these tiny patches of cultivation looked forlorn. The maize was wilting for lack of moisture and leaf edges already had that brown, scorched look that is dreaded by farmers. Trees had obviously been felled in quantity and I passed hundreds of women carrying firewood on their heads as they wandered home.

The great gum plantations that once bordered the road on the way through Marondera and Macheke had gone and instead of looking warmly welcoming, the countryside appeared bleak and unhappy. This was not the Zimbabwe that I remembered and I wondered what horror stories were waiting to be told in that barren looking landscape.

The road through Headlands was not quite as bad, but this was cattle country and even here, the ubiquitous mud huts and straggly maize crops were visible in what had once been lush grazing land. I could only wonder what had happened to the cattle and resolved to find out on my way back.

As I drove in to Rusape, I was recording my impressions into my tape recorder, but in the town centre, I was pulled up by a police roadblock. Dropping the little machine on to the seat beside me, I covered it with my hat, fervently praying that the vehicle would not be searched. I need not have worried, as all the young constable was interested in was the fact that the tax disc on my windscreen had expired the previous month.

"You have forgotten to renew it perhaps, Sir?" He was a polite young man and obviously wished to spare my blushes. Cursing my own stupidity for not checking and the owner of the Ganja Bus for not warning me, I agreed that I had indeed forgotten.

"I am just going up to Nyanga for a couple of days, Officer," I am always prepared to grovel in such circumstances. "I will ensure that it is renewed as soon as I return to Harare."

"Please make sure you do that, Sir."

He waved me on and I turned off the main road and headed into the mountains, singing tunelessly in enjoyment of my escape. Two kilometres out of Rusape, I spotted a weary looking hitchhiker beside the road. Over the preceding week, I had been fed a diet of horror stories on the dangers of picking up passengers and regaled with lurid tales of what could – and presumably did – happen to those who ignored good advice. However, this little guy looked so forlorn in his heavy jacket and it was a hot and sticky day. Besides, I often feel that a great deal of resentment is unnecessarily stirred up when motorists in virtually empty cars flash past poor folk who might wait in the blazing sun for hours before a bus or a friendly driver comes along. I did not want to add to the tension between races in my country, so I stopped to offer the young man a lift.

His name was Todi Katande and I gathered that he was heading for Nyanga. I was not going quite so far, but the Nyanga Mountains were so spectacularly beautiful that driving was a pleasure and I eventually took Todi all the way into the village. I can never understand why motorists hurry to get through these wonderful mountains. This is magnificent countryside and the road winds between mighty crags and cliff faces, rocky grey hillsides and verdantly beautiful pasturelands on every side. The whole area is normally a paradise for tourists, but it was obviously going through hard times. For thirty-five kilometres, we did not see another vehicle. There wasn't even a cyclist and those few pedestrians we passed looked forlorn and listless. Lonely eagles circled slowly above our heads and after an initial awkward silence, Todi and I began to talk. Like travellers everywhere, our talk immediately centred on the weather and the drought that was crippling an already crippled country.

"The Good Lord must be angry with our government," Todi said sagely. "Neighbouring countries have all had good rains, but we have seen nothing for many weeks and everyone is now starving."

It was certainly true that Botswana, Zambia, Mozambique and South Africa had enjoyed excellent growing seasons, while those convergence zones that reached the borders with Zimbabwe, would inexplicably wither away and disappear. Perhaps God really was angry.

But Todi had more important matters on his mind.

"See that store," he jerked a thumb contemptuously at a small forecourt shop outside Brondesbury Park hotel. "They have mealie meal in there, but unless you have a Zanu PF party card, you are not allowed to buy it."

Feeling that this was possibly unlikely, I later told local housemaid, Martha Chidondo about the mealie meal, allegedly available at Brondesbury Park. In high excitement at the possibility of proper food for her family – they had been living on potatoes and beans - she hurried off, only to return two hours later with a long face.

"I do not support the government or MDC," she told me. "But because I did not have a Zanu PF card, I was turned away."

With an election due in the not too far distant future, I wondered what the outside observers would make of this bit of blatant coercion, but from what I had seen of those worthies in previous elections, they seemed more interested in buying souvenirs than sorting out what skulduggery might be occurring.

Having dropped Todi off in Nyanga village, I decided that with time on my hands, a visit to Troutbeck was called for. I had stayed at the Troutbeck Hotel on many occasions and at one time, my son had worked there, so it held special memories for me. At first glance, only the position of the entrance gate seemed to have changed.

There was the wonderfully difficult golf course, criss-crossed by mountain streams and small dams. Why is water such an irresistible magnet for golf balls, I wondered to myself as I remembered many a shanked drive sending the ball inexorably into the Troutbeck waters. There was the lake, brimming with fat trout and sapphire-blue in the sunshine of early afternoon. There was the fire in the foyer, which traditionally is never allowed to go out and there were the lush green lawns that I remembered so well. The air was as crisply enervating as dry Champagne and everything was spotlessly clean, but there were no people.

I looked in the bars; I looked in the lounges; I looked outside on the terrace and I looked in the dining rooms and toilets. Apart from shyly smiling members of staff, I was the only person in that magnificently spacious hotel.

Barman Apros Chibvongodze shrugged wearily when I asked where everyone was.

"It has been like this for weeks, Sir. I spend my time polishing glasses and the maids and kitchen staff clean and polish until they are fed up with it. Unfortunately, we have few guests to appreciate our nice clean hotel and if this goes on, soon we will have no hotel anyway."

On my second cold beer, I broached the subject of politics and the farm invasions. After casting a quick glance over his shoulder at the man behind the reception desk, Apros was openly belligerent.

"I don't know who will win the next election," he answered my question. "But if Zanu PF remains in power, there will definitely be violence afterwards and this time, Zimbabweans are ready to fight. We have had enough of corruption and want power for the people. If that means *hondo*, then so be it. We are ready and we will die if we have to. The farmers and their people will back us, I'm sure of that."

Apart from a few gung-ho Harare whites talking about fighting their way to the border, Apros was the first person I had met who felt that violence was inevitable. In general, Zimbabweans are peaceful souls, but here was one man who had definitely had enough of the status quo. Still doubtful, I pointed out that the farmers – apart from Martin Olds – had shown little inclination to fight so far.

"Mugabe is clever," Apros went on. "He keeps the people hungry and frightened so that their will to resist is quickly broken. Take me for example; I am one of the lucky ones with a regular job, but my parents and my brothers live in the communal lands. They are starving and rely on me to keep them fed, but nowadays, I cannot find the food even if I have the money to pay for it. I have the energy to fight but in normal times, the ordinary people are too weak and brow beaten. Next time though, they will be desperate and that is when blood will flow."

I mentioned the forecourt shop at Brondesbury and he grinned without humour.

"That hotel has recently been taken over by one of the Zanu PF chefs," he told me, casting yet another glance at the apparently bored receptionist. "I don't know what his position is, but he has good connections, which is why he is able to get mealie meal.

'It gives Mugabe yet another lever to use on the *povo* who have to support him and buy party cards or starve. It is not fair, but when has Mugabe or his party done anything that was fair or straightforward?"

It was a rhetorical question and I left a healthy tip on the counter when I took my leave. Apros thanked me gravely and his eyes were twinkling as he bade me farewell.

"Be careful, Sir," he admonished. "You ask too many questions and with a white skin, that is dangerous in Zimbabwe. You must hide your camera too."

I had been carrying an ordinary family video camera, thinking that it was something that any tourist would have, but not according to Apros.

"If the Youth Wing stop you and see that, you will be beaten and the camera will be stolen or smashed up.

'Please be careful, Sir.'"

Assuring Apros that I would, I left Troutbeck, feeling a little like a passenger, who had been allowed a free lift off the Titanic as it sank. I soon cheered up however. I was on my way back into the mountains to see one of my oldest friends.

* * *

She didn't want me to write about her but is an integral part of my story, so I will call her Mary Jane. She has been a close friend of mine for over thirty years and our reunion was as fondly boisterous as ever. Well into her seventies and not in the best of health, Mary Jane nevertheless carried her age well and when I enveloped her tiny body in a fond bear hug, it was wonderful to hear her bar room laugh ringing through the wild, mountain countryside.

Mary Jane's home in the Nyanga foothills consisted of two thatched *rondavels*, one of which served as living area with a lounge, bedroom, bathroom and kitchen, while the other was her own *en suite* bedroom. It was all very rustic and in happier times, was often let out to holidaymakers or tourists, keen to sample the joys of Zimbabwe mountain life, but when I visited, all was very quiet.

For me, the finest part of Mary Jane's little homestead was the garden and the view. Walking down from the front step that first afternoon, I enjoyed the feel of rough grass under my feet, while I looked down a long, wide valley, bordered by towering hills and crags. It seemed as though we were alone in the world, yet less than a hundred metres away were other houses, other people. Truly, it is a magical part of my wonderful country and I breathed in that clear mountain air with a feeling that I could work well in this enchanted place.

Back in the house, Mary Jane made me smile in gleeful anticipation.

"Do you want a nice story to send back?" She asked quizzically. "You must be fed up with tales of woe and disaster."

In truth I was. I had only been in the country a week, but continual stories of hardship and violence were beginning to wear me down. Agreeing eagerly to her plans for the rest of the day, I was soon loaded into the passenger seat of her little white pick up and off we went along an abominably dusty road to meet new friends.

Take a widowed Harare businesswoman and a computer development officer from Exeter University, put them in one of the loveliest valleys in Africa and you have a real-life version of Tom and Barbara Goode in that television comedy, 'The Good Life.'

Gill and Rob Ashmore were farming thirty acres in the spectacularly beautiful Cumberland Valley, set deep in the foothills of Nyanga and Mary Jane had already told me that not only had they sunk all their capital into the place, but that they were totally self sufficient. As we pulled up outside a large, thatched homestead, I wondered what I was going to find. How could anyone be completely self-reliant in the twenty-first century? What about things like cooking oil and butter? Surely stores and supermarkets were needed for everyday items.

Rob Ashmore proved to be a burly, bearded man who still had a broad Devonian accent, while Gill was an elegantly pretty blonde who looked anything but the outdoor type. Their home was big and sprawling and after exclaiming over the view from their lounge, I accepted a cold beer and made myself comfortable. My doubts about the proposed story were growing. These folk were obviously 'townies' and I could not imagine either of them looking out for themselves. From computers to compost, and boardroom to bush life seemed a bit of a tall order to me.

After five minutes of ritual small talk, I asked the Ashmores to tell me their story.

"We have been here about three years now," Rob was obviously enthusiastic about the place and my sense of cynicism increased. "I can hardly remember what life was like in my previous existence. Exeter seems a million miles away and the university might well have been on Mars.

'Of course, only half the land here is workable," he went on. "The rest is made up of steep-sided hills and rocks, where we can't grow anything and even the livestock can't feed. Nevertheless, we do what we can with our workable fifteen acres and I don't think we have done too badly so far."

He went on to tell me about their enterprise and as my ready cynicism waned, I came to think that his comment about not doing too badly was a considerable understatement. On what for Zimbabwe was a tiny plot of land, Rob and Gill were raising pigs, chickens, sheep, rabbits and goats. With a staff of four, they also grew maize, wheat, soya, fruit, sunflowers and vegetables, had fish in a small dam and spent a great deal of time in trying to keep livestock out of the vegetables. They made their own wine from the grapes and although I am no connoisseur, we had some with supper and it tasted pretty good to me.

"We also make our own beer," Rob said proudly. "If I could find barley in this country, I might even try my hand at whisky."

"We hadn't intended farming originally," Gill chipped in with a mischievous grin. "I owned the plot next door and with my life pretty much at a loose end after the death of my husband, I went overseas where I met Rob. One thing led to another and he came to Zimbabwe on holiday the following year. I brought him up here and after one look, he suggested that we buy this plot, because it already had a house on it. At that stage, we hadn't looked at the house – it turned out to be an awful mess - but it was an extra fifteen acres to play with, so Rob sold everything in England and we somehow drifted into breeding chickens. From there, things developed and we moved into rabbits, then goats, sheep and now pigs. After only three years, we feed most of the neighbourhood and people come from miles around to buy our produce. Although we don't make much money, we have a pretty good turn over and it really is fun."

Although glamorous in the extreme and looking very much a city lady, I could see the enthusiasm bubbling over in Gill's eyes and couldn't help smiling inwardly as she spoke. Born and bred a Zimbabwean, the spirit of the pioneers obviously still beat deep within this lady's frame and I could not help but admire her enthusiasm for everything, she and Rob were trying to do.

"We try to produce absolutely everything ourselves," she went on earnestly. "Our dairy products come from the goats and I make our own jam. We bake bread from the wheat we grow and everything seems to taste that much better when it is from our own stock or we have made it ourselves."

And cooking oil – surely I had them there? Gill smiled and I knew that I had lost.

"We have tried pressing sunflower seeds, but it is a laborious process, so if we need oil, I strain some of the goats butter. It leaves a bit of an after taste, but is not too bad."

At the inevitable question about war vets and squatters, Gill laughed mischievously. The story she proceeded to tell was pure Rider Haggard and could only have happened in Zimbabwe.

"Some years ago," she waved her glass at me. "I worked at the Sheraton Hotel in Harare with a chap I only knew as Gono. My daughter Vicky married a young hunter called Allan Moodie and not so long ago, they were working in the Lowveld, (South Eastern Zimbabwe) when they came up against a local war vet leader, calling himself Black Jesus. This was Gono himself and he recognised Vicky. After asking how I was, he gave her his phone number with the instruction that if ever any of us needed help, to ring him and he would provide. Poor Rob had only been out here a short while when he fired one of the staff and was promptly confronted by an excited mob of these so-called war vets.

'Before he quite knew what was happening, he was pinned against a wall, so he yelled at our cook to 'go and see the Madam and tell her to ring Black Jesus.'

'The effect was almost miraculous. His attackers moved back and after regarding him with considerable suspicion, asked whether he really did know Black Jesus."

"I was pretty relieved," it was Rob's turn to cut in. "and when they asked this damn fool question, I assured them that Gill was a personal friend of the Great Man and that they should watch their steps. The whole lot of them promptly moved off and since they have ascertained that we really do know this bloke, we haven't had any trouble at all."

With much of their produce, the Ashmores ran a barter system, taking eggs or chickens down to a neighbour in exchange for vegetables, or importing mangoes from other farms on condition that a few of them were returned in the form of chutney. Rabbits were popular with the local population and there was always a queue of prospective customers waiting to buy or barter for something that they had raised.

"I get very angry about the current situation," Gill said fiercely, when the dinner talk inevitably came around to politics. "When our neighbours had serious problems on their farm, I wanted to ring Tony Blair and ask him what he intended to do about it. After all, Rob and many other Zimbabweans have paid a great deal of tax in Britain, so why shouldn't we be entitled to a little protection from their spineless government. Anyway, Blair was away in Mexico, but I eventually got through to the Foreign and Commonwealth office in London. I asked for Baroness Amos, but was inevitably fobbed off, although eventually, I was put through to one of her aides, called Jane Fidnall.

'I was pretty overwrought at the time and told her that folk in Zimbabwe were desperate. I said that we were crying out for some sort of help and promptly burst into tears, but that didn't phase the woman. She listened quite sympathetically to my moans, but while I was speaking to her, Rob came around the corner, carrying the first pig he had ever slaughtered. Tears were streaming down his face as well and I had to hang up on the lady without explanation, so I don't know what she thinks about Zimbabweans now."

"I wasn't made for the killing bit," Rob affirmed. "I had to fortify myself with a few whiskies first. Our abattoir consists of a water drum, a hook for hanging the carcasses and a few bits of rag for cleaning up so it can get awfully messy, but it was the shock of having to kill something that I had reared from a tiny baby that nearly did for me. You'd never believe I was a vegetarian for ten years, would you? I am better at the killing process now, but that first one...."

He left the sentence unfinished as if to emphasise the horror, but I was still smiling at Gill's story. Almost hesitantly, I asked for details about butchering their stock and Gill laughed uproariously.

"I do most of it," she told me. "Rob is too much of a wimp, but he has to kill them. We started off with a book called The Complete Book of Self Sufficiency that we bought in Britain. It was written 'for realists and dreamers' by a chap called John Seymour and it gives step-by-step instructions for cutting anything up. Of course, it is aimed at an English readership, but we have adapted it for our own needs. It was all terribly messy at first, but we are definitely getting better at it and I've even got to the stage of packaging individual cuts of meat before I sell them."

Messy or not, the Ashmores had developed their little butchery into a thriving business and they used absolutely everything in a carcass. Nothing was wasted. Even stomach contents went to feed the chickens and Gill made superbly spicy sausages with bits and pieces in her kitchen.

"We call them Cumberland Valley sausages," she smiled, "and I reckon they are every bit as tasty as the real thing."

Among their white neighbours, the Ashmores were looked upon as mildly eccentric, while local blacks regarded them as saviours of the people. In those times of desperate shortage, their produce kept everyone going and their reputation for good works was enhanced when a maid gave birth to a daughter in the back of Rob's brand new car.

"We couldn't reach the hospital in time," Gill explained. "The only lights I could find were outside the casino at Montclair Hotel, so I pulled into the car park and that is where the birth took place. It didn't do much for Rob's nice new upholstery, but after killing chickens, pigs, goats and rabbits, it was nice to bring a life into the world for a change."

At a time when so much was going wrong in Zimbabwe and so many people were leaving the country, it was refreshing to meet a couple who were doing something to help themselves and had actually invested in the land instead of sending their money out. As we drove back to Mary Jane's house in the starlit darkness, I felt a sudden sense that all was not really lost in my tormented little country. With people like Gill and Rob Ashmore around, Zimbabwe will always be – if nothing else – an incredibly interesting place to live.

* * *

My evening with the Ashmores had been a magical interlude in my journey, but the following morning, I was back to earth with a bump. My first visit was to Richard and Ann Lamb, who ran a fruit farm on the edge of a communal land. This would have worried me, but Richard was adamant that it was the best place to be.

"I employ a number of people from the reserve," he told me over coffee and homemade biscuits, "and when there is casual work to be done, I send word into the communal land and they come running. The local chief knows that I do a lot for his people and if the war vets were to descend upon this place, they would have him to deal with first."

Richard and Ann had farmed in the same area throughout the bush war and he smiled tightly at the memories.

"All my neighbours moved out, but we were determined to see it through. Our packing sheds were burned down and one day when we were packing fruit in the open, there was a battle just over the border of the communal land. Helicopters were flying low overhead and bullets were flying every which way, but we carried on with what we were doing and nobody was hurt. After surviving that sort of nonsense, Mugabe's war vets are not really too frightening."

A slender man in his middle seventies, Richard had the stern visage and washed eyes that seem so typical of Zimbabwe farmers. He spoke slowly and chose his words carefully, but every one was delivered with the quiet confidence of a man who knew exactly who he was and what he was doing. Ann was a little round lady with abundant good humour and I enjoyed the couple of hours I spent in their lovely, sprawling homestead.

"We built it from an old shed," Ann told me on the way out to the Ganja Bus. "It was hard work, but we have put our lives into this farm and do not want to leave. If only there were more folk around like you who are prepared to tell the world what we are going through."

It was a sentiment I was beginning to grow accustomed to as I travelled around the country. Zimbabweans – both black and white – seemed pathetically grateful that somebody was actually interested enough in their troubles to listen to what they had to say. At times, it made me feel an awful fraud, because I knew that little of what I wrote would actually be published, but at the same time, it was heart warming to think that I was helping these folk, even if only by listening to their woes.

Walking through the shady garden, Ann pulled me to one side. She was a Christian Scientist and earnestly explained that the only way out of Zimbabwe's predicament was through the power of prayer. Having long lost most of my belief in religion, I was not overly convinced, but when she put her hands on my arms and exhorted me to 'pray with all my heart,' I was lost. She really was a sweet lady and I did not want to disappoint her.

"I will try, Ann Dear," I told her a little reluctantly. "But I do not really believe any more."

"That doesn't matter," she said firmly. "The more people who pray to the Lord now, the more chance we have of getting out from this mess we are in."

Approaching the Ganja Bus, I shook hands with Richard and thanked him for his hospitality as well as the box of peaches, he had pressed upon me.

"Come back again," He said gravely and I promised that I would, although I did not think that promise would be kept. Turning to Ann, I gave her a peck on the cheek, but she wasn't having that.

"Kiss me properly," she commanded and throwing her arms around my neck, gave me a big kiss on the mouth. It was lovely, but surely God would not approve of her kissing a complete stranger so intimately?

"Oh yes He will," she chuckled. "God looks after us all the time and he told me to kiss you like that, so it has to be right."

"Thank you, God," I murmured as I drove away and felt sure that my memories of a brave and lovely couple would stay with me for a very long time. The Lambs of Juliasdale were the sort of people who typified Zimbabwe farming stock.

When I visited them again a year later, they were living with neighbours, having lost their farm. Surrounded by packing cases, Richard looked drawn and old.

"We will join our children in South Africa, I suppose," Even his voice had lost its strength. "I don't know how we will manage but perhaps something will crop up."

The difference in Ann was even more marked. The lovely, bubbly lady I remembered had changed into a gaunt, silent woman with haunted eyes. She had lost everything and to me, she seemed to be a dead woman walking. I took her in my arms – no objective journalist me – and was horrified to feel her shoulder blades prominent through the back of her dress.

My heart was breaking when I left that wonderful couple for the last time. They seemed to symbolise all the madness and horror that was taking place in my beloved country.

* * *

Allan Langan was another displaced farmer living in the Nyanga foothills. At first, his story sounded like all the other Zimbabwe farming stories I had heard over preceding weeks. His farm had been occupied by squatters, calling themselves war vets. Initially there had been little trouble, then the original invaders had moved or been moved away and the situation deteriorated rapidly.

Allan and his lovely wife, Ann had both been born and bred in Shamva and at the time things had fallen apart, they had been running two farms as a family concern.

"I left my son in charge," heavily built and appearing always on the verge of laughter, Allan told the story over cold beer, "while I came up here for an early retirement. At first, he used to send me money, but then he was no longer allowed to farm, so he moved into town and now, nearly five thousand acres of prime farming land is going to waste.

"Do you remember," he went on slowly, "when the world ploughing championships were held at Harare South Country Club in 1981?"

I did not, but motioned with my glass for Allan to go on with his story.

"Well, the chief comrade, Bobby Mugabe came along to pay us a visit and I spoke with him in the bar. He was only Prime Minister then and very affable. I can remember him saying to me, 'You know, Mr Langan, this country needs you commercial farmers. Agriculture has always been the backbone of Zimbabwe and without you, the economy will collapse.'"

Shaking his head in baffled wonderment, Allan stared into his glass for a moment before continuing.

"Now here we are, twenty odd years later, Mugabe is still in power, my farm is abandoned and producing nothing, while I live in the mountains on twenty-five acres of useless land that I am scared will be occupied by these bloody war vets any day now. 'Section eights' (orders giving farmers thirty days to leave their farms) 'have been served on most of our neighbours and we will surely be next. My land is all mountainside and rock, but these blokes don't seem to care whether it is workable or not. They think that if they have land, they can be farmers."

It certainly seemed that the land resettlement scheme was being extended to take in mountain plots like Langan's twenty-five acres and for most Nyanga residents, this seemed like the beginning of the end.

"After this, then what?" Allan asked helplessly. "Will they start taking over suburban gardens in the city? Will they settle on land belonging to schools and hospitals or is Mugabe only trying to drive the whites out of this country?"

These were all unanswerable questions, but just before I left Nyanga, Ralph and Tanny Barret did a little to restore my faith in the strength of beleaguered Zimbabweans.

"We are not moving," Ralph told me firmly. "Times are difficult and trying to bring our children up in this atmosphere of uncertainty is stressful, but we will hang on. We tried a new life in Australia during the nineties, but six months later we were back with our tails between our legs. It wasn't that Oz was so bad, it was just that it wasn't a bit like home and the people were not as nice as Zimbabweans.

'Whatever happens over the next few weeks, this is still the best place in the world for all of us."

A few other Nyanga residents were equally confident and MDC signs were painted over trees, in the road and on the many rocks that bordered the highway. Most of the pedestrians I passed gave me the open-handed wave, even though for many of them, the period leading up to the next election promised to be a worrying one. They all seemed convinced that Tsvangirai would win, but I was beginning to have my doubts. As far as I could see, there were too many powerful people hanging on to Mugabe's coat tails and if he went, they would lose everything. That might have been regarded as par for the course with politicians in the Western world, but in Africa, I could not see it happening. In my heart, I felt sure that contingency plans would have been made and that Mugabe would retain power, whatever the voters of Zimbabwe might say.

It was with a heavy heart and a feeling of deep foreboding that I said goodbye to Mary Jane and took the long winding road back to the city. I had promised to return, but at the time, I had no inkling of the troubles that would bring me back again and again.

Chapter Five

(Another Needless Killing)

Terry Ford was dead. He had been the first farmer I interviewed in my role as a wandering journalist and his death hit me hard. My report on the original interview had been 'spiked' by my editor as not being particularly newsworthy, but with his death all that changed and I was inundated by emails, phone calls and texts from Phil McNeill.

"We need more details," he told me and I forbore from pointing out that he hadn't wanted to know while the Norton farmer was still alive. "I want pictures, quotes and something about his dog. Apparently it went everywhere with him."

Subsequent reports in the British media harped on about Ford's little terrier and its devotion, but it certainly had not been with him at our original interview. Nevertheless, I set out to discover what I could.

At seven o'clock one Sunday evening, Terry had appealed for help on the Norton farm radio network, saying that the war vets and their supporters were breaking up his sheds, chanting *chimurenga* songs and threatening to kill him. Zimbabwe farmers are quick to respond to such appeals, because they know only too well that they might find themselves in a similar situation. A neighbour immediately offered to take Terry in for the night, but he declined, saying that he would try and sort things out himself.

For four hours, Terry Ford endured the tormenting of those who had already taken over his farm and cost him his livelihood. He did not fight back because he was not that sort of man and in any case, he had nothing to fight with even though police reports later described his death being as 'the result of a gun fight.'

Eventually realising that the situation was deteriorating, Ford climbed into his truck and tried to escape from the farm that had been his home all his life. He did not make it. The war veterans or squatters or illegal settlers – call them what you will – dragged him from the vehicle, tied him to a tree and bludgeoned him to death. One can only imagine the fear and despair of this simple, kindly man as he faced brutal death in the dark at the hands of callous thugs.

The day after Ford's murder, Norton police reported that three men had been arrested for the killing, but eight other white farmers had already been murdered in Zimbabwe over the previous two years and nobody had been brought to book for their deaths. There was little reason to believe that Terry Ford's case would be any different. The men who killed him – if indeed they were the ones in custody – would be quietly released or perhaps pardoned in yet another presidential amnesty. White farmers were fair game in Zimbabwe and it was one of the ironies of this particular case that in spite of Robert Mugabe's oft repeated claims that land was being seized for the peasants who had none, Terry Ford's three hundred and fifty hectare property was being claimed by a former Army colonel. This man already owned businesses in Harare and had two fine houses in the city suburbs, so he was hardly of peasant stock.

For him at least, the minor obstacle of having an owner in residence on the farm that he wanted for himself had been removed. Any arrests made would be politically expedient and would not help Terry Ford or do anything for the image of a country that was rapidly descending into anarchy.

At the time of Terry Ford's death, violence was spreading through the farming areas. I had reported on some of it. Friends of mine, Iain and Kerry Kay had been chased off their Marondera farm, John Rutherford was beaten to a pulp in mistake for a neighbour, while his security guard was killed;

two elderly ladies were being held hostage in Hwedza and in Chinhoyi and Doma, farms were being trashed by mindless youths, bent on destruction. Killings were becoming ever more commonplace and while blacks were more often victims than whites, it was not the colour of Terry Ford's skin that made his murder so poignant for me. I remembered only too well his animation as he talked about his beloved Gowrie Farm and I remembered his obvious distress when he told me how his lorry driver had been beaten the previous day. Terry was a nice man and did not deserve the fate that was dealt out to him.

There were many others like Terry Ford in Zimbabwe and as I wandered among the farms and listened to their stories, my heart burned with anger at the politicians of the western world and even in other African states who could see for themselves and ought to have been only too well aware what was going on.

Thabo Mbeki and General Obasanjo, the leaders of South Africa and Nigeria respectively were paying a brief visit to Zimbabwe when Ford was murdered, but I don't suppose they were told about this latest act of violence. Even if they were, I knew that it would not make the slightest difference to their claims that everything was going well in my tormented little country. Their reports later reflected a picture of good governance and peaceful stability in the country so that - like Terry Ford - Zimbabwe and her people would be left to fend for themselves in their hour of greatest need.

* * *

They came from all over the country. All ages colours and stratas of Zimbabwe society flocked into Highlands Presbyterian Church to pay their last respects to Terry Ford. Ruddy-faced farmers sat beside besuited city businessmen, farm workers in patched clothing were cheek by jowl with matrons dressed in all their finery and babies vied with octogenarians for attention. Former Prime Minister Ian Smith was helped up the aisle by a friend and I was horrified to see how old and frail he looked. This was the man who had defied the world and who had been correct all along about the evil of Mugabe. I couldn't help wondering whether anyone had ever thought of apologising to him.

Also present was the old Jack Russell terrier, which had been pictured so often beside Terry Ford's dead body in the British media. The article I had done for my own newspaper had the dog as its main picture even though I had never seen the animal. The terrier, apparently known as Squeak obviously had no idea as to the solemnity of the occasion however, as it wriggled and yapped through the service, eventually having to be carried out half way through.

The church was packed far beyond its capacity, but faces were grim and unsmiling as people contemplated the fate dealt out to a man who had done nothing wrong but to live on a farm that had been in his family for three generations.

Four days after Ford's murder, police spokesman, Assistant Commissioner Wayne Bvudzijena gave the official line to waiting journalists.

"There are some household items missing from the farmhouse and this seems to suggest that the crime was criminal rather than political." Bvudzijena said glibly, but Zimbabweans knew only too well that this was a long way from the truth. Not only was Terry Ford under siege from war veterans and squatters for months, but many of them had been or were in the same situation and it was only through chance and good luck that more had not suffered the same fate as the Norton farmer.

My friend, David Bradshaw was in sombre mood when I spoke with him in his office.

"Over the past three weeks," he told me. "Eight of my sixty-five tenant farmers have been beaten up by squatters, four of those were hospitalised and two were put straight into intensive care wards – one of them for five days."

It was a horrifying statistic and one that was backed up by the Commercial Farmers' Union who stated that fifty farmers had been driven off their properties in a matter of days. The violence of the land resettlement programme had increased dramatically and I could only marvel at the courage and fortitude shown by those who remained on their farms. They were in constant danger, their families were being traumatised and they had no guarantee that they would be able to make a living from the land in years to come. None of them knew if they would even be allowed to keep what was rightfully theirs and this must have been a terrible way to live.

"I will plant seedbeds and do the land prep," Brett Rowlands told me. "However, I have no intention of planting a crop till we get some assurance from the government that we will be allowed to continue farming."

Brett was another one who had fallen foul of the squatters since Terry Ford died and it was not even on his own farm.

"I went to help my neighbour," he said simply. "He had been under siege for three days and yesterday morning, his wife came on the radio, pleading for help. She said that their ten year old was traumatised and screaming. I crept through the bush and managed to get into their house without being seen, but when I saw my neighbour being pushed around by these people, I had to do something."

What Brett did was attempt to stop the manhandling of his neighbour, but it resulted in him being seized, handcuffed, stripped of most of his clothing and pushed down on to the floor of the barn.

"I was bloody terrified," he admitted. "There were about twenty of them and they accused me of bringing a bomb across and placing it in the house. They didn't beat me, but there were lots of threats and waving of sticks. It only needed one of them to start hitting me and I would have been badly hurt. All I could do was keep talking and eventually five of them took me off into the bush, where they discussed what to do with me. I told them that I was a Zanu PF supporter, as were all my farm labour and eventually they changed their attitude completely and let me go."

Brett was incredibly lucky and he knew it. I couldn't help thinking back to my interview with Terry Ford.

"I don't have a weapon in the house," Norton police claimed to have confiscated a .22 pistol 'belonging to the deceased' and a neighbour stated that Ford fired shots in the air to scare the intruders away. I didn't believe either story. "I don't want one," Terry had said. "I only hope that I can talk my way out if things get bad. The trouble is that these blokes have made my life a misery for so long now that I am at my wits end and there is nobody I can turn to for help."

Those were the words of a peaceful man, but he was right. There was nobody he could turn to and so he died alone. Looking around at the mourners attending his funeral, I wondered how long Zimbabweans would be expected to hold their feelings in check and keep talking their way out of trouble when threatened and harassed by government-sponsored squatters on their land. Brett Rowlands and his neighbour's farm were in Trelawney, but even as we sat in Church and listened to tributes paid to the murdered Terry Ford, other household sieges and assaults on farmers and their staff were being reported from Marondera, Hwedza, Ruzawi River, Banket, Chinhoyi, Mhangura and Chivhu. That was only in Mashonaland and I could only wonder how many more were taking place in other provinces of this vast, farming country. Zimbabwean farmers have always been a tremendously brave bunch of men and women, but they could only take so much. Surely someone would snap and fight back before the situation brought the entire country to its knees. Despite having spoken with farmers throughout the province, I still could not understand their meek acceptance of the status quo.

Mugabe's thugs were deliberately trying to scare them off their land and already, there were murmurings from many about emigration. If these people were to leave the country, there would be no food crop for many years and a crippling famine would be inevitable. It was a difficult prospect to accept.

The last hymn of Terry Ford's funeral service was 'Our Zimbabwe,' a song written by local Test cricketer Henry

Olonga. As the congregation swayed and hummed to the tune, I couldn't help wondering how soon it would be before they were gathered together again, in order to mourn the passing of yet another of their number. I didn't think Terry Ford would be the last farmer to die.

As the congregation moved quietly out of the church, I followed the lean, stooped figure of Ian Smith into the car park. Stopping beside an elderly Mercedes, he turned to me and there was a familiar glint in those grey/brown eyes.

"How are you Sir?" I ventured. Smith was the one person in the world I still addressed as 'Sir.'

"Creaking a bit but determined to outlive that gangster Mugabe," he told me fiercely. "This country is being run entirely by bandits and they will not be happy until we have all gone."

At my gentle question, he shook his head emphatically.

"No, the average Zimbabwean of whatever colour is a sensible bloke and knows where his food is coming from. It is only Mugabe and his thugs causing all this trouble. The British could have prevented it, but they were too lily-livered for that."

I tried not to smile at this pithy comment on Perfidious Albion. Smithy's views on the Mother Country obviously hadn't changed over the years.

"This country is my home," He added as he started the car. "If Mugabe's bandits want to be rid of me, they will have to carry me out. You take care hey. Keep that notebook hidden. We don't want to be reading about you next."

I was aghast. How did he know what I was doing? It was supposed to be a well-kept secret, but in the close confines of white Zimbabwean society, I suppose it was inevitable that word would get around and Smithy and I shared quite a few friends and acquaintances in common. He smiled at the look on my face.

"Just be careful Boy." Was his advice and he drove out of the car park, waving back to the crowd, all of whom had broken off their conversations to wave farewell to the former leader.

It seemed that the man who had been known as 'Good Old Smithy' in the days of Rhodesia was still 'Good Old Smithy' to most citizens of the country he loved.

Ian Douglas Smith is dead now and never did manage to outlive Mugabe, but on the few occasions I spoke with him, he left a lasting impression. History will not be kind to him or his policies, but like so many others, I would have followed him anywhere and among Zimbabweans of every colour, he will always be fondly remembered as an honest politician, a man of principal and a leader who was not afraid to take on the world.

He was also a Zimbabwean farmer and although they left him alone at first, it was inevitable that eventually, his beloved Gwenhoro Farm in Shurugwe would also be occupied and in time, abandoned to people who did not know what to do with it.

* * *

While white commercial farmers of Zimbabwe were enduring invasions, loss of their homes and livelihoods and in some cases, death at the hands of ruthless militiamen, it was the farm workers themselves who were really in trouble. The majority of them were uneducated and unemployable in other professions, but they worked hard and were a huge part of Zimbabwean agriculture. Most of them lived with their wives and families on the farms and at times of the year when extra labour was needed, these wives and children would be employed on a part time basis. They were not well paid by international standards but they were fed and in many cases educated by their employers. They were transported to hospital and treated when necessary by the farmers or their wives and even buried on the farms in which most of them had spent their lives. Farmers would provide beer for the men on weekends and in general, most farm labour forces were a big, happy family, their welfare discreetly overseen by their employers.

With the invasions and the closing down of farming operations, their lives had been destroyed and suddenly there were two hundred thousand of them unemployed and with no future at all. They worked for the white man, so in the eyes of Zanu PF they were traitors and beneath contempt.

A study carried out by the Farm Orphan Support Trust of Zimbabwe (FOST) showed that by the year 2002, two hundred and fifty thousand families had been left vulnerable to poverty and general abuse. Lynn Walker, the Executive Director of FOST told me that eighty-two percent of households surveyed by her organisation indicated that they had always relied on farm wages for their food, security and other needs.

"The loss of income has severely hampered the ability of many households to support their children and fewer extended families are taking in orphaned children, as has always been the custom among rural people," she said.

Ms Walker estimated that in 2002 there were more than one hundred and fifty thousand orphaned children in former commercial farming areas throughout the country. She went on to point out that female children were particularly vulnerable to general abuse and transactional sex. I had seen this for myself in urban centres where prostitutes of fourteen years or less were plying their trade on every street corner. In the farmlands, they would merely be passed from household to household in order to do menial work and provide sex for the men folk.

"Where the household is headed by a girl, she will often resort to early marriage in an attempt to support herself and her siblings," said Ms Walker. "FOST knows of many households where children have engaged in transactional sex in order to obtain food and other needs.

'Previously, households such as these would have been supported by the farmer, who would have provided shelter, health facilities and education as well as financial security. Work would be found for older household members and for children during the school holidays to enable them to support themselves. These options are no longer available."

Lynn Walker went on to give me some horrifying statistics. According to figures released by her organisation, there was an average of one orphaned child on every farm in the country in 1995. In 2001 when the farm invasions were beginning to hurt the agricultural sector, the figure rose sharply to twelve orphans per farm and by 2002, the figure was a horrific seventeen. It got worse. In 2005, there were on average, twenty-five orphaned children per farm throughout the country and the figure kept rising. I was supposed to be a detached journalist, but I couldn't help wondering how the world could sit by and watch this carnage taking place.

The FOST study also reported that seventy-two percent of vulnerable households in farming areas were headed by women, ten percent by orphans and nearly thirty percent of schoolchildren were no longer receiving any education.

There will never be official figures available for the number of farm workers displaced during Mugabe's violent land grab, but from the people I spoke with, I can only estimate the number as being in excess of half a million. Most of the incoming settlers could not afford to accommodate the workers on farms they took over from white owners, so living quarters as well as livelihoods were lost by the workers. Many who resisted the land reform exercise were accused of siding with the whites and were forcibly evicted from their homes and left destitute.

Wherever I went, I saw them sitting in small clusters by roadsides, their eyes blank as they waited for they knew not what to happen. Many of them had their life possessions scattered around them and despite my efforts to remain detached from the situation, I felt a sense of deep sorrow, as well as acute anger toward those unfeeling politicians who had forced them into lifelong penury and probably early death.

To me it seemed ironic that although the land reform exercise was aimed at ousting white farmers from their properties, the majority of those whites soon made new careers or started farming elsewhere in the world. Their workers were not able to leave their homeland and so, despite their black skins became the main victims of President Mugabe's blatantly racist policies.

Some of them also suffered from extreme violence at the hands of marauding farm invaders.

*　　*　　*

The township of Mbare is a place of contrasts. A city in its own right, it sprawls untidily adjacent to the Southern sector of Harare and in fact, was the original Harare when the city itself was Salisbury.

There are some fine buildings in Mbare. It is the home of magnificent Rufaro Stadium where the Zimbabwe flag was first raised at midnight on 18th April 1980. The old police station is built in spacious colonial style and the local hospital once had far more in the way of equipment than the more modern Parirenyatwa hospital in The Avenues. In the more secluded corners of the township, large houses shelter behind leafy gardens and testify to the presence of hardy folk who have done well financially, but see no need to move into the more affluent suburbs. For them, the old township has always been home and home it will remain.

There are also some pretty squalid areas of Mbare and as I drove past the walls of Rufaro, my nose wrinkled at the overpowering smell of sewers. Blocks of flats – originally built for the single men and women of the township – had been allowed to decay and the question of sanitation was obviously not high on the priority list of the local authority. The roads were deeply potholed and small, box-like houses on either side of the main thoroughfare were devoid of paint or ornament. In the western world, places like this would be looked upon as terrible slums, but only a short distance away from these dingy streets is 'shanty town'- a genuine slum where families huddle in makeshift shelters and single people make do with a piece of cardboard or plastic. There is no sewerage system at all and the water supply for a couple of thousand people often comes from just one tap. Shanty Town at Mbare is no place for the faint hearted, but it was there that I had tea with Phineas Chifaka.

Phineas used a homemade crutch to walk with and I had spotted him hobbling along Samora Machel Avenue one hot and sticky morning. I was back in the country to cover a forthcoming election and needed something for my weekly story. When I offered Phineas a lift, he looked amazed, then doubtful, then finally very pleased.

"If you are sure, Sir," He hauled himself laboriously up into the front of the Ganja Bus. "I live close to Mbare, but you can drop me somewhere near."

"Nonsense; I will take you home and you can tell me about yourself on the way."

I didn't know what I was letting myself in for, but I was keen to speak with as many ordinary Zimbabweans as I could and I didn't think they came more ordinary than my new passenger. I studied him as I drove.

I always find it difficult to estimate age, particularly in Africa, but I put Phineas at about fifty-five. His sparse hair was very grey and there were deep lines on his face, but – apart from the injured leg - his demeanour was that of a much younger man. His eyes sparkled with interest as he examined the furnishings of my vehicle and he willingly answered my questions.

"I come from Hwedza, Sir. I was educated at Mount St Mary's mission and I am an agricultural worker. At least I was until last year, when my life changed."

Phineas had been directing me as he spoke and as we moved into Shanty Town, I had a moment of misgiving. If anything went wrong here, I was in trouble. Not only would there be nobody to help me, but nobody knew where I was. For the first – but not the last – time in my life, I cursed myself for not carrying a mobile phone.

Phineas obviously saw the doubt on my face and kept urging me to drop him off, but I was eager to hear his story. I had played cricket for Hwedza in happier days and knew most of the district personalities. When Phineas indicated his home, I pulled up outside and stepped into the open air.

If I had been aware of the smell from the flats outside Rufaro Stadium, it was nothing compared to the stench that assailed my nostrils as I alighted from the Ganja Bus. It was foul – miasmic and almost primeval. Made up of raw sewage, sweat, wood smoke and a variety of cooking foodstuffs, it niggled at the nostrils and made breathing an unpleasant experience. To take my mind away from its horror, I studied my surroundings with interest.

The street in which I was standing was little more than a narrow gap between hopelessly cluttered buildings that had to be houses, although few of them would have been allowed as dog kennels in the Western world. Emaciated children played listlessly in oozing black mud and I shuddered to think what they were actually covering themselves with. There were none of the dogs – always painfully thin and cowering away from any human contact – that are usually to be seen in African townships. I wondered if they had all been eaten and from the sad air of deprivation that seemed to hang around me that seemed eminently possible.

My reverie was interrupted by my companion, desperately trying to get himself down from the high front seat of the Ganja Bus. Landing on the ground with an undignified thud, he hurried around to my side of the vehicle and welcomed me to his abode.

"Will you enter my house, Sir?"

His use of English grammar was inclined to be old fashioned, but the invitation was genuine and I smiled my thanks. In fact, the 'house' was no more than perhaps a dozen sheets of corrugated iron – rusted through in places and blackened with wood smoke. The roof was made from torn plastic sheeting and could not have kept a mouse dry when it rained. Yet for all its primitive and unsanitary appearance, efforts had obviously been made to keep the place clean and wooden boxes were scattered around the earth floor to act as makeshift chairs. Pictures of Rio de Janeiro had been torn from a calendar and made up the wall furnishings, while strips of coloured cloth had been placed over holes in the wall to act as curtains.

"Would you like to sit down, Sir?"

How often have we all heard that invitation? I have been invited into homes all over the world, but this was surely the most rudimentary hovel I have ever tried to make myself comfortable in. For all that, the invitation was given with such simple dignity that I could not have refused, even had I not been eager to hear the man's story.

A worried looking woman in a faded blue dress and a baby on her back had welcomed me to the house and when Phineas addressed her in Chishona that was too fast for me to follow, she curtsied and bowed her head as though I was a visiting dignitary. I moved across to shake her hand and she looked vaguely embarrassed by the gesture.

"This is my wife, Blessing, Sir. She is a good woman and we have three children. This one is Chipo and she is the youngest. Benade is playing with his friends and the eldest is with my mother in the reserve."

Five minutes later, I had done the ritual admiration bit with baby Chipo and found myself seated on a box opposite my host, who now that he was on home ground, had doubled in self-confidence. The drink I was offered had only a hint of the normal tea taste and it was luke-warm, but it came in a proper tin mug and was presented with another curtsy from Blessing that made it taste all the better. While her husband spoke to me, she was joined by a boy of about ten who I took to be Benade and they sat listening in one corner of the dingy room. When I glanced across at her in the middle of the story, I saw that her eyes were filled with tears, while the boy stared at me from two of the most enormous brown eyes I have ever seen.

"You say you were an agricultural worker, Phineas," I prompted. "Who did you work for?"

"I was working for Mr Edridge, Sir – Mr Tilden Edridge of Tilita Farm who died recently. Did you know of him?"

I did indeed. I had shared many a beer with Tilden and the rest of the Edridge clan over the years, but I motioned Phineas to continue.

"All was going well and I was good at reaping and grading the tobacco, so Mr Edridge told me that he would promote me soon. I enjoyed the job and my wife was working in the farm store, so we were making good money, but when we had the referendum last year, I was one of those who voted 'no.'"

I had already noticed that Phineas' injured limb had been broken and badly set at some time, giving him a permanent limp and a huge lump on one side of the lower leg. With an horrific sense of what was coming, I couldn't help looking at it again. He noticed my glance and smiled.

"We had war vets on the farm soon after the referendum and then the local Zanu PF officers came and asked us all which way we had voted. Many of my colleagues lied and claimed that they had been on the government side, but I am a good Catholic, Sir, so I told the truth. Five of them beat me and knocked most of my teeth out with a screwdriver. When I was unconscious, they held me down and smashed my leg with iron bars, but I was lucky because they didn't kill me. Some of my friends carried me away to a man who had a scotch cart and he took Blessing and I into the bush, where she looked after me for many months. We had to live like animals, but the war vets and Zanu PF had told me that they would kill us if we ever came back, so that was the way it was.

'Eventually, Mr Tilden heard that I was alive and he sent us money to come into town with our children. Unfortunately, there is no work for people like me and the money did not last long, so we came here, where at least we can stay dry when it rains."

I glanced doubtfully at the plastic above my head and Phineas laughed.

"Nearly dry, Sir – nearly dry."

"And Benade," I ventured. "Does he know what happened to you?"

"My family were made to watch my beating," This terrible reply was given in matter of fact tones and I wanted to cry. "Blessing and the children were all there to hear my cries and pleas for an end to my beating. These people of Mugabe's will not allow a man to remain a man and keep his pride. I do not think that my children will ever forget that day. Even the little one..."

He gestured toward the sleeping baby with a shrug of skinny shoulders.

"But what will you do now? How will you survive? What do you do for food?"

"I have friends, Sir and when they come into town, they bring fruit and vegetables, which we sell by the road. Blessing comes from the Mhondoro communal land near Beatrice, so she takes the bus home every week and brings things back to sell. We have enough to keep us alive and for that, we can only thank God.

'What I am worried about the most, Sir is the election for president."

"Why Phineas?"

The man had been deliberately crippled, lived in appalling circumstances and was on the verge of starvation, yet he was worried about an election? That did not make sense. He smiled at my incredulity.

"After all that has happened to us, my wife and I will obviously vote for Tsvangirai, but now we are told that we have no vote at all."

"But why not? Surely everyone has the right to vote?"

Phineas smiled again, but this time it was with sadness at my innocence.

"We are registered as living in Hwedza, Sir and are not allowed to vote anywhere else. I have made enquiries in Harare and Mbare – Msika, but if we want to vote, then we have to do it in Hwedza. I will try to get there, but I don't know about Blessing. If we both leave this place, someone else will move in and then we will have no home at all."

It seemed iniquitous to me and I suddenly realised that if farm workers were being shifted off the farms they worked on and moved elsewhere, they too would not be allowed to vote.

Perhaps this was another reason for the farm invasions – an ideal way to disenfranchise tens of thousands of voters.

Half an hour later, I made my farewells of the sad but lovely Chifaka family and Phineas' eyes twinkled as I pressed a folded bank note into Blessing's cupped hands. She curtsied sweetly again, then looked shocked at the size of my gift, but how was I to explain that to me, it was not much at all. Twenty thousand Zimbabwe dollars at that time was slightly more than two pounds sterling on the parallel market and I reckoned I could spare that? Their life was difficult enough and I just hoped it would give them some slight relief. As I stooped to leave the little house, I turned back to Phineas.

"How old are you, My Friend?"

He smiled again – a friendly, gap-toothed smile that denoted a truly nice man.

"I am twenty-eight, Sir."

It was too much for me. How was this horror being allowed to spread through my country and why was the rest of the world sitting back and doing nothing.

"Don't call me 'Sir.'" It was all I could think of to say and I drove away from that horrible little house far faster than I had come in.

*   *   *

Other than the fact that they are both Zimbabweans, there would appear to be little in common between Phineas Chifaka and an old friend of mine, Ray Deller. Ray has two houses and makes a good living cultivating granadillas on a smallholding outside Harare, while poor old Phineas – well I have told you how he lives. Nevertheless, both Phineas and Ray were effectively prevented from voting in the presidential election and there was nothing that either of them could do about it.

She was sixty-three when she told me her story, but Ray Deller had come to Zimbabwe from England over forty-five years previously. For a long time, she had dual nationality, but on 27th September 1996, she renounced her British passport and proudly proclaimed herself to be a true Zimbabwean. It was not good enough, even though she received a letter from the Zimbabwean Authorities on 7th October that same year, confirming what she had done and wishing her well.

"I did not feel that I had a choice," Ray told me angrily. "This is my country and I wanted to have a say in how it is run. I certainly wasn't sorry to renounce my British citizenship. The Brits have never done anything for me and anyway, I have held a Zimbabwean passport for years and always use that in preference to my British one."

Giving up her birthright for the country of her choice ought to have ensured that Ray had all the voting rights of any Zimbabwean, but the government of President Mugabe obviously worried about her political leanings. Perhaps their worries were because she was white. A few weeks before the Presidential election, my proud-to-be-Zimbabwean friend, Ray received a cyclostyled letter from the Registrar General's office informing her that she no longer had a vote and so was not entitled to a say in whether Robert Mugabe or Morgan Tsvangirai became president in future elections.

'You are not qualified for registration as a voter,' the form pronounced, 'on the grounds that you have in terms of schedule 3, section 3 (3) of the constitution of Zimbabwe, ceased to be a citizen of Zimbabwe.'

No further details were given and Ray was allowed seven days in which to appeal against the ruling, but she was distraught about the matter.

'Sure, I can appeal," she said tearfully, "but then what? They will take months to deal with my case and by the time it is sorted out, the election will be over and probably the one after that, so that is another vote against Mugabe lost. I shudder to think how many other folk are in the same boat."

Over succeeding weeks, I was to see that same cyclostyled letter again and again and hear from many distraught people how their own country was not allowing them their basic rights as citizens. Some appealed, some went to Court, but the end result was that none of them were allowed a say in the making of a president. Like Ray, I could only wonder how many votes were lost in this simply effective manner to Morgan Tsvangirai.

I don't know whether Phineas Chifaka managed to make his laboriously painful way back to Hwedza in order to cast his vote, but he and thousands of other displaced farm workers like him were also victims of a corrupt and devious electoral system.

Whatever else elections in Zimbabwe might be and no matter what hand-picked teams of international observers might say, they are never free and fair.

PART THREE

(Politics and its Victims)

Chapter Six

(Election Fever in Zimbabwe)

With his eighty-first birthday behind him, his country devastated and his party in disarray, President Mugabe obviously felt supremely confident of victory in the forthcoming general election.

He opened his election campaign with a blistering attack on Tony Blair and Condoleeza Rice, the new American secretary of state. In a ninety minute birthday interview, the ageing president described the alleged relationship between Blair and Zimbabwe's opposition party, the MDC as 'treasonous.'

"That's the worst betrayal there can ever be. You can't eat with the enemy," he said of MDC leader Morgan Tsvangirai. For Blair, he had harsher words.

"You can never ever convince an Englishman that you are equal to him. He is always superior, it doesn't matter what circumstances, it doesn't matter what education, it doesn't matter what power, you are always inferior."

Asked what he would do if he was to meet Blair, Mugabe said, "I would tell him that he, Tony Blair is a liar; that on Zimbabwe he has lied; on Iraq he has lied."

There he was hitting a sore point with many expatriate Zimbabweans. Iraq had oil while Zimbabwe had very little to offer the voracious modern world. Had the situation been reversed, would Blair and his friend George W Bush have been more intent on toppling Mugabe than Saddam Hussein? It was an unanswerable question but it worried me as well as many of my countrymen.

Mugabe went on to accuse the British Prime Minister of falsely claiming that Zimbabwe was undemocratic and lacked transparency or the rule of law. Asked if he was not running away from issues at home by adopting an anti Blair theme for his party's electoral campaign, the president said that Blair had interfered with Zimbabwe's domestic affairs through his 'agent,' the MDC but refused to elaborate.

Blair had been a target for Mugabe's barbs since Zimbabwe was suspended from the Commonwealth in 2002 after its observers reported problems with his re-election to yet another term in office. Robert Gabriel Mugabe was never one to forget a slight.

He also launched a diatribe against Rice, the most prominent African American in George W Bush's administration, saying she was a slave to white masters in Washington for branding Zimbabwe an 'outpost of tyranny.'

As for the looming elections, Mugabe seemed determined that they would be held his way and as always, he brooked no interference. Only thirty-two observer missions were invited for the March 31st ballot. Twenty-three of these were from African nations, five from Asia, three from the Americas and one from Russia to represent Europe. Britain, the United States and the European Union were to be conspicuous by their absence. I read in Britain that the election would be closely monitored by the outside world as a test of government commitment to free and fair polls, yet Mugabe did not seem to care what anyone thought of him.

According to principles laid down by the Southern African Development Community, a team of SADC observers should have been allowed into Zimbabwe at least ninety days prior to the election date, but even though this was only thirty-two days away, no invitation had been forthcoming. Interested parties from the Congress of South African Trade Unions and the Democratic alliance had been turned away from the country, yet the South African President, Thabo Mbeki appeared unconcerned about the situation.

"We will probably have them there next week." He commented about the SADC observers.

Zimbabwe Opposition spokesman Paul Themba Nyathi complained, "The list of observers is ridiculous. If the government has nothing to hide it should have allowed everyone who wanted to come and observe the elections to do so.

'We are not surprised that they are avoiding people who tell the truth."

Vilified by most of the world and hesitantly shunned by many of his African colleagues, Mugabe still had the wholehearted support of two of the continents leading figures.

"There is no reason why the forthcoming elections in Zimbabwe should not be free and fair." Said South African Foreign Minister, Nkosozana Dlamini-Zuma, while Benjamin Mkapa, the president of Tanzania and a protégé of Tony Blair was even more supportive.

"I don't see Zimbabwe as an illustration of bad governance at all. I don't buy it." He told the BBC.

If President Mugabe did have any doubts as to the outcome of the election, he made sure of the result by awarding massive pay rises to the armed forces, while recruiting fifty thousand militia from the notorious Youth Brigade to monitor polling stations. This was blatantly provocative but once again, the outside world allowed him to get away with it.

In theory, Zimbabweans had the chance to vote his government out of office on 31st March, but everyone knew that wouldn't happen. In spite of Mr Mkapa's remarks, they had little food, no money and a ruined economy, but their votes would be governed by fear and that is above politics or poverty.

Elections in Africa are seldom straightforward, but the opportunity for human interest stories was too good to miss, so off I went again. Unofficial correspondent, Bryan Graham was back in business.

*   *   *

This time, I had obtained my entry visa from the Zimbabwean Embassy in London. It had cost me five quid more than it would have at Harare airport, but it gave me a clear six month stay in the country. It had also been issued with smiling efficiency and even though an airport official tried to spoil my mood, it was again good to be home.

"You have three months," the immigration officer told me and when I pointed out the dates so clearly logged in my passport, he shrugged with withering contempt.

"Those people in London are diplomats, not immigration officers. They do not know what they are doing. You have three months."

In truth, I didn't think I would need six months, but as the official had left my shiny new visa untouched, resolved to ignore his instructions. There was another shock to my system awaiting me on my way out of the airport. As I made my way through the green route, a customs officer stepped in front of me. He was polite but very firm.

"May I look through your luggage please Sir?"

That could prove upsetting to all concerned. Once again, I had loaded up with the necessary tools of my new trade as well as foodstuffs and little luxuries for friends in Harare and Kariba. I didn't think the luxuries would cause a problem, but a laptop, dictaphone, miniature camera and numerous notebooks might well seem out of place on someone coming into the country on a family visit. Searching desperately for an explanation, I fumbled with the straps of my luggage. The Customs man was chatty.

"Are you here on a visit, Sir?"

"Yes I suppose so," I told him. "My younger son has just presented me with a brand new grandson, so I am coming to see the baby and wet his head a little."

It was a blatant lie but an inspired explanation. Children are very important in African society and this fellow was delighted with my good fortune.

"Ah, you have become a *sekuru*," He pumped my free hand enthusiastically. "That is excellent news and I hope you will be overjoyed when you see the baby."

I hadn't mentioned that my most recent grandson, Dougal was already a year old and I knew him well, but didn't suppose that mattered.

"Don't worry about that," the Customs officer indicated that I could stop struggling with the straps. "I am looking forward to the day when I can also be a *sekuru* so I will be thinking of you."

I was through and feeling slightly shell-shocked, I wandered out of the terminal and breathed deeply on the crystal clear air of Zimbabwe in early February. The sky was blue, the sun shone and it was good to be home.

With such an important election looming and violence escalating, the atmosphere in Zimbabwe was pretty tense, but more than any other centre in my troubled country, the city of Harare had the fevered air of a community on the brink of war.

Apart from the occasional political demonstration in the centre of town, life appeared to go on as normal – street kids were still hassling motorists to look after their cars, vendors hawked their tawdry wares and beggars wailed high-pitched entreaties to passers by. In the avenues, ancient jacaranda and flamboyant trees cast precious shade over flats and a few old fashioned houses, but in the more affluent suburbs, the pre election atmosphere was rapidly developing into one of acute paranoia.

While most folk seemed to firmly believe that Morgan Tsvangirai's Movement for Democratic Change would win easily in the city, talk around suburban dinner tables centred on the possibility of reprisals and mass violence after the voting was over. Men spoke glibly about fighting their way in convoy to the border with South Africa, while their womenfolk chattered nervously about the latest vehicle hijack in town and the fearful possibility of being raped in their own homes.

The rumour mill was working overtime and just before Valentine's Day, there was mass panic when it was 'reliably reported' that the Le Patourels of Beatrice, who were the major rose producers in the country, had been given thirty-six hours to get off their farm. This was an absolute disaster and disappointed suitors rushed around city florists to find red roses, but a telephone call confirmed that for the Le Patourels at least, business went on as usual.

"For the moment, our district is quiet," I was told; "and we will fulfil all our orders on Valentine's Day."

In the event, they must have made an absolute killing, as virtually every woman in Harare was heavily laden with red roses on the day itself.

However, most of the rumours were concerned with the escalating violence and were not so amusing. Harare in the early years of the twenty-first century was certainly a far more violent place than it had been twenty years previously, but the same could probably be said for every major city in the world. In fact, although violent crime was on the increase and would obviously get worse as the food shortage took effect, this was still one of the safest cities to be in. The economy might have been crumbling around their ears, but people still moved around at night and the general populace seemed perfectly prepared to lend a hand in order to catch a mugger or thief. Firearms were much in evidence both on the streets and in suburban homes, but even at that time, there were many more crimes of violence committed each day in London, Manchester, Birmingham or Bristol.

"I work two nights a week in a restaurant," suburban housewife, Lesley Corbett told me, "and although people say that I am stupid, I drive home alone and seldom even see anyone along the streets. My house is well locked and it takes me minutes to open the gate, but I have never felt scared about it."

As is so often the case in nervous times, it was the pubs and the churches that were doing the most business. From lunch time onwards, almost every bar or tavern in the city was thronged with well dressed, managerial types and there were daily queues for morning mass at both the Dominican Convent and the Anglican Cathedral. When I asked a prominent local businessman what he was doing in the Keg and Maiden in mid afternoon, he laughed.

"The economy is in such a state that business is virtually at a standstill," he said. "I can sit in my office and worry or come out for a few grogs with my *shamwaris* and forget my troubles. What would you do?"

That seemed fair enough, but although Zimbabweans have always had the reputation of being heavy drinkers, I found myself continually amazed at just how much alcohol they could consume. Afternoon sessions lasted well into the evening and offices were left virtually unmanned while executives and their secretaries partied the hours away.

In church, the atmosphere was hardly so congenial. The general theme among all religions was to pray for peace and even among the white-robed Apostolic sect who conducted their services on any piece of open land they could find, faces were sombre and worried. On Sunday mornings, the Harare showground was thronged with worshippers from dozens of different churches and the haunting sounds of their singing could be heard all around the city centre.

"Our country is in desperate trouble," Nelson Mandizva told me sadly. "We have to vote Mugabe out in March or we will all be dead. The man is a monster and I come here to pray that he will be defeated and Zimbabweans can once again look to the future with hope rather than despair."

That was a commonly expressed prayer throughout Harare, but elections in Africa are never free and fair and the more people I spoke with, the more my own doubts mounted.

*   *   *

Bobby Sithole is a Zimbabwean businessman who has worked his way to the top. Starting as an office clerk in an International company, he had been Managing Director of that same company for over twenty-five years when we met in his downtown office. Bobby's job takes him all over the world, but it was the situation in his own country that was worrying him. Over tea and biscuits, he told me of his concerns.

"Our problem is that we rely a great deal on aid from the European Union, but since all the violence started, that aid has been withdrawn and we are struggling. To give them their due, the government have done their best to assist, but ours is a critical industry and we need more.

'Of course, a great deal depends on what happens in March," he went on thoughtfully. "If Tsvangirai wins the election, I have no doubt that aid will pour into the country, but if the status quo remains, much will depend on what the election observers report."

"And who will win?"

I couldn't resist the question and Bobby frowned. For a moment, I thought he wouldn't answer the question or would fob me off with a platitude. Most of the Zimbabweans I had spoken with were wary about airing their true feelings, but he and I had been friends for two decades.

"At the moment, it is probably fifty/fifty, with perhaps a slight bias towards Mugabe." He sounded thoughtful. "I think it is going to be desperately close. Although he is over eighty, the Old Man is determined to remain in power and it will take a great deal to unseat him. After all, Kamuzu Banda in Malawi went on well into his nineties.

'The military leaders will support Mugabe and he is loved in the rural areas. In town, his support is less, but intimidation will be rife and many people will be too frightened to vote at all. The Youth Brigade will be out in every township and the people are scared of them. These are hand-picked, carefully vetted young men and their mandate is to place Robert Mugabe back in power. They have been given *carte blanche* to do this by whatever means are at hand and as most of them are illiterate and uneducated, their preferred method for getting things done is by using extreme violence. We need election observers here now, not in four weeks time."

We went on to talk about personalities in government and Sithole brought out some fascinating facts.

"We hear a lot about Mugabe's bad health," he told me, "but most of this is rumour based on false hope. He is an old man and tends to forget things, while some of his speeches have been rambling ones. On the other hand, he keeps to a rigorous schedule and has the energy of a man half his age."

So who could take over should he win the election and fail to complete his term?

"There we have a problem. Muzenda and Msika (the Vice Presidents at the time) are older than Mugabe and he keeps younger ministers firmly in line."

I was intrigued and Bobby smiled at the naiveté of my question.

"It is the same with all African leaders. When an up and coming politician does something wrong, Mugabe doesn't throw him out or prosecute him. He encourages the corruption and warns the individual that he knows exactly what is going on. This means that those who yield to temptation – and many of them do – are forever in Mugabe's power and have no choice but to support him. They are afraid of losing their jobs and even being imprisoned, so most of them will defend Mugabe with their lives.

'Our president also surrounds himself with the most unlikely acolytes. Jonathan Moyo (the Information Minister) used to be rabidly anti Mugabe, yet now he has gone the other way and is virtually a praise-singer for the President."

Since that interview in 2002, Moyo has switched his allegiance on two occasions and for a while wrote fulminating diatribes against Mugabe in the local press. Then he was either forgiven by Mugabe or saw the light on his own account and in 2011, is once again doing his praise-singing act on behalf of the president.

"Joseph Chinotimba was a municipal policeman," Bobby sipped his tea and lit a cigarette. I noticed that like many Zimbabweans in fairly high positions, he had taken to chain smoking. "His job was to chase vendors off street corners, yet he is now a man of considerable power and wealth. The late Chenjerai Hunzvi was the same and nobody knows whether Mugabe is merely using these people or feels some sort of genuine friendship towards them. In the main, they are thugs, but they obviously serve some use to the president."

My next question was on the economic situation and here, Sithole was pessimistic.

"The government have taken to printing their own money and that is a recipe for disaster. Such is the work involved that they have opened a new factory in Matabeleland to cope. They hold the official value of the Zim dollar, but on the streets it sells for eight, ten or twenty times that value. We cannot go on like this or we will all be out of business. Even if Tsvangirai gets in, it will take us years to recover from the mess and if he doesn't, things will get considerably worse."

Zimbabwe is an agricultural country and my concern was for the farms.

"I don't think that will be too much of a problem," Bobby said. "The incompetent settlers can be moved off to less arable areas, while those who have proved themselves can be given assistance to expand production. With luck, we can have large scale commercial farming back again, this time with as many black farmers as white."

And like most citizens of this troubled country, Bobby Sithole was upbeat when we parted.

"Whatever the result in March," he smiled, "I pray it will reflect the wish of the People and allow us to rebuild our lives."

I didn't think it would but his optimism was infectious and we parted with smiles and a firm handshake.

Chapter Seven

(The Crocodile's Den)

There is something about driving in Africa that soothes my soul and as the huddled squalor of Harare's high-density suburbs fell away behind me, I relaxed for the first time in days.

I was on my way to Bulawayo and it felt good to be leaving the capital city with its hurtling traffic, confused politics and desperately worried citizenry. I had nothing against Harare. I had been to school there, so knew the city well, but the stories I was being told were all the same and the propaganda war going on in the media would have brought effusive congratulations from Dr Goebbels himself, had he been able to see it.

The state-sponsored, Herald newspaper only reported news that reflected well on President Mugabe and they were sycophantic in their praise for him and downright libellous in what they said about his political opponents or the British. Most daily editions had at least two – and sometimes three or four – full page advertisements, extolling Mugabe's virtues and making Morgan Tsvangirai, George W. Bush and Tony Blair out to be colonial stooges, acting in concert to the detriment of all Zimbabweans. They called Blair 'Bliar' which made me smile, but in general their coverage of what purported to be news, left me feeling ashamed for these people who claimed to be journalists. I had written features for the Herald in the past and could only wonder how any self-respecting editor would allow his paper to be used in this horribly ingratiating manner.

Not that the Daily News or the Zimbabwe Independent were much better. They merely saw everything from the opposite perspective to the Herald. The men and women running the Daily News were obviously brave and resourceful people and determined to say what they wanted, no matter what trouble it brought down on their heads. The only problem was that they leaned so far toward MDC values, that I was forced to read both newspapers in tandem, just to get some idea of what was happening. The Daily News also ran full page, political advertisements and while the MDC did not have as much coverage as Zanu PF did in the Herald, what there was seemed equally partisan.

Another big difference between the newspapers was the price. With government backing, The Herald could afford to sell copies at vastly reduced cost and this meant that the rural poor – that hugely influential section of society that probably held the election result in its hands – tended to buy it, rather than go for one of the more expensive papers.

The independent journalists were also very brave. Basildon Peta who wrote for the Independent in Britain unfortunately blotted his copybook shortly before the 2002 election by filing different versions of the same story to his British and Zimbabwean employers. By doing this, he played right into government hands and duly received the expected lambasting in the Herald and the Bulawayo Chronicle. His credibility destroyed, Peta then made matters worse by heading for South Africa and reporting from there. He had done a good job and his voice would be missed, but he had also dealt a serious blow to the credibility of his colleagues. Mugabe's verbose Minister of Information, Jonathan Moyo lost no opportunity of ridiculing Peta and the other independents like Jan Raath or Peta Thornycroft.

There were also a number of unofficial scribblers like me wandering around the countryside. I met a Canadian gentleman in Gweru and after a little verbal sparring over a beer in order to establish each other's credentials, he turned out to be 'on holiday,' but filing copy on a weekly basis. There were sure to be others and although I had no schedule to adhere to,

I tried to file at least two, eight-hundred word features per week. My editor would fit me in where he could and the arrangement worked very well.

But neither journalism nor propaganda was on my mind as I drove the Ganja Bus past the turn off to Lake Chivero and thought about the long road ahead with considerable pleasure. I loved Bulawayo and I loved Matabeleland. This huge, hospitable province had been good to me in the past and although I had collected a few nasty memories in Entumbane during the riots of the early eighties, I remembered that sprawling landscape with considerable nostalgia. I had a few telephone numbers and addresses in my pocket and a few old friends to look up along the way.

An added bonus was the fact that my transport was now ostensibly legal. No more kow-towing to police officers for this scribbler. I had somewhat rudely told the Ganja Bus' owner of my troubles in Rusape and he ruefully admitted that he had lost all paper work for the vehicle, so was not able to relicense it.

"So what do we do now?"

I am always nervous of getting on the wrong side with policemen and didn't fancy having to explain myself away at every road block.

"I'll ask a friend of mine," and the friend duly sorted matters out by providing me with a blank tax disk on which I had only to fill in the vehicle number.

"Marvellous what you can do with a good scanner," He laughed as he handed me the disk. "It will look legal, so you won't have any more difficulties."

I have always been a law-abiding person, but have to confess that I almost looked forward to fooling the next roadblock with my illegal tax disk.

Even the problem of the missing vehicle documents was being sorted out while I trundled down to Bulawayo. This was being done through the good – but expensive – offices of a Mr Fixit from Chitungwisa. Henry Ndhlovu (I dare not use his real name in case of future need) had the reputation of being able to produce any document at a price and when he had learned where I came from, Henry had even offered me a Zimbabwean passport for fifteen thousand zim dollars (less than a fiver at the time) which I thought was incredibly cheap. I declined the offer, but kept Henry's address and telephone number in my wallet – just in case.

*   *   *

The road between Kadoma and Kwe Kwe is uniformly drab, with thick *msasa* forest growing right to the roadside and long, straight sections where there is absolutely nothing to make the drive any more interesting. It was along one of these straights that I spotted a man working on his bicycle beside the road. He looked hot and flustered, so having cycled through this part of the countryside myself, I pulled in and asked whether he needed help.

"I have a puncture," He was young and sweat poured off his face as he held up the rear wheel for my inspection. "My home is four kilometres that way," he pointed toward Kwe Kwe, "so you can give me a lift."

Moments later, the bicycle was ensconced in the back of the Ganja Bus and my new companion was lighting a newspaper-rolled cigarette beside me. He seemed a cheerful soul and was full of questions.

"Where do you come from?"

This one was a bit of a minefield where I was concerned and I seldom explained my mission in life before I was sure of my audience.

"I am from Kariba," I told him and it was not really untrue. "I am on my way through to Bulawayo where I want to see some friends."

"Myself, I am from Kwe Kwe," he volunteered and for the first time, I noticed that he was wearing a Zanu PF sweatshirt under his tattered pullover. "I was working as a clerk for Bata Shoes, but I am now a farmer."

"You are a war veteran then?"

He shook his head.

"I am not old enough to have been in the *hondo*, but I am one of Comrade President Mugabe's new settlers. Our leader in this area was an important man during the struggle and he has given me eleven hectares of land. Already, my crop has been planted. I was on my way back to my farm when I had the puncture. Meanwhile, my wife will be tending the crop."

This seemed like too good an opportunity to miss, but when I asked if I could see his new 'farm,' my companion looked suddenly doubtful.

"You would need to have permission from Comrade Ngwenya," he frowned. "He does not like you *warungu* and I am not sure if he will allow you to visit my farm.

'I could invite you into my home and give you tea though."

The thought of being able to offer this simple hospitality obviously pleased him and I guessed that he had never had a home of his own before. He nodded briskly when I asked the question.

"No, in Kwe Kwe I lived with my parents. There were many of us in a very small house, but now, we are two and I can build more rooms whenever I want to."

"So where do we find Comrade Ngwenya?"

I brought him back to practicalities and the frown immediately reappeared.

"He lives very close to me on the same farm," he sounded doubtful, "but he occupies what used to be the *mabunhu's* (a derogatory term for white farmer) house. He might not like it if I bring you to see him."

"Ah come on," I was not to be put off now, "let's tell him that I used to work with you at Bata and we met by chance, so you want to show me your farm and introduce me to your wife."

Somewhat reluctantly, he agreed and told me that his name was David.

"That is an easy one to remember."

And suddenly, we were friends. His doubts seemingly forgotten, David directed me along a rough farm track to a battered old farmhouse nestling behind a security fence that was hanging forlornly from rusty support poles. I had seen no signpost to indicate the farm I was on and all I knew was that it was about twenty kilometres East of Kwe Kwe – a place with an evil reputation.

The town had long been a Mugabe stronghold and was ruled by the Youth Brigade who had based themselves in the municipal swimming pool.

"They strut about the streets and do exactly what they want," attractive widow, Elizabeth Masson had told me only a few days previously. "I have reached the stage where I am nervous about going into the supermarket, because even if these thugs aren't there, I am likely to be jostled or verbally abused by the local women. It is not a nice situation in Kwe Kwe and I am not sure why any of us stay there."

And Kwe Kwe was just down the road, while I was going into the lion's den with this hesitant young man. In fact, not quite the lion's den as Ngwenya means crocodile in Chishona, so this could perhaps be called the crocodile's lair.

The thought made me smile and my companion looked across at me, obviously misinterpreting the gesture.

"It is a nice house?" He queried and I nodded enthusiastically.

"Very nice – very big too."

It was certainly large and must once have been a delightful place to live, but there was an air of decay about the place and the house showed signs of traumatic treatment. Most of the windows had been broken, 'Zanu PF' had been daubed across every spare scrap of outside wall in black paint and what must once have been a magnificent lawn was knee deep in grass and weeds. Under a lone *msasa* tree, four people were sleeping and it was to this dormant group that David led me. As we approached, he put one finger to his lips.

"It will be better if I wake Comrade Ngwenya and explain who you are," he whispered and I hung back while he leaned over the nearest supine figure. The man was quickly roused and my confidence took a severe knock when I noticed his hand go straight to the stock of an AK 47 that was lying on the ground beside him. Sitting up abruptly, he glared at me through bloodshot eyes, before lumbering to his feet.

Comrade Ngwenya was a big man, running to fat around his waist, but still powerfully built. Probably in his middle to late fifties, he wore a small beard and had that indefinable aura about him that only a few men possess. It is usually called 'charisma' and I couldn't help wondering whether I really had given myself a problem by arriving so precipitately on his doorstep.

"What do you want?" He stood with his belly almost touching mine and looked down on me with a surly expression on his face. We do not want visitors here – particularly *mabunhu* visitors."

"I am here with my friend, David," I spoke soothingly in my laboured Chishona and having been through the story, we had agreed upon, smiled winningly at the big man. For a moment, he looked on the verge of anger, but my use of the vernacular probably relaxed him and he let out his breath in an explosive sigh. I had an urge to do the same, but it would not have looked good, so contented myself with breathing out very slowly.

With a booming laugh, Comrade Ngwenya stuck out a meaty paw while keeping his grip on the kalashnikov with the other hand.

"We must be careful, My Friend," he boomed. "There are too many British spies in Zimbabwe these days. But you speak our language, so you must be a Zimbabwean and if you are friends with Comrade David, then you are welcome on my farm. David is one of my tenants, you know."

I almost chuckled. The Zimbabwe Tobacco Association had carefully vetted 'tenants,' whom they financed for their first few crops, yet this oaf who had obviously stolen an entire farm had set up a similar scheme – without the finance – himself. If it hadn't been so tragic, it would have been funny. Looking around me, I wondered how many families had grown up in that sad old house; how many dreams had been dreamed there and how many children had played out their happy adventures on that neglected lawn, never dreaming that one day it would all be taken from them.

Comrade Ngwenya brought me back to reality.

"I will accompany you to Comrade David's farm," he announced grandly. I sighed inwardly at the thought that my promised cup of tea would not be forthcoming. At a barked command, poor David led us somewhat sheepishly down a path that went past obviously derelict tobacco barns. We passed open machinery sheds where burned and battered trucks and tractors were lined up in forlorn rows. Tyres were flat, windscreens were smashed and oil had been splashed over previously whitewashed walls. Careful not to show undue interest, I glanced at the various vehicles, but didn't think any of them would ever be driven again. It seemed ironic that although these people were occupying the land and calling themselves farmers and settlers, they were wantonly vandalising the implements that might have helped them set themselves up as true users of the land.

Comrade Ngwenya did not appear to notice the damaged equipment and kept up a rumbling monologue as we walked along. I gathered that he had fought on the side of Mugabe in the liberation struggle and been a great hero. With his own hands – he showed them to me – he had killed many hundreds of Smith's cowardly soldiers. The people in this area apparently loved him and he was content to look after them as their new master. It was all rather sickening, but the assault rifle looked like a toy in his meaty fist and I was not prepared to argue.

Inevitably, David's farm was a disaster and I felt a sudden surge of pity for this earnest young man who obviously had dreams of making something of himself. Like so many others, he had been duped by government agents and this massive thug beside me into giving up steady employment for what must inevitably mean eventual penury and starvation.

A pretty little woman came out of a flimsy hut at our approach and looked immediately disconcerted when she spotted my white skin. David spoke rapidly to her and she relaxed slightly, but kept darting anxious glances in my direction.

"Here are my lands and my crop," David seemed eager to show me his handiwork, but I struggled to keep a smile on my face. The 'lands' were a strip of half cleared ground where the 'crop' – a few wilting maize plants - had been planted in rows that were a long way from straight. With the lack of rain, the plants were wilting and many of them had that scorched look that I had seen so often during my weeks in Zimbabwe. An effort had been made to keep the plants free from weeds, but they needed water and sustenance or they would undoubtedly die. We were at the end of February and even with a generous dose of fertiliser and a couple of weeks of excellent rain, I did not think they stood any chance of producing a crop.

David and his shy little wife waited anxiously for my reaction and I fixed a friendly smile on to my face.

"You have both worked very hard," I complimented insincerely and at their twin smiles, I felt a burst of angry indignation at the way simple youngsters like these were being manipulated by heartless politicians and war lords just to keep one old man in power.

Ten minutes later, David and his wife Esinati had disappeared and I was sitting on the ground beneath the *msasa* tree, where I had first seen Comrade Ngwenya. The three elderly men, who had been sleeping beside him when I arrived, now sat a short distance away, following our conversation, but not saying a word for themselves. Ngwenya opened a bottle of warm Lion beer with his teeth and we passed it back and forth between us like old friends meeting after a long interval. Dire thoughts about the AIDS epidemic and spreading of other diseases flitted through my mind, but I had gone too far to back out now, so I drank heartily from the bottle.

"Do you know, Bryan," we had quickly developed a first name relationship and I learned that he was Amos. "I have spent my whole life in this district and everyone knows me.

They speak of Comrade Ngwenya with respect, but I am still a man of the people, even now that I have a big house and a farm of my own. My friends are always welcome to visit me and I look after them."

"That is good."

I deemed it prudent to say as little as possible and let my host chatter away. He still had one hand firmly clamped on the AK and that disturbed me.

"I can see that you are an educated man, My Friend," he went on. "and I like educated men. Myself, I did not have much time for education, but the teachers in Rimuka (a township outside Kadoma) did try to make me learn when I was very young. In later years, I punished them for it.

'Did you fight in the struggle?"

The sudden change of subject was disconcerting and momentarily, I wondered how to answer.

"I was in the police Support Unit."

The truth seemed politic in the circumstances and my companion let out a great roar of laughter.

"Ah yes – good fighters those Black Boots, but not as good as the men of Amos Ngwenya. Perhaps we might once have fought each other hey and then I would have killed you. That would have been a great shame for then we would not have been here, sharing this beer."

Opening another bottle, he passed it to me and I duly sipped and passed it back. It was warm and treacly, making me feel quite light-headed and I realised that I had not eaten since early that morning. The sun was already beginning to sink and I knew that I must get on and find a bed for the night.

"Do you know why we fought you people, Bryan my friend?"

I confessed that I was not sure.

"For freedom I suppose."

"We fought you for land. All Zimbabweans treasure their land and without land, a man cannot be a true man. Myself, I love this land so much that I can even eat it."

Suiting actions to the words, he grabbed a handful of soil, put it into his mouth and chewed heartily. In spite of the circumstances and my gathering nervousness, I could not resist the comment.

"If it doesn't rain soon, Amos old chap, that is all you will have to eat."

For a moment, I thought I had gone too far. My companion did not appear to be of humorous bent and his eyes clouded as he tried to read some obscure meaning into my words. Then he laughed again and my heart clattered its relief against my ribs.

"Ah, you are right, My Friend. If God doesn't send us rain soon, we will all be hungry. But when you are hungry," his eyes narrowed and he leaned toward me, wafts of beery breath enveloping my senses. "When you are hungry, come and see me. Amos Ngwenya looks after his friends and I will not let you stay hungry. You and I are brothers, so we must help each other. Is that not right?"

"It is indeed."

Over the years since the liberation war ended, I have met many men who fought on the opposite side to me and without exception, we have got on well together. Perhaps it is the innate respect of fighting men for each other, but even though I had a feeling of deep contempt for Amos Ngwenya and his delusions of power, in a sneaking sort of way, I couldn't help liking the man. He was a buffoon and a bully, but there was something about him that appealed to my sense of the ridiculous.

I had seen how young David and his wife had cowered before him and that had been terrible to witness, but I couldn't help feeling that Amos was as much a victim of circumstances as they were. Not only them, but all of us who loved our wonderful country. We were being manipulated and used, not only by the Zimbabwean government, but also by those leaders of the Western World who could generate votes by crying out against the excesses of Robert Mugabe while at the same time doing nothing to curb those excesses.

It was with decidedly mixed feelings that I left that battered farm and its outlandish warlord and headed for more comfortable climes. In one of his more serious moments, Amos had told me that he had originally had twenty-five 'tenants' on 'his' farm, but David and Esinati were the only ones left. I wondered how long they would remain with the wreckage of their dreams and could only hope that the world would not be too harsh on them when they finally packed in their farming venture.

CHAPTER EIGHT

(Frustration in Matabeleland)

By any standards, Bulawayo is a lovely city. The buildings are solidly comfortable without being modern monstrosities of glass and steel, the streets were built wide enough for a full span of sixteen oxen to turn around in and the city gardens are always a riot of colour. The people are as innately friendly as their surroundings and if I ever had to live in an urban metropolis, Bulawayo is the place I would choose.

The original name, *'Gubuluwayo'* meant 'place of killing' and was awfully apt in the days when Mzilikazi ruled the warlike Matabele nation and had his Royal k*raal* on the nearby rock of *Ntabazinduna*. Anyone who disagreed with the king was violently killed and in those days it was often a lottery as to whether an individual would survive the day. The name again took on awful significance during the Entumbane riots of the early nineteen-eighties and my stomach tightened as I remembered the rockets, rounds and mortar bombs that had come our way in those hectic days. On this occasion though, everything looked supremely peaceful as I drove into town in time for a late breakfast. I wasn't sure where to begin my search for stories, but I had a beautiful, sunny day ahead of me and while strolling through a shopping arcade that had sprouted since my previous visit, I spotted a fellow traveller.

He was small and his clothes looked threadbare, but his head was adorned with one of the most spectacular hats I had ever seen. I have always enjoyed hats and have a sizeable collection of the things myself, but this was something special. It had probably been some sort of Stetson originally, but repeated washes and the addition of a red ribbon around the crown and a multi coloured thong to tie beneath the chin had given it an air of panache that I could only envy. As we passed, the man beneath the hat cast a brief look at my own floppy green and I fancied that his upper lip curled slightly. Again, it was too good an opportunity to miss.

"I like your hat," I said and ten minutes later, we were sitting on a bench in the city gardens and enjoying a chat in the sunshine.

His name was Kenneth Chikoro and he was in town looking for mealie meal. This is the ground maize that forms the basic ingredient for the fluffy white porridge that is the staple diet of Africa. In East Africa, it is known as *ugali* or *posho*, South Africans call it *pap*, in Botswana it is *pollichi* and in Zimbabwe it is *sadza*. The mealie meal is boiled with water into a thick, sticky mess that is eaten with vegetables or meat. Extremely nutritious, it tends to be tasteless to the western palate, (my English wife says that it tastes like wallpaper paste) but is eaten for breakfast, lunch and supper in Africa.

For most of the twentieth century, Zimbabwe exported maize to neighbouring countries, while keeping a healthy stockpile for herself in case of drought or other disasters. Now that had all gone. A great deal of maize was sold to Zambia and when the farm invasions began and many farmers were no longer allowed to plant a crop, there was nothing with which to replenish the National stockpile. In the first eight years of the twenty-first century, people were suffering for this government profligacy. Maize was in desperately short supply and with the lack of rain during the first few years of the decade, seemed ever more likely to run out altogether. A little was being imported from South Africa, but every time mealie meal appeared in the stores and supermarkets, the prices were considerably higher than the time before and ordinary people were becoming ever more desperate.

I bought him an ice cream from a passing vendor and my new friend Kenneth gave me some idea of the problems experienced by the ordinary working man. He was the gardener for a white, suburban family and had lived in Bulawayo since 1971.

"I am lucky," he told me wearily. "My boss likes hunting and fishing, so sometimes there is *nyama* that he has brought back from Tuli or the Zambezi Valley and we can store it for future eating. But mealie meal is the problem. Last week, I heard that there was some available in Pumula, (eight kilometres from where he worked) so I took time off and cycled right across the city. When I got there, I found a long queue and by the time I came to the front, the mealie meal was finished, so I cycled all the way back again.

'When I told her what had happened, my employer telephoned around the supermarkets and shops for me. Eventually, she found some mealie meal, but I was only allowed to buy five kilograms and that cost me nearly two thousand dollars."

Out of a monthly wage of fifteen thousand Zim dollars – much less than a fiver at parallel market rates of the time - that was an enormous chunk and I was curious to know how long five kilograms of maize would last.

"I have no family here," Kenneth told me, "so five kg will keep me going for maybe eight or ten days if I am sparing with it."

I did not need to be a mathematician to work out that almost half his monthly salary would go on basic food – provided, he could find it.

"Next year, it will be worse," Kenneth went on. "These politicians have driven the farmers off their land, so there will be no maize crop for us and now another drought is coming and even small scale farmers will starve."

As he spoke, I looked up at the sky. From horizon to horizon, it stretched blue and unblemished and it had been that way for days. I remembered poor David's maize on that awful farm in Kwe Kwe and when I told Kenneth about it, he shook his head in weary resignation.

"It will all burn away if the rain does not come soon," he said, "These new settlers are not farmers and even with good rains, few of them will have a crop to reap, but for people like me, that means we will go hungry.

'February is the month for rain," he went on, "but our government have ignored God's wishes and he has taken the rain away. When it returns, it will be too late for Zimbabweans. We need food and we need it now. The government is importing maize, but they have no foreign money, so that will not last long. In Zimbabwe, we are proud people, but we will have to ask Britain and America for help and they have never wanted to help us before. I do not think there is much future for ordinary Zimbabweans like me. Only God can help us now."

That was the third occasion, I had heard those very words and I could only marvel at how people turn to God in times of crisis. However, I was not at all sure that He could help even if He wanted to and therein lay the tragedy of the situation. Whether through God's intervention or not, successive droughts had come at a particularly bad time for the people of Zimbabwe. After flying over the farming areas of Mashonaland, the Minister for Agriculture, Joseph Made had glibly told Zimbabweans that there was no maize shortage, but even the most menial citizen knew full well that he was lying through his teeth and the growing hunger in so many bellies merely confirmed that the politicians of Zimbabwe were no longer in touch with reality. Nor could they be trusted.

In the past, Zimbabweans have always consoled themselves with the thought that 'next year will be better,' but sitting on my bench with Kenneth, I couldn't help reflecting that he was right. The next year would be worse – far worse – for ordinary citizens. No matter how strong they are, people need food to keep them alive and without an immediate and massive aid programme from Western donors, there would be no food for Zimbabweans like Kenneth Chikoro.

"Have you children?" I asked and he nodded vigorously.

"I have five, but they are all at my home in Gwanda district, so I have to send money back to them whenever I can."

"And school fees?"

He nodded again and his face was suddenly sad.

"Two of my children have now finished, but I have to find school fees for the others and they also need money for books and clothing. I paid nearly five hundred dollars for a small bottle of cooking oil last week and truly, life is becoming difficult for Zimbabweans. I have not tasted sugar for many months and we don't even see ration meat any more. I do not know how we will survive."

Who would he vote for in March, I wondered quietly.

"Ah, that is easy. I will vote for Morgan and everybody else in Bulawayo will vote for Morgan, but after the elections, Mugabe will still be president. That is for sure."

How could that be when support was all going the other way? Kenneth laughed, but there was little humour in the gesture.

"Mugabe has support in the rural areas and even here in the city, many people are too frightened to vote against him. In Mberengwa, Tjolotjo, Nkai and other areas of Matebeleland, there have been many deaths, many beatings and many rapes. The people are scared and will do what the government tells them to do. Even the MPs in Morgan's party are scared and even they are being beaten and harassed."

I found it strange that Zimbabweans of all colours often referred to Tsvangirai by his first name. In the case of whites, this sounded vaguely patronising, but it was a measure of the support this former Trade Union leader was developing throughout the nation.

"Will you be assisting MDC at election time?" I asked, but this time Kenneth vehemently shook his head.

"Oh no, not me. I have my family who need me and I do not want to die or be beaten so badly that I can no longer work. In the last elections, MDC won all the seats in Matabeleland, but the government know this and they will be beating and holding *pungwes* with the people, so that this time things will be different.

'Listen to me, my *makhiwa* friend and note well what I say. President Mugabe will be President Mugabe next year, the year after and the year after that. Morgan will soon be forgotten even here in Matabeleland."

It was a depressing thought, but I was inclined to agree with my hat-wearing friend. As we went our separate ways, I offered him money 'for a beer on me,' but he waved it away with a smile.

"We all need our money for the difficult times ahead, so you keep yours, My Friend."

With a jaunty bob of that magnificent headgear, he walked away through the flowerbeds and I watched him go with a certain amount of envy in my being. Like so many Zimbabweans, Kenneth Chikoro had a boundless faith in his own destiny and his ability to endure whatever fate dealt out to him. For all the crude injustices that were being inflicted on them, Zimbabweans were an optimistically resolute bunch who took each day as it came and tried hard to make the best of everything.

I couldn't help feeling that they deserved a great deal better than they were getting. Mugabe was an old man clinging to power through violence and intimidation whereas Tsvangirai, for all his undoubted powers of leadership, was proving himself singularly naïve as a politician and man who would be president.

*   *   *

Something wasn't quite the same in Bulawayo since my last visit to the city and it took me a while to put my finger on it. When I did, I was surprised to realise that the Matabele people had changed from being a self-confident, warrior race and become dispirited and fearful instead. I had witnessed the early part of *gukuruhundi* and could have understood it then, but since those dreadful years, residents of Matabeleland had pulled themselves up and shown Mugabe that they would not be cowed. Yet with the presidential election less than two weeks away, nobody wanted to speak with me for fear of possible consequences.

I discussed this phenomenon with a man who had been in the police with me and his words gave me pause for thought.

"It is alright for you, Bryan," we were speaking over tea in his spacious house and I had asked him to stick with my new name. He had retired as a very senior officer and was obviously doing well in the security industry. "You can come and go as you please. People here cannot and at present, they are under almost unbearable pressure from Mugabe's Youth Brigade. These thugs are bussed into the city from other provinces and then allowed to run riot over the local population. The murder of Cain Nkala has given the government the excuse they were after and the situation even around here is really terrible."

Cain Nkala had been the leader of Mugabe's war veteran rabble in Matabeleland in 2000. He directed both the violent invasion of white farms and the ruling Zanu PF party's campaign of savage intimidation before the parliamentary elections in June that year. He was also heavily implicated in the abduction in Bulawayo of veteran opposition activist, Patrick Nyabanyana, the day before the election. A year later Nyabanyana had still not been found and in 2010 he was to be declared officially deceased. However, back in 2001, the authorities had somewhat reluctantly charged Nkala with kidnapping and then murder.

Suddenly insecure and frightened for his future, Nkala admitted abducting Nyabanyana but said he had handed him over to one of Mugabe's cabinet ministers. He spoke to friends and colleagues of fleeing to Britain, but that was a mistake on his part. The government could not allow that and on Guy Fawkes night in 2001, Nkala himself had been kidnapped from his home by eight men with AK47 assault rifles. A week later police announced that his body had been found. He had been strangled and left in a shallow grave outside Bulawayo.

Nobody was ever arrested for his murder but the police repeatedly claimed that they were making rigorous enquiries.

"Rigorous enquiries indeed!" My companion scoffed. "All they are doing is letting the Youth Brigade run riot. They spend their weekends beating, burning, raping and generally laying waste to one township at a time and the people are afraid. In the rural areas, it is even worse. Perhaps this is not as big or as well organised as *gukuruhundi,* but only because not as many people are being murdered. Nowadays, government forces are more subtle. They torture and intimidate, using threats of more painful destruction to ensure that people will vote for Mugabe."

"And will they?"

For a moment, he was silent as he pondered my question. When he spoke, my normally cheerful friend sounded extremely sombre.

"I don't know, Bryan; I just do not know. I think Tsvangirai will win here in Bulawayo, but in little places like Tjolotjo, Lupane, Gwanda and Beit Bridge – not to mention the tribal lands - I think the people will be too scared to vote for him. They are frightened of the consequences if they do."

When I mentioned my intention of travelling around the province for a few days, my friend was adamant.

"Do not do that, Bryan – I am asking you as your friend. We have known each other for a long time and you know that I am not a cowardly man, but there is too much danger out there and as a *makhiwa,* you will be too easy a target. Even here in town, you stick out horribly and I fear for your safety."

"You could arrange an escort for me – not a bodyguard as such, but someone to show me around and gain me introductions?"

He shook his head with a smile.

"Oh no – you don't get around me like that. I will not assist you to get yourself beaten up, tortured or even killed. I would suggest that you confine your activities to Bulawayo for the moment and head back to Harare as soon as you can.

'If I have to, I will take you to see a couple of people in the townships who might be able to give you something to write about."

He also offered to introduce me to David Coltart and other senior MDC officials, but I was not overly keen. My brief was with the little people and I was quite prepared to leave the politicians and high profile figures to proper journalists.

That evening, we waited for the onset of darkness before heading into Magwegwe Township and we travelled in my friend's nondescript pickup truck, rather than the Ganja Bus.

"I am not travelling in that thing," I was told in no uncertain terms. "We might as well take megaphones and let everyone know who we are and what we are doing."

Having parked the truck outside an obviously official building, my companion took my arm to guide me and we walked up a narrow, muddy alleyway before he knocked urgently on the door of a house. The door opened a crack and a whispered conversation ensued before I was hurriedly bundled inside. By the light of a flickering candle, I found myself in a small room, bare but for a metal-framed bed and two wooden boxes, one of which was pushed towards me as a chair. The only occupant of the room was a young man who was obviously nervous about my presence.

Twisting the bottom of his sweatshirt in his fingers, he smiled somewhat hesitantly at me and muttered something in Sindebele.

"What did he say?"

My friend smiled.

"He welcomes you to his humble home and has told his wife to prepare tea for us both. His name is Callistus Shumba and he was recently taken into custody and tortured by the CIO."

"Why?"

The young man obviously understood the question and spoke to me in halting English.

"I still do not know why myself please, Sir. I was coming home after seeking work and was surrounded by...."

He looked at my companion and lapsed back into Sindebele.

"Tell him to stick to his own language," I urged. "That way, we will get our facts correct."

Callistus had been pushed against a wall and beaten by members of the Youth Brigade who asked him to produce a Zanu PF party card.

"I am an MDC supporter, Sir," we were back with English. "I do not like Zanu PF but I was too scared to tell them this."

Eventually, the youths had dragged him to a government land rover standing nearby and a bewildered and very frightened Callistus had been thrown into the back, where he found four other young men cowering against the walls.

"They had all been beaten too, Sir."

In the dim light, he showed me a white scar below one eye and started to take his shirt off. I gestured to him that I didn't need to see his wounds, but my friend who had been watching quietly, immediately intervened.

"Let him show," he growled. "You will need to see before you can write about it."

While Callistus was undressing, we were served with tea by his wife, Maria. She was small, thin and looked very scared, but she curtsied to me and clapped in ritual greeting before shaking my hand with fingers that were as light and delicate as drifting feathers.

Producing a government-issue torch, my companion flashed it on to Callistus' bare back and I felt vomit rise in my throat. Great white ropes of scar tissue criss-crossed the shiny black skin and an ugly lump under one armpit looked like a badly-healed broken rib to my untrained eye.

"Who did this, Callistus?"

Shrugging gently, he spoke to my companion in the vernacular and I waited for the translation.

"The green bombers took me to the police post at Tshabalala Township, where I was handed over to policemen in plain clothes. They accused me of being an MDC official and stirring up trouble against the government. I denied this, but they beat me with small rubber clubs like those that are issued to policemen. I cried and pleaded with them to stop because I knew nothing, but they kept going.

'The other boys were also beaten, but the policemen seemed to single me out as the ringleader. When I couldn't tell them anything, they took me into another room and made me take off my clothes. Then they wrapped my wrists and ankles in plastic bags and I did not know what they were going to do. I was very afraid and cried for mercy, but they were laughing now and beat me around the face to make me shut up."

He paused for breath and sweat streamed from his face. His body was trembling with memory and I frowned at my friend, who smiled somewhat sardonically at me.

"You wanted something to write about," he reminded grimly. "This will give you some idea of what is going on without putting your life into extreme danger by wandering blindly around the country."

"But who beat him? Surely they weren't policemen? And what did they want to do with the plastic?"

Shaking his head at my naiveté, my friend turned back to Callistus and told him to go on with the story.

"When they had tied my hands and legs together with the plastic, they ripped my underpants off, so that I was naked. Then I was thrown to the ground and while the others laughed at my nakedness, one of them wrapped my private parts in the plastic. He was rough and the pain was terrible, but by now I was really scared. I struggled to get back on to my feet, but two of them held me down while another one, who I had heard the others address as Ncube lit a match from a box he had in his pocket."

For a long moment, there was silence in that bare little room. Callistus was obviously lost in terrible memory, while my companion and I felt our spirits cringe at the thought of what we were about to hear. Callistus held his hands close together and extended them in my direction. Once again, the torch beam illuminated the scars of terrible injuries. Dead white skin hung loosely from the meat of the young man's arms and I could feel my stomach cringing again as I thought about the agony he had endured.

"They set alight to the plastic on my wrists first," he explained simply. "The pain was terrible and I screamed for mercy, but then it was my ankles and knees and then they were all laughing as they set my private parts alight.

'I think I must have fainted because the next thing I remember is lying on the floor with water being poured over me while another man kept kicking me like a dog that was in his way.

'Later that night, they told me that I could go, but the pain was too much and I couldn't walk. Two men then picked me up and dumped me in the road outside the police post. They threw my clothes into a puddle on the road and I don't know how long I lay there naked in the mud. Eventually, two strangers stopped to see that I was alright and they took me to a clinic where my wounds were tended to.

'I was in serious pain for many weeks."

Those last few words were said with such simple honesty that I felt tears springing to my eyes. Turning to my friend, I demanded to know what had been done about the cruel torture inflicted on the young man. He laughed, but there was little humour in the sound.

"Remember that this is Robert Mugabe's Zimbabwe, Bryan my friend. There is no justice and in this case, it was undoubtedly the Central Intelligence Organisation who were responsible. When you and I were policemen, there were rules that we had to abide by, but for CIO and the police of today, there are no rules or regulations except those that our president feels like imposing. The courts are powerless; honest police officers are powerless; we are all powerless. Incidents like this should be broadcast to the world, which is why I brought you here, but I don't know if the world really cares about Zimbabwe.

'Still, I know that you will do your best."

The morning after that terrible meeting with poor Callistus, I drove the Ganja Bus out of town and headed East toward distant Harare. My eyes were scratchy from lack of sleep, as we had sat up late that night, discussing the ruination of the country we both loved and demolishing a bottle of whisky in the process. It was a sad and depressing evening and even though I tumbled into bed very late, I could not get the mental picture of Callistus Shumba's terrible injuries out of my mind.

Passing what had once been Brady Barracks, I felt somewhat ashamed of my own cowardice in not wandering further afield. After all, I wanted to speak with ordinary people. I wanted to write about the problems they were facing, yet here I was turning my back on simple folk like Callistus. They were living in conditions of intimidation and violence that were as bad or even worse than they had been when Zimbabwe was being torn apart by civil war. These people needed somebody to tell their stories, so why was I abandoning them?

It was not a nice feeling, but I knew that my former colleague had been right. As a white man, I was far too conspicuous and might well put the people I wanted to help into even more danger by visiting their homes. I would also be putting my own safety at risk and while that might add to the excitement of life, I had a family who worried about me and if anything did happen, they could also find themselves under scrutiny from an already paranoid authority.

Thinking about my family, reminded me that although I had been in the country for nearly six weeks, I had yet to see my eldest grandson. He was doing his first term at boarding school – at the grand old age of eight - and his trips home had not coincided with my visits.

"Oh to hell with it all!" I growled at my lumbering transport. "Let's head back to Kariba and see the Kids."

Chapter Nine

(A Day to Remember)

Wearing no hat and a grey shirt that hung outside his uniform trousers, he was hardly the sort of young man to inspire confidence in the Zimbabwe Republic Police service, but I stopped to offer him a lift in any case.

I had spotted him beside the road, waving a languid hand in appeal and although my initial reaction was to drive on by, the chance of speaking with a serving policeman was too good to miss.

"I am going to Chegutu, Sir," he answered my question. "I have to be there by thirteen hundred hours or I will be late for my work."

As it was already after midday and we were at least fifty kilometres from Chegutu, I thought that was pushing things a bit, but he climbed into the passenger seat and we were soon on friendly terms. I kept a packet of cigarettes handy in the glove compartment for unexpected visitors and he was soon puffing smoke around the cab with gay abandon. I lit up my pipe to counter the cloud and almost immediately, the conversation veered around to politics and land resettlement.

"We are having great trouble with the white farmers," he told me with obvious concern. "They beat up the settlers and steal their property. They even take the farm equipment and send it out of the country. That is not a good thing to do for true Zimbabweans. These things are needed for the new settlers to grow their crops."

"But surely the machinery belongs to the people who bought it? Those farmers paid hard cash for their equipment, so they must be entitled to do whatever they want with it."

"But they are not helping the settlers," my companion was unimpressed with this logic. "These new farmers are trying to save Zimbabwe by planting crops and that is because the white farmers have refused to plant anything themselves. They are all rich, so do not have to worry but for poor people, food is needed badly."

As diplomatically as I could with memories of Terry Ford's anxious face in my mind, I pointed out that the farmers gave a different version of events. Many of them were not allowed to work their land and others had lost everything to the settlers, while the police had done nothing to help them.

"But we cannot," My companion was emphatic on the matter. "These white farmers are all politicians and they tell great lies. Like the British, they are on the side of MDC, but all thinking Zimbabweans know that Comrade President Mugabe is the man who led us out of slavery and made us free. Now we must support him or Zimbabwe once again will fall under the colonial yoke."

"But what about the farm workers?" I stifled an urge to throw him out of the vehicle. "Thousands of them are being beaten and dispossessed of everything they own. How can that be justified in a free society?"

"They are puppets of the white man," he looked suddenly doubtful as he remembered the colour of my skin. "The farmers have brainwashed them into believing bad things about the Comrade President. Our commissioner, Comrade Chihuri has told us that we must not listen to lies from the farmers or their workers."

I was moved to protest.

"But Mr Chihuri is now a farmer himself. What happens to his workers?"

Only a few weeks previously, Augustine Chihuri had kicked a Shamva farmer off his land and taken over the unfortunate man's thriving business for himself. A recent report in The Herald had shown the policeman inspecting 'his' tobacco crop and praised him to the skies as being an excellent farmer, bringing great credit to Zimbabwe and great benefit to the economy through his hard work."

The constable laughed.

"All the chefs must have land first," I struggled to believe what I was hearing. "After that, it will be shared among officials in government and business leaders who support the Party, then it will go to soldiers and people like me before the remainder will be shared out among the *povo*."

"So you want to be a farmer too?"

His eyes lit up with an enthusiastic gleam.

"I already know the farm that I will be settled on. It is not yet ready for occupation, but one day it will be mine – and others of course."

The last phrase seemed to tail off a bit and I realised that even in his incredible naiveté, this young man harboured doubts of his own. Brainwashed, he might have been, but he needed a modicum of intelligence to be accepted into the police service and even his enthusiasm was tempered by the harsh reality of the situation.

"Who runs the farm now – a white man?"

Suddenly angry, I was determined to cut him down to size. He nodded warily, probably sensing my change in attitude.

"So what will happen to him? Will he be thrown off his own land so that you and other people can live on it? Will he lose everything he has worked for all his life? Will he and his family be made homeless? Or will you just have him murdered as so many others have been murdered?"

He shook his head vigorously, a sullen look coming over his face.

"It is not like that. Land in Zimbabwe belongs to the people, not to the white man or the British. It must be shared out among all Zimbabweans."

"But the best bits must go to Mr Chihuri and the important people first?"

"They have earned the right by supporting our Comrade President through the bad times."

"But I supported the Comrade President too. I fought for his government in Bulawayo. Without the help of my troops and others like us, he might well have been thrown out even then. Can I also have land?"

The constable looked doubtful and my anger turned to pity. It wasn't really his fault. He was merely a young man, shaped by the system and no longer able to think for himself. As far as I was concerned, he was a disgrace to the uniform, I had once been proud to wear, but even more of a disgrace, were those men in power who had moulded him into thinking this way.

However, the conversation as such had come to an end. My passenger was obviously aware of my anger and he retreated into a sulky silence. I felt a sense of deep relief when we pulled into the main street of Chegutu and I could drop him off. Climbing out of the Ganja Bus, he looked somewhat doubtfully at me.

"Zimbabwe is only for Zimbabweans, Sir. We shall make it into a great country. You will see."

"If you can find enough to eat over the next few years, you might be right."

Shaking my head in weary resignation, I waved my hand and drove on, leaving the young constable gazing wonderingly after me. It was only when I had gone that I realised the cause of his bewilderment. Although I hadn't intended it as such, my wave had been the open handed gesture of an MDC supporter, which accounted for the fact that he had begun to wave back, then abruptly pulled his hand back to his side.

I was not sorry to leave the policeman, but an hour or so later, I wished I hadn't let him go as I was driving directly into trouble.

*　　*　　*

Known as the Gadzema Road, the main highway from Chegutu to Chinhoyi cuts out a great deal of mileage between Bulawayo and Kariba and it was a road, I had often used in the past. With my mood lightening by the moment, I sped along its smoothly tarred surface and headed for Kariba.

The only minor drawback to taking that road was the fact that it went directly through the heartland of Mugabe country. On either side of me was the Zvimba communal land and here there were no open-handed salutes from pedestrians, nor were there many smiling waves of welcome. The people I passed gazed at me with deep suspicion or raised their arms in the clenched-fist salute of Zanu PF and I knew that Tsvangirai would get no votes in this area.

Nevertheless, Alec Kay lived at the other end of this road and he had invited me to drop in so it seemed an excellent opportunity to experience for myself, life on a farm that had already been invaded.

For seventy kilometres, nothing went wrong and I was singing softly to the Ganja Bus as we came out of the communal land and entered Chinhoyi commercial farming area. Bare and barren looking land gave way to patches of forest and verdant fields, tractors chugged back and forth and whitewashed tobacco barns could be seen on both sides of the road. Feeling a tension that I had not realised I was experiencing ease from my shoulders, I looked for Alec's farm sign to the left of the road. He had told me that his property came right down to the tarmac and I 'couldn't miss it,' but he was wrong on one count at least. Driving very slowly, I peered at every gate, my frustration mounting by the moment.

Had I been paying more attention to the road itself, I would have seen them in good time, but before I quite realised what was happening, I found myself wrestling the Ganja Bus to an untidy halt. In front of me, a pile of *msasa* branches had been placed right across the tarmac. Around this makeshift barricade stood a group of youths and I didn't need to see the clubs and axes in their hands to realise that these were members of the notorious Youth Brigade and this was one of their infamous roadblocks.

Carefully ensuring that the vehicle doors were locked, I wound my window half up and waited for them to do something. At first, they were too fascinated by my vehicle to pay attention to me, but eventually two of them wandered around to my side, while the others clustered around the bonnet, exclaiming in delighted tones about the 'Malawi Gold' stencilling.

"Where are you going?"

The larger of the two on my side began quite politely. He wore a green jacket over his Mugabe sweatshirt and it was only the heavy stick in his hand that marked him out as anything but a pleasant young man seeking a lift.

"I am heading for Kariba."

"Why do you come this way then? This is not the way to Kariba."

"It is if you come from Bulawayo and that is where I have come from."

Obviously nonplussed, he held out a hand.

"Do you have money for me?"

I shook my head. There was no way that I would pay for the privilege of being stopped by these young thugs.

"No."

In an instant, the atmosphere changed. In spite of the circumstances, everything had seemed quite relaxed, but palpable tension suddenly filled the air. My questioner scowled and kept his hand out.

"Where is your party card?"

I tried to sound reasonable, but could feel the nervousness building in my stomach and knew that there was a risk of my voice cracking with fear. These young men were unpredictable and extremely dangerous. A number of farmers and other innocent motorists had been dragged from their vehicles and made to dance, chant political songs or humiliate themselves in other ways and I did not want to end up in the same predicament.

"I am a visitor to your country and do not support any political party, so I don't have a card."

"This is President Mugabe's road, so if you use it you must have a card."

"I didn't know that. Where can I get a card?"

I felt sure that my question would calm things down a bit, but it seemed to inflame the young man and he struck the front tyre of the Ganja Bus with his stick.

"Do not be clever with me," he snarled. "Give me five thousand dollars or you will be beaten."

There was a murmur of excited assent among the youths who had drifted up to his shoulder in order to witness the humiliation of another white man. They were clad in an assortment of torn and scruffy clothing, many of them wearing the ubiquitous Mugabe sweatshirts with the president's unsmiling features plastered across their chests. Apart from the one who wanted the money, they all seemed absurdly young and I wondered why I was allowing myself to be harassed by this collection of children. Two of them were still crouched over the front of the Ganja Bus, chortling at its paintwork and seeing that I had no intention of paying up, my questioner changed his tack.

"Out – get out of the car now or you will be beaten."

"Fuck off!"

I had definitely had enough and suddenly slamming the Ganja Bus into gear, I accelerated into the branches across the road, scattering wood and the two stragglers in the process. The dear old truck lurched, the engine screamed momentarily and we were over the obstacle and away. Behind me in the road, two young men howled their pain and I smiled grimly at the thought that with heavy bull bars, reinforced by a large winch on the front of my vehicle, they would be lucky to have escaped without broken bones. Somehow it did not seem to matter.

I was not out of trouble however. After a moment of consternation, the rest of the mob started out in howling pursuit. Sticks flew and I heard one thud against the rear of the vehicle, but I kept my foot hard on the accelerator and trundler or not, my lovely machine soon outdistanced the pursuers.

I had escaped the roadblock without injury or ritual humiliation and for that I was thankful, but the consequences of running down two of Mugabe's hand-picked troops could be dire if the incident was reported to the police. My nerves were fluttering and I was a worried man as I drove for Karoi, my intention to stop off with Alec Kay forgotten as I tried to put distance between myself and those loathsome young men who had stopped me.

In the event nothing happened. The police never came looking for me and I could only think that either the Youth Brigade had been too embarrassed to call on mere coppers for help or they had not managed to get my number in the confusion. Mind you, the Ganja Bus was hardly inconspicuous and would not have taken much finding, so perhaps the first option was the correct one. The Youth Brigade were a law unto themselves and even in the political climate of modern Zimbabwe, I could not think that local policemen would look on them with any favour.

Vowing never to even consider stopping at an unofficial roadblock again, I put my foot down and my grand old vehicle fairly rushed me along the road to Karoi and relative safety.

Chapter Ten

(Laughter and Local Leaders.)

I couldn't believe my eyes. It was only an hour since my confrontation with the Youth Brigade roadblock and here was a man in the middle of the road, waving a red flag. Surely, it could not be happening again?

This time I was not going to stop. Hauling the big engine down a gear, I accelerated past the flag-waver, yet even as he leaped to safety, I realised that there was something different about this road block.

To begin with, there was no obstacle in the road and although I caught a glimpse of figures in the verge and heard a despairing yell, there was no crowd of hostile youths confronting me. Secondly, something about red flags in the road struck a chord of memory. Where had I seen them before?

It didn't matter. I was clear of any possible trouble and I gunned the Ganja Bus into ever faster movement, while something important kept niggling at my brain. Replaying the scene with the flag bearer over in my mind, I tried to visualise the figures I had seen at the side of the road. Surely there had been a pram or a wheelchair of some sort over on its side? I was aware of two people, apart from the flag-bearer and one of those had been sitting or lying down. Hadn't that cry I heard had been something like, 'Help us please.'

It was too much. Youth Brigade roadblocks or not, my conscience would not allow me to go on without checking out the man with the red flag. Sighing with deep exasperation, I laboriously turned my transport around.

They were waiting for me at the side of the road. Two young men with red flags and the wheelchair jockey himself – a tiny, wizened man with a badly twisted leg and a beaming smile.

"Hello Sir – we knew you would come back."

Still a bit shaky from my run in with the Youth Brigade, I greeted him somewhat curtly.

"What is the problem?"

"It is my chair; a bolt has sheared off."

He held up the offending bolt and I wondered what they expected me to do about it. Barely two minutes later, I knew. With the handicapped one ensconced in the seat beside me, his acolytes on the rear seat and what seemed like a mountain of kit and equipment, plus the damaged wheelchair in the boot, we were on our way again to Karoi. I was in no mood for idle conversation, but felt that I had to make the effort. Besides, this twisted little man intrigued me. Where was he heading for on a hot day like this? How far had he come on a very battered wheelchair that had seen better days? He then made me feel churlish by introducing himself.

"I am Jack Moyo," he announced grandly. "I am from Gweru, but presently living in Chegutu."

"You're a long way from home, Jack," was all I could think of to say. "What are you doing out here?"

"I am travelling from Plumtree to Kariba in order to raise money."

It was said without fuss or elaboration and I turned my head to look at the man. Plumtree was in the far South West of the country and at least one thousand kilometres away. At that stage, we were less than two hundred kays from Kariba, so most of his journey was done, but it must have been a tremendous slog in his unusual transport.

"How long has that taken you then?"

His beaming smile was guileless and in spite of my precarious mood, I found myself warming to the little fellow.

"Many weeks altogether," he told me. "I need to find out about chickens, so we have paused wherever we have seen them being reared."

"Chickens?"

I have heard many unlikely reasons for adventure, but learning about chickens must surely have been the most original. Jack hastened to explain and it seemed that he had dreams of starting up his own business of large-scale chicken rearing in Gweru. He had done his homework and knew what it would cost and how long it would take before the business was viable, but I wondered if he had thought about the competition. A farming friend of mine had tried poultry rearing a few years previously and although he had done reasonably well at first, the major producers soon cut him out and he had gone back to growing tobacco. Jack smiled when I told the story.

"Ah but your friend was trying to be too big," he said gently. "Even if I raise a lot of money from this trip, I will not be able to supply shops or supermarkets. My market will be among people in the townships and those who work on the farms."

That comment brought back memories of what had not been a pleasant morning and I wondered how long anyone would be left working on the farms. Jack shook his head at my comment.

"It is true; it is true," he said mildly. "To be a farm worker in these times, you need to be very brave and very strong. All over the country, they are being forced off the land and I have even been in trouble myself during my journey."

"You?" I was surprised. "What on earth for?"

"For being there I suppose. Because I am crippled, people know that I cannot fight back, so they are mean and nasty with me. Most people are very good, but I have had troubles from the Youth Brigade and even some settlers whom I asked for water."

In spite of his handicap, Jack Moyo seemed to laugh at the vicissitudes of life and his problems made my run in on the Gadzema Road seem pretty mild. I felt immediately ashamed of my churlishness when I had first met these intrepid young men. In contrast to my feelings when dropping the young constable in Chegutu, I found myself disappointed when we drove through the main street of Karoi, so I suggested that we stop for a coke at a garage before I sent them on their way.

"We need to be left at a garage anyway," Jack told me. "If they cannot fix this bolt or get me another one, I shall have to dash across town to another place I know."

It provoked an incongruous picture in my mind and Jack smiled when he realised what I was thinking.

"I can dash," he told me solemnly. "I have crutches in my kit and can go as fast as anyone, but only for fifteen kilometres."

"And then?"

I knew a fair number of able-bodied folk who would struggle to 'dash' fifteen kays, but Jack was unabashed.

"After fifteen kays, my hands get blistered and I can go no further."

Over our cool drinks, he told me that he was thirty-three years old and had been stricken with polio when he was four. He took this as God's will and assured me that he could do everything that anybody else could do. He led a full life and although he was not married, he had been thinking about getting himself a wife when he raised the money for *lobolo*.

"Have you a lady in mind? I asked innocently and he roared with laughter.

"There are many," he assured me. "Wherever I go, they all want to see Jack Moyo."

With his infectious good humour and obvious zest for life, I could well believe it and when I drove on again, I realised that the meeting with Jack had restored my good humour. I couldn't help reflecting that people with nothing, so often set an example for those of us who can get almost anything we need.

I was to see more of Jack Moyo and his acolytes, but I didn't know that when I took a couple of photographs of the trio and drove on to see a local farmer.

*   *   *

I had been given Chris Sheppard's name as a leading light in the Karoi community and we met at the Twin Rivers Motel just outside the town. I had to wait a little while and watched with interest as a South African election monitoring team sat down on the lawn and ordered lunch. They were obviously enjoying life and I wondered why they weren't out in the communal lands or even on the Gadzema road, watching out for my roadblock friends. My reverie was interrupted by Chris' arrival. Thick set and fair haired, he was dressed in the regulation farmer's gear of shorts, casual shirt and calf length boots over baggy socks. After we had shaken hands, he regarded me with obvious doubt.

"I was told you were coming up," he said. "I don't know what I can tell you though."

I had been given the impression that he was in charge of security for the area and as Karoi had been taking a real bashing from war veterans and squatters over the previous weeks, that seemed a good place to start. But Chris had other ideas.

"I tell you what, I have a meeting with the local MDC boss at two o'clock. He was involved in a pitched battle with Zanu PF thugs last night and we need to make a plan of action. Would you like to come home for lunch and then we can meet him?"

I had tried to avoid politicians of any sort on my trip so far, but Chris was so obviously enthusiastic that it seemed only polite to agree and besides, the thought of lunch appealed. Leaving the Ganja Bus in radiant splendour on the motel forecourt, I jumped into Chris's truck and off we went.

Lunch was a delight. The Sheppard residence was an elegant, double-storied building, surrounded by fields and paddocks. Birds sang in tall trees around the house and a magnificent stud bull gazed impassively over a small fence as we alighted from the vehicle. Inside, I met Chris' lovely wife, Elly and a friend who brought a three hundred percent improvement to my day, by asking if I was my elder son's brother.

"I am not, but I'll tell him that you thought so," was my comment and realising her mistake, Peta McDonald laughed uproariously. To give him his due, so did Brian when I carried out my promise to tell him.

At the table, Chris very much held court and his views on the presidential election were somewhat depressing.

"If Mugabe and his thugs get in again, he will have every white man out of this country within two weeks."

It was a somewhat dogmatic declaration and when I queried this, Chris assured me that he had it on excellent authority from people who were in the know with government ministers. I concentrated on happier subjects and complimented Elly on the food. It was possible that Chris was correct, but after knowing him less than an hour, I had him down as one of those men who delights in intrigue and likes people to think that (a) he is in the know and (b) he is a very important man. I could have been misjudging him, but I cannot say that I was overly impressed on either count.

After lunch, it was back to work and I was amazed at the sudden change in my host. From being a genial family man, he suddenly became a would-be secret agent of note and I had the distinct impression that he was enjoying himself. Even though there were only the two of us in the truck, he held a number of low-voiced conversations on his mobile phone and eventually told me that we had to meet the MDC man on the dot of two o'clock. If we were late – as seemed distinctly possible - he would 'think we had been taken by the CIO.'

None of it made much sense to me, but I was prepared to humour him, so hung on to my hat as we hurtled through town. We made it, but only just and I looked around me with interest as we approached a group of thuggish looking men, all of whom were wearing dark glasses in the car park of Karoi Golf Club.

*   *   *

There have always been many brave people in Zimbabwe and I met a number of them in the course of my travels. There were journalists like Jan Raath, Peta Thornycroft and Geoff Nyarota who risked their lives and liberty to get reports out to the rest of the world. There were farmers like Iain Kay and Pat Ashton who continued working their land in spite of continued harassment, violence and intimidation. There were women like Kerry Kay who had devoted her life to victims of AIDS and ignored spurious arrest and constant intimidation to keep going. There were of course, many thousands of farm labourers who were determined to vote in the presidential election, come what may and there were the MDC workers from Morgan Tsvangirai downward who seemed determined to get a change of government and make Zimbabwe a safer place for everyone.

Among the last category was Biggie Haurove who was the local chairman of MDC in Karoi. He also seemed to be something of a war lord and I resolved to be fairly cynical where he was concerned. After many searching glances over his shoulder and a whispered warning to keep my eyes open and be prepared for a quick getaway, Chris introduced me to Biggie and the story he told was not a pleasant one.

"They hit my house last night," He was indeed a very big man, but he seemed remarkably calm for one who had been under attack so recently. My own knees still felt a little shaky after the roadblock episode that morning. "During the afternoon, there were truck loads of Mugabe youths coming in and they surrounded the house until there were close to three hundred. We were but six to start with – my wife and children plus two domestics and myself. Others joined us when their own houses were hit by stones and all the women and children hid under furniture while the attack went on."

Leaning against a nearby car, he talked quietly into my tape recorder while Chris and a collection of hard-faced bodyguards wandered around the vicinity, no doubt looking for concealed policemen. When I asked where the bodyguards had been when the attack was on, Biggie smiled slowly.

"My men were outside," he explained. "We realised very early on that there was going to be trouble and so we armed ourselves with many stones. When the Zanu men started throwing their rocks, we retaliated and kept them back with our own missiles."

The thought of a battle with sticks and stones in this age of ICBMs, smart bombs and other assorted heavy weaponry tickled me, but Biggie was very serious and I kept my face straight as I listened to his story.

The attack on his house had started well before midnight and continued for over four hours. Somehow, he and his bodyguards kept the mob at bay, but when the local police arrived to sort out the problem, they were chased away by the Zanu PF youths.

"The police were too scared," Biggie said gleefully. "One rock hit the windscreen of their truck and they ran away like frightened women.

'Do you want to see the house?"

At the question, Chris became visibly agitated and urged me not to go into the township, but I was becoming a little fed up with all the melodrama and more to annoy the farmer than through any real urge to investigate the story, I agreed to visit the house.

In spite of the apparent ferocity of the four-hour rock battle, there had been little damage caused. The walls of Biggie's small, township house were heavily scarred, while there was a hole in the asbestos roof and a broken French window, but that was all. Nobody had been hurt in the fray, but Biggie's family confessed to have been terrified while it went on.

"The police returned this morning," he told me scornfully. "They were brave now that it was daylight and wanted to search my house for guns. They would not believe that I only had my seven men with rocks to help me and kept on and on about illegal weapons. They eventually left me alone, but they will be back again tomorrow. Because I am MDC, I am marked and either the police or Zanu PF will get me eventually."

As if to prove his point, we were forced to move when Chris hurried up to tell us about a man who had been loitering nearby and had suddenly disappeared.

"He has probably gone to call the CIO," Biggie told me as we drove back to the Twin Rivers, where the South African election monitors were still at their garden table. "Wherever I go, I am under surveillance from someone."

I wasn't sure whether to believe him or not, but watching the observers was an education in itself. They sat around a couple of tables on shady lawns and seemed unaware that they were under close scrutiny from two groups. Biggie pointed them out with a scornful laugh.

"Those two are CIO," he explained. "They look to see who will meet with the observers. And those ones," he indicated another pair of hard-eyed 'heavies,' "are bodyguards for the observers themselves. They look to see who the CIO are watching."

It all seemed terribly complicated, but the politics of Africa are both complicated and dangerous. Biggie Haurove had no doubt that his house would be under attack again that night.

"We shall be ready for them," he said heavily. "When they come, we will fight them off again and when Morgan wins the election we will have our revenge."

In the parliamentary elections of 2000, Karoi had the largest Zanu PF majority in the country, yet Biggie and Chris seemed convinced that this would be overturned and Tsvangirai elected with a landslide majority. If that were to happen, Biggie Haurove would be in a position of power and although I could not help admiring his courage, I was a little disturbed by his cold-blooded certainty that the time for revenge was getting closer.

Somewhat to my horror, Chris suddenly brought one of the South Africans over to me for an introduction. Whose idea it was, I didn't know, but I had the feeling that the farmer was merely trying to show off his own importance. Whether to the election observer or to me, I was not sure, but meeting these chaps was the last thing I wanted.

Quickly making my excuses, I drove on for Kariba, leaving Biggie telling his story to the South Africans and Chris bustling around and being important. He was actually a very nice chap, Chris Sheppard and invited me to watch the election from his lovely home – a prospect that definitely appealed.

"Come out for the weekend; we have a nice little outside *rondavel* where you can work in peace. There will be an ops room set up in the house and I shall be out most of the time, but Elly will look after you."

It was a tempting offer, but I have probably had enough of operations room for one lifetime and when I pulled out on to the main road, I pondered uneasily on the violence that had already hit the Karoi community. It was probably illogical, but with all their intrigue and cloak and dagger activities, I couldn't help wondering how many of the reports I had heard were genuine and how much was make believe. It was not fair thinking on my part, but in the event, Mugabe won fairly comfortably in Karoi, Biggie Haurove survived to vote another day, while Chris and his delightful family remained in their magnificent farmhouse for another few months, despite his prophecies of immediate gloom and doom.

The farm, Nyamanda consisted of a thousand hectares of beautifully maintained and extremely profitable land. It was eventually taken over by the Minister for the Environment, Francis Nhema, who not long afterwards was almost unbelievably elected to head the United Nations commission on sustainable development. He couldn't even sustain the farm he stole from Chris Sheppard.

Chris used to produce a hundred hectares of maize and another hundred of tobacco, as well as beef, cattle pigs and sheep. He had employed two hundred and fifty workers and housed both them and their families. During the season, he would take on another two hundred and fifty contract workers and they were also supplied with housing, food and various benefits. Under Nhema's dubious ownership, the entire set up quickly degenerated into a wasteland. Flying low over the farm some weeks after it had been taken from him, Chris Sheppard was horrified by the change.

"There was about thirty hectares of wilting maize which will produce nothing," he told me angrily when we met up in Harare. "It hasn't been irrigated. Nhema rents out some of my land to a couple of white farmers still in the district. There is nothing else. The place looks dreadful. Two of the tobacco barns which burned down after Nhema moved in have not been rebuilt. I could hardly believe my eyes when I saw the destruction. Within a few weeks of our leaving the place, thirty percent of male workers on the farm had moved on and only about ten of them are still there."

I had heard similar stories from other dispossessed farmers. Many of the workers taken on by Mugabe's cronies reported that they were grossly underpaid and exploited by their new employers and most of them walked out in disgust.

"You must speak to my farm manager about anything related to the farm," Nhema said fatuously when I phoned him in New York. He denied that the farm taken over from Sheppard had as much as one thousand and sixty-seven hectares. "I didn't know that. I don't own that much land."

Sheppard was understandably furious."When Elly and I were so violently evicted," he told me, "it took the Zim NSPCA several days to negotiate their way onto the farm. We left more than four hundred pigs that had not been watered for a week and were killing each other. It was too terrible."

When Francis Nhema was voted into the chair of the UN commission, the voting was twenty-six votes to twenty-one, with three abstentions. Needless to say, the votes for him were all from the African bloc. The body was supposed to be responsible for promoting economic progress and environmental protection and Nhema was elected despite opposition from human rights organisations, the United States and European nations. Sigmar Gabriel, Germany's Environment Minister, said the European Union had imposed travel sanctions among other penalties on officials in President Robert Mugabe's government, so it would be impossible for the EU environmental authorities to have contact with Nhema. I couldn't help the sour thought that he was as out of touch with reality as the rest of Europe's politicians – including Tony Blair.

A jubilant Boniface Chidyausiku, Zimbabwe's ambassador to the UN told the BBC after the vote that he was very pleased with the result: "What has sustainable development to do with human rights? The post rotates among regions and Africa nominated Nhema as chairman of the commission."

Nhema himself was more prosaic.

"I think this is not the time to point fingers." He said blandly. "There is never a perfect method; it's always a method which is appropriate to each country, so it's important not only to look at Zimbabwe, but to look at each other and see what we can learn."

He had obviously learned nothing about farming despite having taken over one of the most prosperous and well managed farms in Africa and as Minister for the environment he had already proved himself a complete failure. Under his tenureship of the post, poaching in Zimbabwe had reached unprecedented levels and scores of conservancies had collapsed.

So had Nyamanda Farm and the people who really suffered for the takeover were not only Chris Sheppard and his family, but all his workers and their families, as well as thousands of other Zimbabweans being driven ever faster down the road to eventual starvation.

* * *

But the loss of Nyamanda Farm was still in the future and as I drove up to Kariba Heights that evening, I looked somewhat ruefully back on what had been the most eventful day of my trip. It had also been a day of extreme mood swings. That morning, I had been depressed in Bulawayo, while my chat with the police constable from Chegutu had made me angry. Events at the Youth Brigade roadblock had frightened the life out of me and left me weak and trembling with reaction, while my spirits had been lifted immeasurably by the infectious humour of Jack Moyo – a man who had so little in his own life to make him cheerful.

Then of course there had been the high melodrama of my afternoon in Karoi and now I was on my way to spend time in the bosom of my family. When a trio of young elephant bulls stood in the middle of the road and dared me to pass, I laughed aloud in sheer good humour. Kariba is surely a magical place and I was determined to have a couple of days off. I had been travelling and working for nearly six weeks, the election was ten days away and I felt that I deserved a break.

Chapter Eleven

(Troubles in Paradise)

If there was one place in Zimbabwe where all the ills that were afflicting my country could really be seen, it was Kariba. I have lived in this lovely little resort town on an 'on and off' basis for nearly forty years, my family lived there until very recently and I love the place with a passion. Where else in the world can visitors have water sports, spectacular scenery, endless sunshine and elephants walking across hotel lawns or plucking foliage outside bedroom windows? Quite apart from the excitements on offer, the people of Kariba are traditionally a laid back lot and always willing to help a stranger in difficulty.

In early March, Kariba is fiendishly hot, but even then the place should have been bustling with foreign visitors. However, when I breezed thankfully into town after my eventful journey, the hotels were virtually empty, luxury leisure craft lay idle in the harbours and day-hire boats were lined up like city taxis, while their drivers waited for clients who obviously were not coming.

After my problems in Bulawayo and on the road, I was particularly pleased to switch off and relax, but the journalistic bug had taken over my soul and even in the bosom of my family, I was looking for human interest stories. Friends greeted me as though they saw me every day however and I had the feeling that I would not get much to file from my home town.

I needed a break though and for a couple of days, I relaxed in well-remembered bars, chatted with old friends and allowed the hot sun to ease the kinks from my body and beer to dull the worries in my mind.

My first working stop in Kariba itself was at Caribbea Bay, a pink-stuccoed holiday complex, built in the Sardinian style and run by my eldest son. We arrived there early in the morning as befits the General Manager of a leading hotel, but once there, Brian had little to do.

"It is normally quiet from January through to March, Dad," he told me thoughtfully, "but this year the whole place seems completely dead."

The reasons certainly were not difficult to work out. In the run up to the parliamentary elections in 2000, violence in Kariba made headlines around the world. Two supporters of the MDC were beaten to death in the Zambezi Valley Hotel and their bodies were left in Nyamunga shopping centre as dire warning to any locals who might have been thinking of voting for Morgan Tsvangirai's party. A woman from the Kariba banana farm was chased naked through the streets of Nyamunga township, while chanting youths beat her with sticks and two other men just disappeared. The perpetrators, led by a thug, calling himself Comrade Jesus were arrested and promptly released under a presidential amnesty, but few overseas visitors were going to risk being caught up in that sort of violence before yet another election. I didn't think visitors were likely in Kariba until the Mugabe regime was voted out and a new president was installed. If Mugabe remained in power, it was highly likely that visitors would not be seen in Kariba again.

"It is pretty worrying," Brian confirmed. "Our average daily occupancy is about twelve and this is a six hundred and fifty bed hotel."

The sad thing is that Kariba is one of the most beautiful places in the world and with the Zimbabwe dollar changing hands on the parallel market at well over seven thousand to the pound – five years later it would going at seven million to the pound and would rise to staggering numbers before it was finally abandoned – the place should have been a major tourist destination. Standing on a veranda at Caribbea Bay, I could only sigh in wonderment at the view before me. The great lake stretched blue and vast into the distance, the hills of Matusadona looked hazy in the sunshine and I might well have been on the edge of the Mediterranean Sea. But this is how Kariba is and has always been. Luxury hotels and lodges are scattered almost haphazardly around the shoreline and not only elephants, but lions, leopards, buffalo and a host of smaller but very wild animals can often be seen ambling through the town itself.

Before settling down to some serious work, I had promised myself a break and this came in the form of a magical four days on the lake. I travelled in Queen Two – my favourite vessel – with friends, Barry Simpson and Danie Coetzee, plus a pretty New Zealand girl, Miriam Eyles who was out from London. We wandered the waterways of the Matusadona National Park, watched elephants, rhino, hippopotami and a variety of smaller animals in their natural surroundings and enjoyed each other's company in that magical ambience that is surely peculiar to Lake Kariba. The trip was over far too soon and Miriam was bubbling over with enthusiasm when we finally parted at Kariba Breezes Hotel – also suffering from an acute lack of trade.

"It was just breathtaking," she said sincerely, "I cannot remember when I have enjoyed myself so much and I can't wait to come back again."

But it looked as though Miriam and I were the only visitors in town and for the locals, the good life seemed to have come to an end. Quite apart from the absence of tourists, food was desperately short. Cooking oil and sugar were no longer available in the shops and when Blue Water Charters brought in thirty-four tons of maize meal one Saturday morning, over five hundred hopeful customers stood patiently waiting for hours in the blazing sun.

"It was pretty chaotic," Dave Webster owned Blue Waters. "We struggled to serve them all and by Monday we were almost out of stock again. God only knows when we will have another delivery and if these people have nothing to eat, wild life will suffer. Thousands of impala in this area have already been snared."

Dave was a former fruit farmer and his mother was the last surviving member of the Pioneer Column, so he spoke Chishona like a native. He was popular in Kariba and his harbour-side shop was always crowded with customers, many of them coming just to enjoy a chat with this white man who sounded so black. But like so many other Zimbabwean businessmen, Dave Webster had already been threatened by the local branch of Zanu PF War Veterans. Not any old war vets mind you – these ones were definitely supporters of the ruling party. When Dave dismissed a worker for stealing a boat engine, Mr Mudede, the local chairman of the War Veterans Task Force Labour Committee (think of an acronym for that!) sent him a letter demanding that the man be paid forty-five thousand Zim dollars within three days 'or we will come to your place to stop you operating your business.'

"I called the police and it was sorted out, but this sort of petty bullying is becoming ever more commonplace," Dave was philosophical. "They didn't dare try anything with the queues this weekend though. At one stage, a couple of thugs moved up toward the head of the line, but you could hear the grumble in the crowd and they thought better of it. If they had tried to jump their turn, I reckon the people would have torn them apart. The need for mealie meal is desperate now and supplies are getting ever more difficult to come by."

Taking a bit of a risk, I visited the Ministry of Works office at the other side of the harbour. This government building was where the so-called war veterans had made their headquarters and I was curious to see some of those who had so laid waste to my country. I need not have bothered. Even though I came with a spurious story about wanting to fire my garden worker, Mr Mudede refused to speak with me.

"He is too busy," I was told by a gum-chewing youth in jeans and a torn Zanu PF tee shirt. "He cannot see you."

"What will happen when I sack this man and he complains that I have underpaid him?"

"Then you will be summoned to see Mr Mudede." The answer was unequivocal and I marvelled at the power these completely unofficial officials seem to hold over ordinary people.

But my main interest in Kariba was not so much in how the white business community was faring, but what was happening in the townships. Mahombekombe is the smaller of the two high-density suburbs, but this seemed very peaceful when I drove through, so deciding that I might as well be hanged for a sheep as a lamb, I headed out to Nyamunga in the Ganja Bus. The sun was fiendishly hot as I pulled up outside the Zambezi Valley supermarket and ambled into the store itself.

At first, everything appeared normal and I greeted old friends such as the Lake Captain and James Gumpo who owned the entire Zambezi Valley set up of hotel, supermarkets, transport and mining companies. Everyone was friendly and when I came out again, there was the inevitable crowd around my vehicle.

"Lovely colour," a young man named Fanwell ventured and I solemnly agreed that it was indeed a lovely colour. I didn't even cross my fingers as I said it and to be truthful, that garish gold was beginning to grow on me. I chatted for a while with Fanwell and his friends, but they were obviously nervous and as soon as I broached the subject of politics and violence, sidelong glances were thrown to all points of the compass and a few of my companions pointedly drifted away. Nobody wanted to talk, but over a beer in the nearby Zambezi Valley Hotel, Fanwell told me that he and his friends were all supporters of the MDC.

"We have to keep it very quiet," he went on seriously. "Those people from the Border Gezi Youth Movement come into Nyamunga every weekend. They hold *pungwes* and they terrorise the people. On Saturday or Sunday mornings, they set up road blocks near the shopping centre and everyone who goes by must produce a Zanu PF card."

"And if they don't have a card?"

Fanwell shook his head.

"Then they will be beaten or fined by those people. If they have any money in their pockets, it will be taken and if not, they will be hit on the face or body with sticks before being chased away to get themselves a card.

'Those people hold parades through the streets of Nyamunga and they drag passers by and children along to support them. If we do not go and watch, we are in trouble. Nobody has been killed yet, but everyone in Nyamunga is fearful about what will happen before the election. There will be much bloodshed, Sir; I promise you."

There was one person who could surely tell me more about life in Nyamunga and when I called in at the offices of Lemon and Carey Safaris, Verna Mangiza gave me a big, welcoming hug.

"Why didn't you let us know you were in the country?" She bubbled, but when I tried to gently pump her for information, even Verna clammed up.

"It is dangerous to say too much," She told me and I adopted my most cajoling manner.

"Come on Verna Dear; you know me of old. Whatever you tell me is going no further."

This time I did have my fingers crossed and couldn't help wondering whether regular journalists lie as much as I seemed to have been doing over the previous few days. Firmly quashing all twinges of conscience, I took Verna to lunch at the nearby Kariba Breezes poolside restaurant and after a glass of wine, she loosened up a little.

Verna was an elegant, highly educated lady and she made an excellent companion. She had already worked for Lemon & Carey for many years, but her house was in Nyamunga Township and she had deep reservations about the weeks ahead.

"I suppose I support Tsvangirai's crowd, but I am not really politically minded and we keep a low profile at home," she said. "I am well paid and the youths do not like that, particularly as I work for a white man. Kariba is my home and I don't want to leave, but I need to work and if we do not get an influx of visitors soon, there will be no work for anyone. Then what can I do?"

It was an unanswerable question, but one that I had heard all too often throughout Zimbabwe. In Kariba, tourism was the local lifeline and without it, this sparkling little resort would inevitably become just another African shantytown. Folk like Verna obviously did not want this but I had no ready answer to her question.

She had her own ideas however and had obviously been entertaining them for some time. Shortly before the election was due to take place, I wandered back into the Lemon & Carey office for another chat and my query as to her whereabouts was greeted with roars of laughter from the office staff.

"She is now an asylum seeker, refugee or whatever you want to call it in your country," Steve Carey is a very big man and I looked up at him in perplexity. "She told us that she was having a holiday in Cape Town, but then we received a frantic call from one of our London agents. Verna had pitched up at Heathrow and given them as references. They didn't know what to do and the upshot of it all was that the silly fool was given a week in the UK, which expired yesterday. She was not on last nights flight, so God alone knows where she is now."

"But why did she do it?" I had visions of my friend Verna skulking in some Brixton council flat or being forced to ply the streets of Soho to make a living. "I know she was worried about the lead up to the election, but not this worried."

"Hah!" The exclamation came from the office clerk who went by the unlikely name of Obedience. "She wasn't scared – not Verna: she just wanted to make some proper money rather than Zim dollars. She was always going on about sterling and how much easier life is in the UK."

I was shattered. I had looked on Verna as a friend and wondered why she hadn't confided in me when we had our lunch time chat. I might have been able to help in some small way and I knew from my own experience that although many Zimbabweans look upon Britain as the Promised Land, life in the West can be very cruel. Now she was a fugitive from justice and would not even be able to get out of Britain unless she had a forged passport.

It all seemed terribly sad, but later in the day I cheered up considerably as I sat with a beer and watched my grandsons playing with a little girl called Precious. The pretty little mite had been found in the boot of a car while its South African occupants tried to smuggle her across the dam wall to Zambia, where she would have been murdered and her body parts used for *muti* or traditional medicine. Fortunately, her tiny life had been saved by an alert Immigration Officer and she was now in the loving care of a Kariba couple. With all the sadness and desperation going on in Zimbabwe, it was reassuring to know that there were still good people in the country and when she went off home, I gave Precious a big hug for restoring my faith in humanity – even if only just a little.

I had been trying to make a plan as where best to be for the election itself. Harare was the obvious place, but Bulawayo was another possibility. Of course there was Chris Sheppard's offer to observe from Karoi and I could always head back into the hills of Nyanga. It was definitely time I moved on from Kariba, but my plans were thrown into further disarray when my grandson, Gareth confided that he and his schoolmates had been given the following weekend off.

"I will be home again, Gramps," he told me seriously. "It is election time and we will all be sent home in case of trouble. Will you still be here?"

I felt a moment of acute guilt. This was supposed to be a family trip, yet I was neglecting my loved ones in the search for people with stories that I could send back to London. I was keen that tales about the ordinary folk of Zimbabwe should be read by the outside world, but that was no excuse for neglecting my nearest and dearest.

"Of course, I will, My Boy."

And so it was settled. I would spend the polling weekend in Kariba and hopefully get a couple of stories from those who had come up to the lake in order to avoid voting. It was fairly obvious that the poll counts would not be announced for a few days, so that would give me time to get back into Harare for the results and be back in Kariba a week later, when I was to give a talk on elephants for a local restaurant. The talk was scheduled for the final Tuesday of my trip and had been pencilled into my calendar many weeks previously.

Three return trips to Kariba in close succession would mean a great deal of solitary driving, but I was growing accustomed to that and the talk was to raise money for elephants, so that was important.

I even debated spending a week – or perhaps the entire fortnight - in Kariba and visiting a safari camp to chill out for a few days. It was a tempting prospect, but events conspired against me yet again. On Sunday evening, I received a call from Mary Jane in Nyanga. I had promised to come up there again in order to photograph the Ashmores for a possible magazine spread on 'the good life' as lived by them.

"If you want photographs, you will have to get here on Monday," Mary Jane told me firmly. "Gill is trying to get her right to vote back in the Mutare Court on Tuesday and they are not sure how long it will take. They are taking a few days off after that, so Monday is the only time they are free."

It meant another long drive, as Nyanga was on the other side of the country and it also meant that my plans to relax in safari camp luxury had to be scrapped, but there was nothing for it.

"Okay," I said. "I will be with you by early evening."

Before I left the following morning, I was cornered by my daughter in law. After she had given me a hug and kissed me goodbye, she spoke very seriously.

"Please give us a call to let us know how you are every so often. We worry about you."

I laughed a little uneasily. I have always enjoyed travelling about on my own, content in the knowledge that nobody knows where I am and I have only myself to worry about if things go wrong. It is a selfish attitude I know and Sarah was pointing this out to me.

"There is no need to worry about me, Sarah Dear. I have been wandering this continent for years without any real mishap."

She is a determined girl, my daughter in law and not to be put off by my false heroics.

"The one who worries most is your son," she said quietly. "He gets into quite a state when we haven't heard from you in a while."

That floored me. My eldest son is a quiet, gentle man who has risen to the top in his own field with a minimum of fuss. Throughout the trip, he had been only too keen to help and I had filed a number of reports from his office computer – a generous gesture on his part, as he could drop into serious trouble with the authorities if we were found out. He was the last person I would have thought of as worrying about a nomadic father, but I was touched and secretly very pleased.

"I will do my best," I promised and soon afterwards, I was driving away from the great lake and heading for distant mountains.

Chapter Twelve

(More Heartbreak in the Hills)

I could not believe my eyes. Rounding a bend, I saw them relaxing in a lay by and if I hadn't recognised the wizened little figure in the wheelchair, the red flags carried by the other two would certainly have told me who they were.

When I pulled into the lay by, I was greeted with beaming smiles and a handshake from Jack Moyo. His acolytes were as silent as ever, but their smiles made me feel that they were delighted to see me.

"What are you doing here?"

The question was not as inane as it sounded. It was only four days since I had left them in Karoi and even if they had made a major dash to Kariba, they would not have had time to return this far. We were between Lions Den and Chinhoyi – a good sixty kilometres further back from Karoi.

Jack laughed disarmingly.

"My chair is still broken," The broken bolt worked one of the small steering wheels in front of the contraption and I could see the hole where it had been. "We tried for a while with a made up bolt, but it did not work very well and the police told us that it was not safe to go all the way to Kariba. We turned back, but now the bolt has gone again and we are stuck. A farmer has taken the bolt away to see whether he can make another one, so now we just wait."

"Why did the police say that the road to Kariba was not safe?"

My mind was on other things. Could trouble have started in Kariba since I had left a few hours previously? Jack shook his head as he spotted the drift of my thoughts.

"They were worried about lions," he grinned. "They said that we would be eaten if we took that road."

And indeed they might have been and would not have been the first. We chatted for a while longer, but I had a long drive ahead of me, so I took my leave of Jack and his acolytes to continue my journey.

I didn't think I would see them again.

* * *

One election gimmick of Robert Mugabe's that had already gone spectacularly wrong was the distribution of computers to rural schools. I was reminded of a visit I had paid to Vumbunu secondary school in rural Manicaland on my previous trip. The school had five computers donated to it by a European NGO, but a former pupil, eighteen-year old Fungayi Chidahuyo told me that the machines had never been used and merely sat in a storeroom, gathering dust.

"The computers were there but we could not use them because there is no electricity at the school," Fungayi shrugged. "Now I cannot get a job because I am uneducated."

Fungayi had failed his O level examinations that year and told me that there had been a suggestion that the NGO who had donated the equipment should come back and put electricity into the school so that pupils could actually use the computers.

"What is the use of that?" The young man sniffed scornfully. "We don't need computers or electricity. What these people should be donating is basic learning materials such as textbooks and equipment for the school science laboratory which is empty and not used.

'Computers and electricity are alright in Europe perhaps, but they are not what we need at Vumbunu school today. The reason some of my friends and I failed was because we did not have basic resources to help with our learning - things like textbooks and ballpoint pens."

He added: "Clearly, if the NGO people had known the situation on the ground at our school they would have given us books first and computers later."

Now Mugabe was making the identical mistake. He was so out of touch with the realities of the country he ruled that he spent time distributing expensive computers that would never be used. He would have gained far more respect from the rural people, had he doled out basics like textbooks, pens and pencils.

It seemed an obvious oversight but was perhaps indicative of the fact that the president was losing touch with reality. A former teacher himself and a man, known for his passionate espousal of the education cause, he had spent weeks travelling the length and breadth of Zimbabwe and donating computers worth more than Z 1.8 billion to rural schools. He told the Press that this was not an election gimmick, but was meant to strengthen the country's education system by providing cutting-edge technology to students.

The teachers and other education experts I spoke with assured me that the president's gifts might be well-meant but they were also a testimony as to how out of touch he was with the parlous state of affairs in the public school system.

"If this is not mere electioneering, then it is a classical case of misplaced priorities," said Moses Nguna, a teacher at a secondary school in rural Mutoko. "At our school a class of up to forty-five children will share a single textbook which is read to the class by the teacher. There are no desks and some children have to sit on home-made stools or on the floor.

'We have no electricity and we cannot even dream of science laboratories, so now you tell me what use are computers to our students?"

The public education sector in Zimbabwe had once taken pride of place among the achievements of Mugabe and his government, but somewhere along the line, the wheels had fallen off.

In my own travels, I saw schools crumbling after years of under-funding and neglect, I saw pupils struggling to learn without equipment that had once been regarded as standard and it seemed a vivid illustration of Zimbabwe's social, economic and political decline. Where education was concerned, Robert Mugabe had completely failed the children of Zimbabwe and his exhortations to schoolchildren around the country to learn from the new computers was crazy. How could they learn anything without electricity?

The acute shortage of books and other learning aids at schools had certainly not been helped by political violence which had seen many teachers accused by ZANU PF militants of backing the opposition parties. Dozens of them fled their rural schools for the comparative safety of life in towns and cities.

An executive member of the Progressive Teachers Union of Zimbabwe, Macdonald Maungazani had been openly scornful of Mugabe's new-found largesse.

"What our schools need badly now are textbooks," he confirmed what I had already been told. "It is only books that enable students to pass. They also need an end to political violence so that teachers do not run away from rural areas.

'Even in schools with electricity, there is no student who is going to use the computers productively to pass O-levels when our basic resources are lacking."

But Mr Maungazani obviously saw the broader picture with far more clarity than President Mugabe, as in the weeks leading up to polling day, he continued with his doling out of useless computers. I couldn't help wondering what out of touch NGO or Aid Agency had given them to him, but as pre election tension mounted, I didn't have time to find out.

*   *   *

I spotted him outside the Grain Marketing Board in Nyanga. There was no mistaking that burly figure and shining pate, even though his shirt was black with sweat and he was one of a line of men, manhandling grain bags into the back of a battered farm truck.

"Hey Allan," I called. "What are you doing."

Allan Langan's face lightened with relief at being able to spare a moment from the toil.

"Good to see you, Bryan" It was strange how I had grown accustomed to being known and introduced as Bryan Graham. "GMB had a load of maize in, so I am loading up our quota for the workers. It will keep the poor sods happy for a while."

We were joined by Ann and she looked almost as tired as her husband. Wearily, she wiped a smudge of grain chaff from her forehead.

"This is the part of Zimbabwean life that the rest of the world doesn't see," she smiled wearily. "White Zimbos are depicted as racist colonials, but our labour force expects us to give up an entire day out of our lives, just to bring their food back from town. We do it gladly, but I often wish we would be given a little more credit for it."

"If you weren't here, who would get the grain out to them?"

She laughed shortly – a small, feisty woman.

"Nobody: they would not get it unless they clubbed together and hired a truck…"

"For which they would probably need a Zanu PF card," Interrupted her husband with a broad grin. "Nothing is for free in modern Zimbabwe. 'Vote for me and I will see you are fed,' is our revered leader's catch phrase nowadays.

'Anyway, what are you doing back here?"

I told him about my photographs of the Ashmores and of the excellent – entirely home produced – dinner I had enjoyed the previous evening and it was Ann who interrupted my story.

There is an old couple near us who you should interview. Jack and Trish are in their late eighties and really good people. They have lived here for years and are loved by everyone – black and white alike. They work all hours of the day and supply the locals with fruit, veggies, jam and even furniture. Over the years, they have built Silver Rocks into a little holiday complex and it has proved a real attraction for tourists, wanting to get off the beaten track.

'Now they have been served with a 'section eight,' so they have three months to get off their farm and nowhere to go. It is really tragic and the shock has put poor old Jack into hospital."

So it was that I drove through the hills on a dusty farm track until I came to the Silver Rocks holiday complex, where I was met by Trish Marshall herself.

At eighty-five, Trish had difficulty in getting around and she greeted me from a battered zimmer frame. Her face was lined from years of sunshine, but her eyes were bright and she apologised for not being able to come out to the truck. Over tea, she told me what had happened.

One of the nicest aspects of African tribal culture for me has always been the way that the elderly are cared for, yet in Zimbabwe, this seemed to have fallen by the wayside. Here was a very old couple who were being hounded and persecuted by Mugabe's government officials.

"My Jack is eighty-seven now," Trish told me with a proud smile, "and it was always our dream to end our days on a little farm in the hills. When Jack retired from the Civil Service in 1972, we came up here and although it is only six hundred and seventy acres, it suits us down to the ground. It was virgin bush when we took it over, but Jack is good with his hands and between us, we managed to build a small homestead, which we have occupied ever since. We made additions as and when we could afford them, then we added a number of basic chalets, which we have rented out to visitors for the last twenty years.

'We cater for the family types," she poured me more tea. "We were among the first in the area to do this and have had visitors from all over the world. We have left a large part of the farm undeveloped so that it has become a little wild life sanctuary in its own right and perfect for family walks and picnics. Almost all our visitors have become friends and they used to come back year after year. It was really lovely, but since the farm invasions began, people have been scared off. We haven't had visitors now for months and it is worrying."

Even more worrying for this lovely old couple were the events of the previous weekend. There were tears in her eyes when Trish told me about it.

"Jack is suffering from prostate cancer and we had been into town for treatment. When we came back, there were these people waiting for us at the door."

"Were they government officials, police or what?"

She shook her head and looked desperately forlorn. I had spoken with a number of farmers who had gone through the emotional devastation of being served with 'section eights' – effectively confining them to their homesteads and giving them three months notice to leave their farm – but they had all been young and strong enough to take it. Poor old Trish Marshall was another matter and I wondered how many others in her age group were going through the same trauma.

"I don't really know, but my Jack was devastated," typically, her first thought was for her husband. "We came back from town and these people were waiting for us. There were four of them – one woman - in an old car and there was nothing to say who they were, but they made us sign a receipt for this bit of paper that virtually takes away everything we own. We have had settlers on the farm for ages, most of them acting for the local CIO chief, the District Administrator and Inspector Majoni at the police station, but they haven't really given us trouble. When they first came, Jack negotiated a deal with them and they now have half the farm – which they don't use – while we work the other half. They often come to us for help or a lift into Nyanga when they know that Jack is going in. Now they seem to want everything and we are easy targets, so they will take it all.

'At our age, we should probably have been put in a residential home long ago, but we have kept going and worked hard. We have brought foreign currency into the country and done a lot of good for the community. Now it is being thrown in our face."

I was hesitant to ask how such an elderly couple worked their farm, but Trish smiled at my worries.

"It isn't difficult really. Jack takes his workers out to the apples and proteas, while I sell my plants and paintings from here. We have eleven labourers, two of whom help me with the flowers, while the others work with Jack. Now they will all lose their jobs and we have no money to pay them off with anyway."

As farmers, forced off their land were required by law to pay each laid-off worker the equivalent of three months salary for ten years, this was not difficult to understand. Even rich farmers were struggling to find the cash and the Marshalls were obviously not rich. When I asked Trish to show me her garden, she readily agreed. We walked out together and I had to restrain myself from helping whenever her wheeled walking frame struggled over rough ground.

"I am quite used to it," she smiled at my confusion. "I can get about with sticks, but this thing is better over the bumps, so don't worry please."

Amid the orderly rows of fuschias, proteas and geraniums growing on a small plot behind the house, this lovely old lady really came alive. Picking at a rusted leaf here and carefully readjusting a stem there, her face was alight with joy at her creations and I wondered what on earth she would do if they had to leave this enchanted spot.

"I don't know," she said sadly. "We can join my daughter in South Africa, but we will have no money at all and it is a bit late in life to grow accustomed to penury. I will have to sell all my flowers before I go, because whoever takes this place over won't look after them and I couldn't bear that."

Back in the house, she showed me some of her paintings of Nyanga scenery and they were magnificent.

"Doing these helps in times of stress," she said. "I sell a few miniatures in the village, but most of my stuff is done for friends and family."

But Trish Marshall's main concern was still centred on her husband's health.

"This nonsense has really knocked him back," she told me sadly. "He has worn a pacemaker for twelve years now and since the section eight was served on us, it has gone haywire. Unfortunately, with the current brain drain from Zim, Mr Fumajena is the only heart man left in the country with any experience of these things and he is trying to do what he can. However, the prospect is bleak and I am scared that any more of this harassment will kill him."

I had heard a lot of sad stories over the previous weeks, but I came away from picturesque Silver Rocks with a definite lump in my throat and anger building in my heart. This was not land reform or reparation for wrongs done in the past. This was harassment of the elderly in order to prove a political point.

My abiding memory of that spectacular little farm is of an indomitable old lady seeing me off on her mobile zimmer and even managing to smile as she waved. Trish Marshall was directly descended from the pioneer settlers of Zimbabwe and like them, she was prepared for hardship, but her future looked desperate. At eighty-five, nobody should be forced out of their home and no matter what the rights and wrongs of the Zimbabwe land issue, a government that does that to its elderly citizens is a government without a soul and does not deserve to be in power.

As I drove away, I wondered whether Morgan Tsvangirai had any chance of upsetting the status quo and perhaps coming to the rescue of folk like Jack and Trish Marshall.

Two years later when I revisited the area, the Marshalls were both dead, the nursery was overgrown and Silver Rocks was virtually abandoned.

* * *

Allan Langan's plot was on my way out from Silver Rocks, so I stopped there for lunch and over a few beers, we discussed the future, should Tsvangirai upset the odds and unseat the president.

"If he does, we might just have a chance," Allan's normally cheerful face wore a sudden frown. "The economy is about as shot as it can be, but without Mugabe in power, foreign donors might pour a bit of money in and that would give us a small opportunity to make things come right again. Without that, everything will just get worse until we have a peasants' revolt or a military coup – either of which will only lead to more bloodshed."

For all the problems surrounding us, lunch was a cheerful affair, enlivened by anecdotes about life in Shamva, where both Allan and Ann had been born and brought up.

"You know, we could have done so much," Allan said at one point. "We were a prosperous district and one that always pulled together. Almost everyone stayed put during the liberation war, even though we took quite a hammering. There was a lot of money about during the early nineties and a group of us decided to build a big dam, so that we could diversify into sugar production. We sited it on the Porta and Mazoe rivers and I think at that stage, it was the largest privately owned dam in the country. We built pumping sheds and refineries with money invested by Hulett Tongaat, who are one of South Africa's major sugar producers.

'Everything was going really well, but before we could start production, a number of local farms were designated by government for occupation and Hulett Tongaat quite naturally withdrew their support. They weren't going to invest in an area which was suddenly in danger of being taken over by war vets. We protested to Mugabe himself and shortly afterwards, the designation orders were withdrawn, but it was too late. The South Africans were scared to invest any more money in the project and when the farm invasions began in earnest, the whole scheme collapsed. Now there are only eight farmers left in the Shamva district, so everything has been wasted. We all lost a great deal of money, but even more importantly, the country lost a major industrial scheme that could have brought in millions of dollars worth of foreign exchange."

We shook our heads at the innate folly of Zimbabwe's political leaders and went on to more cheerful topics. I left the lovely Langans feeling distinctly more pleased with life and even the thought of a long drive back to Harare didn't worry me too much.

Mind you, that was probably due to a surfeit of beer and I should have been worried as for once, the Ganja Bus misbehaved and the drive turned out to be even longer than usual and extremely hard on the nerves.

* * *

There had been an ominous shudder beneath the vehicle for some time, but as it only occurred when the speed went over eighty kilometres per hour, I was not too worried. On my way back from Nyanga however, things worsened and my maximum speed dropped to sixty by Rusape and then forty shortly after passing Macheke. Night was almost upon us and there was light rain falling, so after making a desultory inspection underneath the bodywork – I didn't know what I was looking for in any case – I limped on, the speed reducing drastically as the shuddering increased.

I had forgotten the horrors of driving on Zimbabwean roads at night. The general standard of vehicles had increased over the years with many new models making an appearance, but the standard of maintenance was another matter. There were a number of vehicles with only one headlight and many more with no headlights at all. It was fortunate that I was going slowly as on three occasions, cars or trucks suddenly appeared ahead of me, their rear lights non-existent or merely a notion of what should have been showing. Closer to Harare, cyclists began to appear and none of these had even considered installing lights on their machines, while outside the Ruwa shopping centre, I was forced to brake and swerve around a man I can only assume was drunk. He was lying with his legs across the verge and his body well into the road surface, apparently sound asleep. I only saw him at the last moment and when I drove on, my hands were trembling with reaction.

Never in my life have I been so pleased to see the lights of a city, but at last I was home and after a quick supper with friends in Highlands, dived into bed to dream of fuchsias and a lady whose motorised zimmer frame was falling apart.

Chapter Thirteen

(Misplaced Optimism)

I couldn't help reflecting that the most serious problem facing Tsvangirai if he won the election would be what to do with the illegal settlers on commercial farms. Bobby Sithole's solution to the problem had seemed reasonable at the time, but I had been on many farms since speaking with him and could no longer see it working.

A number of occupied farms had been handed over to government officials, police officers, military men and friends of President Mugabe, but these were not really the people at issue. On most farms, squatters had settled in at the behest of government and I did not think they would move under any circumstances.

Iain Kay was an old friend who farmed Chipesa Farm to the South of Marondera. At least, Iain did farm Chipesa until the war vets descended upon him in March 2000. Since then, he had been engaged in a small personal war, wherein he had been beaten up, ambushed and pinned in his homestead by armed gunmen. His wife Kerry had been repeatedly arrested on spurious charges and Iain had been threatened with death on numerous occasions, but the Kays flatly refused to leave the farm under any circumstances.

"This place is my home. It has always been my home and I am staying put."

That was Iain's comment and I could not help admiring him for his spirit in the face of extreme provocation. He had always been a brave man and even with his house permanently surrounded and his fields occupied by hundreds of settlers, Kay remained openly defiant.

"Kerry and I are both members of the MDC," he told me. "We are focussed on getting political change in Zimbabwe. We still believe there will be a return to law as it was, and international law in terms of property rights. I think we stand an excellent chance of returning to full scale farming once problems are resolved."

I had met Kerry Kay in London toward the end of 2001 and even then, she seemed supremely optimistic.

"Next year will be a good one for Zimbabwe," she told me cheerfully. "It will be a year of change and I can assure you that Morgan will be in and Mugabe out."

As Kerry was in charge of the programme to reduce AIDS in the country and travelled all over the world in that role, I took cognisance of what she said, but even then I wondered whether she wasn't being unduly optimistic. She and Iain had always been MDC members - which was the main reason for their life being made a misery - but I had always felt that Tsvangirai's supporters were clutching at straws. He was a brave and charismatic man, but for one who would be president, he was politically naïve.

Tsvangirai had already been indicted for treason on one occasion when he gave no forethought to what he was saying and shortly before the presidential election, he was in trouble again. A film was shown on the ZTV news wherein two men in deep discussion were reported as being Tsvangirai with Ari Ben Menashe, director of a Canadian Public Relations company and allegedly a former member of MOSSAD. Ben Menashe was a man known for his shady dealings. He was also said to be heavily involved with Zanu PF, so quite what the opposition leader had been doing with him had to be open to serious question. Ben Menashe claimed that Tsvangirai had approached him with a plan to assassinate Mugabe and although the MDC man denied the charge, he had to admit that he had been the man in the film.

For a leading politician to put himself in the position of being alone with a man like Ben Menashe hardly said much for

Tsvangirai's political acumen and I had my doubts as to his suitability for the office he sought. On the other hand, he had to be better than Mugabe and did at least offer a modicum of hope for the future to all Zimbabweans. Kerry Kay thought he was a fine man and as she knew far more about the situation than I did, I could only hope that she would be proved correct.

Another person who had lived on Chipesa Farm all his life was Manyowa Chipanga who was in the forefront of the illegal squatters, occupying Kay's farm. When speaking of Iain Kay, Chipanga was openly scornful.

"He still has the hangover of colonialism in his mind. It has already gone away so he should drop all those minds that are in his one mind and become a man who lives in Zimbabwe."

"It is not that easy," Kay said softly. "We are tobacco farmers and a tobacco crop requires a great deal of land, which has to be carefully looked after. Lands need to be rotated, but these blokes (he was referring to the squatters) don't even think of things like that. Besides, Chipesa has been in my family for a very long time and I do not see why it should be stolen from me as a form of political expediency."

Manyowa Chipanga was not impressed.

"They were the thieves," he shouted. "The British were the thieves who were stealing our fathers' land. They didn't compensate our chiefs. They just came and fought ourselves and chased us from the good land and then they sent us into the rocks. Then they started developing the land in here, but when we came back from that land - from the rocks - to say 'we want land,' they say, 'ah you are taking our land,' but from where do they get theirs from?"

It was a convoluted statement, but I understood what he was getting at and it worried me, for this was where the current problems of Zimbabwe were focussed. Men like Manyowa Chipanga felt – and with some justification - that at last they had a piece of their own country for themselves. The fact that dividing a viable farm into hundreds of totally unworkable plots could only be self-defeating never entered their minds.

"This is my country and my land," Manyowa shouted at me when I met him on Chipesa. "I love this soil and if necessary I will die for it."

Iain Kay was also somewhat unimpressed.

"If we don't get rain soon, what the hell are they going to do with this soil?" He commented bitterly. "I mean – look at their crops. None of these blokes have irrigation or fertiliser and even when they steal mine, they have no idea how to use the stuff. This has been a bad year for rainfall and it will not be long before these alleged settlers are looking for hand outs from the few commercial farmers who have stayed on."

We both knew that Iain was right. With many commercial farmers being forced off the land or not allowed to plant, maize was already in desperately short supply throughout Zimbabwe. Those few people who had money were buying potatoes and rice, but these items are not regular large-scale crops in Zimbabwe and supplies could not possibly last for long. When they were finished, starvation would be rampant.

Even as the election approached, the position was deteriorating by the day. In communal areas where subsistence farming had been the norm for generations, children and the elderly were dying from malnutrition and things could only get worse. Fatuous pronouncements from politicians such as Joseph Made, the Minister of Agriculture did nothing to ease the situation.

In the meantime, Iain Kay and Mayowa Chipanga who were friends as children, shared the same land and could not sort out their differences. Theirs was a problem without a solution, but Chipesa Farm was merely one tiny part of the farming tragedy that had already engulfed my country and threatened to destroy what was once described as the breadbasket of Africa.

I hoped that I was wrong, but for all the optimism of Kerry Kay and other MDC supporters, I could only foresee widespread famine and disaster for Zimbabwe.

*   *   *

The televised news report was pretty shocking. There was a white, commercial farmer from Mhangura apparently setting fire to his maize crop. The reporter alleged that this was an act of vandalism, designed to 'prevent other Zimbabweans from having enough food in their bellies.' The news clip was impressively done and with the escalating maize shortage already bringing starvation to parts of the country, it had been carefully calculated to arouse the anger of the populace.

The farmer was named as Clive Thomas and although I didn't know the man, I just could not believe that any commercial farmer would destroy his own crop for the reasons given. It did not make sense. It did not take me long to discover that the facts were not at all as reported, yet the net result of that news clip was that Mr Thomas became yet another commercial farmer to lose everything he owned.

In fact, the burning maize was inedible 'male seed maize' from the previous seasons harvest. Thomas had been a registered seed maize grower for fifteen years and had produced an excellent crop in the previous season, but was unable to plant in 2002 due to the designation of his farm and disturbances to his programme by illegal settlers.

Stringent conditions governed the operations of seed growers and Zimbabwe Seed Maize Association, rule 28 required that 'male inbred plants be removed from the seed crop by 31st May.' In Thomas' case, the 'male removal' inspection was carried out on 10th May 2001 by a government certified inspector. Most seed maize producers recover some value from the male plants by milling the whole plant as stock feed and Thomas merely confirmed that he had intended to do this.

"I reaped the male lines from my crop in May 2001 and put them in heaps to be shelled later. I had been invaded by war vets in April and because of the uncertainty of the times, I've been short of staff to undertake this and other tasks. Three to four tonnes were milled and offered to my workers in June, but they complained that it was not fit to eat. This was the maize that I eventually burned."

It all sounded fair enough, but events took a nasty turn immediately after the news bulletin was aired. Let Clive Thomas continue the story.

"At around two pm, a delegation of people arrived on the farm. They did not directly identify themselves, but I believe they were from the war veteran leadership, the President's office and the police. None of them were in uniform, but they questioned me about the news report and when I explained what had happened, they went off into a huddle, before telling me that they had reached a decision. One of them who appeared to be the spokesman said, 'We are taking your farm immediately.'"

Thomas shook his head at the memory.

"I just looked at them in total perplexity and then asked what they meant and whether I could at least have the requisite ninety days to finish my tobacco crop.

'I was told, 'You obviously don't understand. We are taking this farm immediately.'"

Shortly afterwards, Clive Thomas and his family left the farm for safety reasons, but his leaving meant yet another dent in the nation's crumbling economy. The maize shortage was worsening by the day and Doug Taylor-Freeme, a vice president of the Commercial Farmers' Union lamented the careless disregard for national food security on the part of government.

"If our advice, given with Zimbabwe's best interest at heart had been acted upon last year, maize could have been imported at a better price then. We understand that the country is now out of stock and in our opinion, imports cannot arrive in sufficient quantities quickly enough to avert a national crisis."

When I asked him about the Thomas case, Taylor-Freeme commented somewhat grimly.

"The burnt maize shown in the film clip was that gleaned from the land to make way for the early planted tobacco crop – a practice common in commercial agriculture. For the Minister to infer that any farmer would destroy his maize merely to spite government is highly irresponsible and should be treated with the derision it deserves."

Taylor-Freeme also said that the CFU was extremely concerned about the ongoing seizure of grain lawfully held for farm labour and stock feed use.

"Farmers have budgeted their grain consumption, including on-farm use and now they find themselves seriously prejudiced. Minister Made when all is said and done, must be held accountable for the current chaos in the agricultural sector and pending mass food shortages. Far from his target of four point eight million tons to be produced mainly by 'new farmers,' we estimate that national production this year under the current dry conditions may not even reach one million tons."

Taylor-Freeme was undoubtedly correct and all thinking Zimbabweans knew this. For every working farmer like Clive Thomas who was forced off the land for whatever reason, the prospect of mass starvation in Zimbabwe came closer. It did not seem possible that mere political victory could be worth that much, but then I was not a politician or running for the post of President of Zimbabwe.

* * *

It was a glorious highveld morning and for once I was not alone. The Ganja Bus was having bolts replaced in her prop shaft and as David Bradshaw was visiting a few of his tenants in Marondera, I was only too pleased to accompany him on his rounds. With us was John Drake – a former tobacco grower from Virginia who having been evicted from his farm was now working on a part-time basis with ZTA in order to make ends meet.

As we drove, we discussed the arrest over the weekend of Marondera farmer, Hans Christen and my friend Kerry Kay.

"As far as I know," Bradshaw told the story. "Hans was arrested for giving fuel to a couple of stranded MDC members doing their rounds and God alone knows why Kerry was picked up. She has been released, but it seems that Hans has been moved and nobody is really sure where he is being held.

'I dread to think what these bastards are doing to him."

The thought was one that subdued us all and as we drove, I wondered at the courage shown by those farmers still on their often very isolated properties. So many of them had been harassed, beaten up, imprisoned and even murdered over the past months, yet still they stayed on their farms and did their best to work the land. In the early days of the farm invasions, I had often wondered why nobody fought back against the so-called war veterans. After all, farmers had been in the front line during the liberation war and had proved their courage on numerous occasions.

Now they were showing a different sort of courage and 'turning the other cheek' to Mugabe's thugs, in the process absorbing more punishment than anybody should have been subjected to. It was somehow sad and admirable at the same time, but I still found it difficult to understand. I have never really believed in turning the other cheek.

Over breakfast in Marondera, I brought up the subject of a newspaper article I had read the previous weekend. The Sunday Mail headline read, **'Remarkable Feat for Tobacco Grower'** and the accompanying feature told how Harare businessman, Maurice Ndenga had planted a wonderful crop on Plymtree Farm in Hwedza. It was all very encouraging for the new land settlers of Zimbabwe, but something about the article did not ring true.

Could he be reaping four tonnes to the hectare for example? I put the question to my companions and they were openly scornful.

"No," was the flat reply from Bradshaw. "The average this year is well below three point five tonnes and while I know there is an excellent crop on Plymtree, it has little to do with Mr Ndenga. The farm was occupied by one of our tenants who went off to the UK last August when his squatters would not allow him to plant a crop. He left behind carefully prepared lands, his seed beds, fertilisers, pesticides and machinery. The only money Ndenga would have put into it is payment for his labour force. That article is pure propaganda."

Tobacco has been the mainstay of the Zimbabwean economy since the first small crop was planted by a Captain Wilson near the Hunyani River in the 1920s. It kept the country going through the desperate years of sanctions and made many a fortune for the growers, while keeping the economy buoyant. As the economic situation in Zimbabwe became critical in the first two years of this millennium, the crop came under ever more serious threat from war vets and settlers. In their thousands, they crowded on to viable tobacco farms and either prevented farmers from planting a crop or hindered their efforts to such an extent that many were forced to give up.

"We produced two hundred and fifty million tons in 2000," Bradshaw told me. "It was down to two hundred and five million in 2001 and has been dropping ever since. Official figures give estimates for this year as still being over a million tons, but I will be surprised if we produce even half of that. If this nonsense continues, the international buyers will soon stop coming here and the industry will die."

John Drake nodded in grim agreement.

Our first visit was to a young farmer named Steve Newmarch and anyone less like a colonial oppressor, I could not imagine. Steve was a serious young man who obviously took pride in his work and as we wandered through his tobacco lands, both Bradshaw and John Drake were visibly impressed.

"I have had settlers on the farm for a long time," Newmarch told the now familiar story. "We had worked things out between us; I had given them a slice of land to use and they were no trouble, but over the past few weeks, the Youth Brigade thugs have moved in and it has become almost impossible to work. My labour force are frightened. They are regularly beaten and bullied, so that work on the farm has become almost impossible. The women don't even sing any more."

Steve's farm was set in magnificent surroundings and as my companions made learned comments about quality of leaf and various types of tobacco seed, I wandered off on my own, enjoying the tranquillity of the morning. The sky was cobalt blue and almost brassy at the edges, while gaunt kopjes glowered down on me from all sides, their massive crags and boulders glowing in the sunlight. Yellow-billed kites circled high overhead, but my pleasure in the moment was spoiled when I realised that Hans Christen farmed in this area and while I was admiring the landscape around his home, he was probably lying in a dank cell, wondering whether he would ever see it again. It was a sobering thought and I felt a sense of relief when we moved on again.

I was to talk with Hans Christen later and he told me about his thirteen days spent as a prisoner on spurious charges of setting fire to a Zanu PF vehicle. The vehicle in question had been in Marondera police station car park at the time, but Christen who campaigned openly for the MDC was locked up and tortured with three of his colleagues before being sent to the local prison while further enquiries were made.

"In most countries," he told me, "the police investigate and then arrest. In Zimbabwe, they arrest and then investigate."

While in the prison, Christen met with nothing but kindness from his fellow inmates and even made friends with a number of the guards.

"I might not have survived were it not for them," He admitted. "The worst part of it all was when a very sick man in my cell died in front of us. The previous day I had given him food but when he asked for a cigarette, I refused because I didn't think it would be good for him in his condition. When he died, I felt terrible about that and wished I had given him the cigarette."

Inevitably, Christen's case was dropped but he was one Norwegian citizen who had learned the hard way how difficult it is to be politically inclined in modern Zimbabwe.

*   *   *

Glen Mirams had a similar story to Steve Newmarch and while we were inspecting his tobacco barns, a surly looking individual in tattered clothing moved closer in order to hear what we were saying. Glen jerked his thumb contemptuously at him.

"Youth Brigade, wanting to know what we are talking about. These bastards are making life really difficult at the moment."

The man had what appeared to be a small radio strapped to one wrist and I wondered what it was. Mirams laughed a little uncertainly.

"A number of them carry those," he explained. "They are either tape recorders, so that their lords and masters know exactly what is being said or they are mock ups to make the locals think they are being recorded.

'That thug will be questioning the workers as soon as we are out of sight," he told me. "These blokes are not afraid of using violence either. My cook was beaten up the other day and his wife had to have sixteen stitches in her head after one of these louts struck her with an axe handle."

When I asked why, Glen smiled somewhat wryly.

"The official reason was that they did not attend a *pungwe*, but the more likely one is that Lovemore is my friend. He has been part of the family for many years and these youths feel he is a sell out."

There were a group of children following us through the barns and when they realised that I was not really part of the official party, they tagged on to me. No conversation took place, but we smiled a lot and when I gave them the MDC salute, they giggled happily and wandered along behind me, sticking out little pink palms whenever they caught my eye.

"Careful," Bradshaw warned quietly. "If those little mites go home and do the same thing, they will lay themselves and their parents open to beatings from the Youth Brigade."

Horrified at my own crass stupidity, I quickly shooed the children away, ignoring them from then on. They looked disappointed and eventually sulked in a dark corner of the barn, glaring at me from time to time. I felt desperately sad at how the cruel reality of Zimbabwe politics could even spoil the cheerful spontaneity of children. It was a tragic reflection on a society that despite the tensions engendered by colonialism and a brutal civil war, has always been famed for its openness and friendly relationship between ages, genders and races.

Our third farm visit of the day did not work out as planned. Kevin Solomon had contacted me a week or so previously with a request that I drop in and see the cattle that had been slashed by settlers on his farm.

"You would not believe the wanton cruelty inflicted on dumb animals," was his message.

In the event, we did not even reach Kevin's farm and I spoke to him at a house in Marondera. Kevin himself was wide-eyed and shaken as he told his story.

"I am not taking you guys out to look at my crop," he told my companions. "I have just come in from the farm and barely escaped with my life at a Youth Brigade road block. These blokes are bloody dangerous, I can tell you. They wanted to kill me and I was lucky to get away."

Kevin had also received a letter from his resident settlers, telling him that unless he acceded to their demands that they take over his house and barns, they (the house and barns) were going to be destroyed. The last paragraph of this badly spelled missive warned him not to tell the police, as they - in the form of the Support Unit -were working for Zanu PF anyway. He shrugged when I asked for a copy of the letter.

"That's no problem," he assured me. "But what good will it do? The rest of the world cannot see what is going on and if they are told about it by blokes like you, they don't care anyway. I have a lot of families on my farm who rely on me for their livelihood, yet these thugs are putting them all in danger of starvation."

On the way back to town, the three of us were unusually silent. The meeting with Kevin Solomon had shaken us and I think we all realised that the future for tobacco farming in Zimbabwe was very limited. Articles like the one on Maurice

Ndenga might fire the dreams of landless Zimbabweans, but they were totally misleading. Small scale farming of tobacco can work, but it is an exacting business and a great deal of capital is needed to fund it. Young men like Steve, Glen and Kevin had the backing of the Zimbabwe Tobacco Association, but only because they had a proven record in tobacco production and could cope with the difficulties of producing a crop. Without that backing, few small-scale growers could possibly survive and all the so-called settlers were doing was wasting land and crippling the national economy.

Yet for all the problems, the three young farmers we had spoken to that day were optimistic about the future.

"Provided, we have the correct result in March," Kevin spoke for them all. "I shall be producing another crop next season. This is my land and I want to use it properly."

Most Zimbabweans were praying that Kevin and the other two would get the result they wanted on 9th and 10th March. If they did not, the economic future for Zimbabwe without tobacco was very bleak.

Chapter Fourteen

(Chaos at the Polls)

In those tense weeks immediately prior to the general election, nervousness in the cities had been stirred up by a number of noisy marches and demonstrations, held by Zanu (PF) supporters. Having been bussed into Harare, Bulawayo, Gweru and Mutare from the high density suburbs, they sang and danced their way through city streets, terrifying pedestrians and threatening all sorts of disaster to anybody who supported Tsvangirai and the MDC. Apart from a few slightly damaged cars, these demonstrations had not produced much in the way of actual lawlessness, but they were unnerving for city residents.

In the course of one such demonstration, a city secretary called Estelle had been walking back to work after lunch when she found herself in the same street as a column of exuberantly chanting marchers. Feeling nervous about being out in the open, she cut across Africa Unity Square in central Harare, only to find herself suddenly pulled to one side by the flower sellers who throng the pavement opposite Meikles Hotel.

"At first I thought I was about to be assaulted or robbed," she told me later. "Only a few weeks previously, I had been mugged outside the Holiday Inn and this felt very similar. To tell you the truth I was terrified, but these blokes meant me no harm. Before I knew what was happening, I was surrounded by flower sellers and the only white faces I could see belonged to a couple of Australian tourists who had also been pulled into the circle. It took us a moment or two to realise that the flower sellers were protecting us from the advancing mob.

'A few of the Zanu PF women spotted our white faces and came running across the road, screaming abuse at us and threatening us with just about every fate imaginable. The flower sellers turned their backs on these women and a number of them took quite hefty blows across their shoulders, just so that we would be safe. It really was frightening and if it hadn't been for those blokes, I don't know what might have happened to me or the tourists."

When I spoke to David Mangwanda, a dreadlocked flower vendor with a Che Guevara beret and Zanu PF sweatshirt, he remembered the incident but was dismissive of the courage displayed by himself and his colleagues.

"What else could we do, Brother? Those white folk had done nothing wrong, but if we had not grabbed them, they would have been assaulted and perhaps killed by that bunch of *tsotsis*. They were innocent people so we protected them. It was nothing.

'It was our duty Bro."

It was a little more than nothing to Estelle and the two visitors, but David's attitude was typical of most Harare citizens. Day after day, they watched the antics of Mugabe's supporters with blistering contempt and did what they could to help those who might become victims of the violence that threatened to erupt at any moment. Later I was to experience something of what Estelle and the Australians went through and it was truly frightening.

* * *

The weekend was to be a vitally important one for all Zimbabweans and was greeted with a mixture of emotions across the country. For MDC supporters, it was the culmination of all their hopes and dreams; for followers of Zanu PF it was a chance to retain power and re-establish President Mugabe in the eyes of both the people and the outside world. For Zimbabweans of whatever colour and creed, it was the moment when they could do their bit toward making a future for themselves in their own country.

In Harare, Saturday dawned grey and drizzly.

"That is all we need," Big Sister Sandra said in exasperation. "Now the voters will get wet and many of them will go home without bothering to vote."

But Zimbabweans are hardy folk and when I went for a drive just after eight, the queue of prospective voters outside Highlands Primary School already stretched nearly a kilometre down the road. This was Ward Eight in the affluent Northern suburbs of the city and the voters I spoke with were determined to have their say.

"I was up at five thirty this morning," I found Lesley Corbett well back in the queue with her son Richard. "We brought books, chairs and refreshments with us because it could be a long day. The one thing we didn't think of was an umbrella."

In drought-stricken Zimbabwe, this was hardly surprising, but by mid morning the sun had appeared and streets began to gently steam in its warmth. More enervating than the weather though, was the slowness of progress. The queue at Highlands hardly seemed to move but everyone seemed resigned to it.

"This is Africa," Titus Mazorodzvi was happy to be doing his bit. "Nothing moves fast and besides, we are accustomed to standing in lines. We do it all the time when we are trying to buy food."

Naturally enough, the Harare rumour mill was in fine form on election day. The morning had barely begun when I was telephoned with the news that a CNN broadcast reported heavy artillery being moved to the centre of town, but all I saw when I drove around the city centre was four bored pedestrians and a few groups of armed policemen. Everyone seemed cheerful and friendly, even the coppers waving to me and there was certainly no sign of trouble.

Polling stations in Mabvuku and Mufakose also had long lines of people waiting to vote and while smiles were few and far between, everyone seemed reconciled to a long wait, but relieved that at last they could have a say in Zimbabwe's future.

Driving out to check on the polling at Borrowdale, I passed State House with its razor-wired walls and phalanx of armed guards, all togged out with steel infantry helmets and fixed bayonets. As I drove past, two limousines were arriving at the main gate and the foremost of these was flying the Libyan flag on its bonnet. I wondered what it meant. Was Mugabe relying on Colonel Gadaffi's friendship to see him through the days ahead perhaps? It was an intriguing question, but I was not going to ask the State House visitors why they were coming to see the Boss. That was a messy way to commit suicide.

I had considered driving down to Bulawayo again but had promised to see my grandson, so after satisfying myself that there was unlikely to be trouble in Harare, set out once again on the long road to Kariba. I had heard on the grapevine of farmers being arrested in Banket and that was on my way, so it gave me the excuse I needed.

There had also been talk of Youth Brigade road blocks set up throughout the Banket area, but when I drove slowly through the little town, all I saw were groups of drunken revellers, so I stopped to see what was happening. My question was greeted with hoots of ribald laughter by a few of the young bloods.

"Ah the voting is taking too long by far," the speaker was a thick-set youth who refused to give me his name. "I came early but they are doing less than three every hour and that is no good. We have all given up for now and will drink beer instead. Perhaps we can try to vote again tomorrow."

Judging from the number of bottles, he and his friends had already emptied, I could only hope that his hangover would allow it.

After sharing a bottle of warm beer with another of the young men, I drove on to Chinhoyi, smiling somewhat wryly at the incongruity of the welcoming sign.

'Welcome to Chinhoyi' it proclaimed in foot high letters. 'Enjoy our friendly atmosphere.'

This was the town that had hit world headlines only a few weeks previously when twenty-two white farmers were arrested and imprisoned on trumped up charges, while Zanu PF youths went on a rampage through the town. Anyone with a white face had been beaten up and advanced age did not exempt one from the violence. Maria Hartmann was in her seventies and had been queuing in the post office when she was attacked and beaten about the face by a government supporter. Another elderly white man was stabbed in the street.

'Friendly atmosphere' indeed!

Only a week previously, David Bradshaw and John Drake had broken down in Chinhoyi and were lucky to be rescued from an angry mob by passing farmers. Once again, the friendly atmosphere had not been in evidence.

On polling day however, the town seemed very quiet and even the queue outside the polling station appeared subdued. Chinhoyi is close to Zvimba, Mugabe's heartland and the area where I had encountered the Youth Brigade road block. This time though, I was not harried, although everyone I passed either ignored me or gave the clenched fist salute of Zanu PF. Meanwhile the car radio told me that there was a large turnout of voters throughout the country, that in Dzvirasekwa, a polling station had collapsed and that in Gweru, former mayor Patrick Kombayi had been arrested for singing MDC songs within twenty metres of a polling station.

It was just another normal voting day in Zimbabwe.

Near Lions Den, the picturesque hamlet where the railway line ends, I stopped to admire an incredible vista of true Zimbabwean farmland. This was Ormeston Farm, run by a man called Les de Jager. I say 'run' because I understood that de Jager had been thrown off his farm by a leading politician, but was allowed to remain in his house provided he kept the farm going as a viable business.

That he had certainly done. As I climbed from the Ganja Bus, my nostrils twitched to the warm, sweet smell of contented cattle. Fat and literally glowing with health, the *mombies* were congregated at one end of a massive, modern dam that must have cost many millions of Zim dollars to build. Standing on the side of the road, I found myself filled with nostalgia. This was how Zimbabwean cattle were supposed to look and in normal times, I would have been able to see similar specimens everywhere. The fact that these looked so splendid that I had to stop and appreciate them was just another indictment of the state of modern Zimbabwe.

The irony of it was that in the course of my travels, I had repeatedly been told that the cattle industry in Zimbabwe was ruined. Three of the five Cold Storage Commission abattoirs had closed down, but those gently bellowing beauties beside the Great North Road must have been worth a small fortune.

I couldn't help wondering who actually owned them and how Mr de Jager felt about his own cattle belonging to someone else while he did the work of raising them.

But it wasn't only the cattle. Beyond the far shoreline of the dam, neatly contoured fields stretched as far as the eye could see. Workers were reaping tobacco in the nearest one while beyond it, I could see cotton and soya plants reaching into the horizon. Irrigation sprinklers whispered their blandishments to early wheat and beautifully ripening maize plants gave promise of a bumper harvest.

This was surely what farming in Zimbabwe was all about. It didn't really matter who owned the land. Ormeston and the farms immediately adjacent were growing the crops that would keep the people fed and the economy healthy. A fine compound of solid looking, brick houses could be seen alongside the road and those workers I smiled at gave me cheerful grins and stuck out large pink palms to indicate their support for the MDC.

Perhaps the change of government they wanted really was coming. With a sudden feeling of optimism for the future, I drove on toward Karoi.

All was quiet there too, but serious-faced farmers gathered on every major junction, their heads bowed over maps spread out on vehicle bonnets. This was surely taking the election a little too seriously or perhaps I was missing something.

"We are trying to work out voting patterns," spotting Chris Sheppard, I pulled over to speak with him. "If necessary, we can take our labourers into centres where they can vote freely and get out safely."

Although obviously sincere, Chris was having fun, so leaving them all to their war games, I drove on for the Zambezi Valley and home.

It was in Kariba that the sheer Alice-in-Wonderland quality of the situation really hit home. I stayed with a friend that night and together we watched the sun rise over the magnificent Zambezi Valley on day two of the election. Elephant trumpeted six hundred metres below Mervyn's veranda and sipping my morning tea, I tried without too much success to identify birds, serenading the advent of a new day. This seemed a world away from the tensions and the grey drizzle of Harare. My companion echoed my thoughts.

"This is such an important time in our country's history," Mervyn had lived in Kariba for nearly forty years; "yet we sit here surrounded by wild Africa and don't really have a clue as to what is going on elsewhere in the country."

It was true and I felt a pang of guilt. Why was I relaxing in peaceful Kariba and not chasing stories in the frenetic bustle of Harare or Bulawayo?

It didn't really matter though and two hours later, we wandered up to the local polling station on Kariba Heights. Here there were no queues and officialdom far outnumbered voters. In fact, there were only three local people there to vote and although all three had received official letters, advising them that their right to vote had been withdrawn, they were still on the roll and a cheerful polling officer allowed them to mark their crosses just the same. Local observers and police spoke quietly outside the old theatre, designated as the polling station and the unreality of the situation was emphasised by hymns, loudly sung at Mass in the church of St Barbara next door. I wondered whether the congregation were praying for an MDC victory.

Having witnessed such extremes of voting conditions, I couldn't help wondering what the next few days would bring to my troubled little country. Would it be the old villain, Robert Mugabe or the young pretender Morgan Tsvangirai who took up the reigns of leadership and would widespread violence follow the declared result?

The questions were unanswerable and it was in a thoughtful frame of mind that I drove across the Mucharara Valley for a few hours with my grandchildren.

* * *

It was not only people who were suffering from years of political mismanagement in Zimbabwe. Taking a dusty drive out to the Nyaodza River, I stopped the Ganja Bus to watch a young elephant bull and it didn't take long to realise that there was something seriously wrong. Kariba bulls are generally docile animals, but this chap was fretful and upset. I could hear his ears crack like pistol shots as he swung his head in annoyance at my presence. Having failed to scare me off, he raised himself to his full height, screamed and took a few dusty steps towards the vehicle in a mock charge. When I still didn't move, he muttered irritably and resumed his laboured foraging.

The problem was easy to identify. Around one rear leg, a piece of thick wire was clearly visible and looking through binoculars, I could see that not only had the snare worked itself deep into the elephant's flesh, but the resultant wound was suppurating badly. The bull must have been in serious pain and in time, the leg would putrefy and become unusable. Because elephant need all four feet to walk on, this young chap would inevitably die – probably of starvation, if the hyenas didn't rip him to pieces first.

Nor were elephant the only victims. As the shortage of basic foodstuffs become ever more critical in the country, local people had little choice but to revert to traditional methods of feeding their families and snares were proliferating at a frightening rate.

"How else can my children survive?" I spoke with Robson Machera in Nyamunga and he shrugged skinny shoulders. "There is no mealie meal and I cannot afford to buy potatoes or rice. I have no job and we must eat. The animals are here and they provide our food."

He was right of course and man's primary responsibility is to keep his family alive, but the Kariba area was once famous for its impala, which used to roam the countryside in herds of five hundred or more. Now they had almost gone, the majority having succumbed to snares or the illegal guns of local poachers. I spent a day wandering the flood plains in the Charara area, but I saw only three young impala rams and they were very wary. I remembered Dave Webster telling me of the poaching that was going on and it all seemed desperately sad. Kudu, waterbuck, warthog and wild pig were also being decimated and in the thick *mopani* forest a short distance from the lake, I found a number of rotting carcasses, snares still in position around necks and legs. Lions, leopard, baboon and even the fearsome crocodiles had been spotted with serious snare wounds in the Kariba area, but the Department of National Parks and Wild Life Management did not seem overly interested in doing anything about it.,

"We do not have the staff," Warden Chikovore told me glumly. "We are engaged in a war against the ivory poachers, so smaller animals are ignored."

We both knew he was talking rubbish and I am sure he did not miss the cynicism behind my smile. I couldn't help comparing the carnage in Kariba with the way wild life seemed to be proliferating in the lush *msasa* forests of the Nyanga foothills.

"I have so much trouble with eland and kudu eating my garden flowers," Mary Jane had told me, "that I am at my wits end. Zebra tear up my lawn as soon as the grass grows and I can't afford to keep it going. The animals ignore my fences and just wander in to feed when they feel like it."

As if to illustrate the point, I came out to the Ganja Bus one morning during my time in Nyanga, to find a fat, male zebra resting in the shade beneath a front wing. He snorted and looked extremely disgusted when I shooed him away.

But Mary Jane and her neighbours were the lucky ones. Perhaps it was due to the more difficult terrain or perhaps it was the fact that locals could barter for food with the Ashmores, but poaching was definitely not as rife in the mountains. There was enough wild life still around to be a nuisance, but in Kariba and the South Western corner of the country, the situation with wild life was desperate. The Save Conservancy was the largest privately owned game farm in the world, but with the influx of war veterans and squatters since early 2000, poaching on the ranch had increased to epidemic proportions. Even the precious black rhinoceros, translocated into the area for their own protection were being found in snares. Forty-two rhino had also been killed in the Bubiyana Conservancy next door. Giraffe, wildebeest, elephant and other animals were being cruelly slaughtered *en masse* and various bodies like the World Wide Fund for Nature, Born Free Foundation, Elefriends and Care for the Wild were ominously quiet about the problem.

Back in England, I had written to the CEOs of all these agencies, describing particular incidents and providing them with horrific pictures and masses of statistics. With the exception of the Environmental Investigation Agency, they had all fobbed me off. My own feeling was that they were too busy spending money on administration and fancy titles to worry about the fate of wild life on the ground and I was not alone in my opinions.

"When we needed to cull elephants a few years ago," Mike Fynn was a safari operator in the Lowveld and an ardent conservationist; "all these august bodies were vociferous in their condemnation. Now they won't say a word while our wild life is dying horribly and in huge quantities. Our hands are tied by government policies, yet these so-called animal lovers don't even protest at the carnage that is going on."

For me, that young bull elephant in Kariba was symptomatic of the terrible malaise that was affecting

Zimbabwe in all spheres of life. Like Mike, I found myself bewildered by the silence of official bodies. Surely they could at least express their condemnation of what was going on in my country. Snared animals face an agonising death and that great beast so close to the Ganja Bus would probably take a few weeks to succumb. In his pain and anger, he might well kill some unfortunate local, which would mean that he would be hunted down and shot by the authorities. That for him would at least be infinitely preferable to dying from starvation or the effects of gangrene.

What a terrible fate that would be for such a wonderful animal and my heart went out to that five ton mass of gentle dignity. Zimbabwe has one of the most incredible collections of wild life in the world, yet it was being rapidly decimated and nobody seemed in the slightest bit interested in halting the carnage.

* * *

The election weekend was coming to a peaceful finish as Mervyn and I relaxed with cold beer on his veranda. Far below us, the lights of Nyamunga twinkled into the darkness and I wondered how much fear and intimidation there had been there over the past two days. Overhead the stars were winking into life, while around us we could hear the shrill chatter of children, playing in the street, a skops owl chirruping in nearby trees and a lone hyaena howling his ode to the world in the distant valley. It was a typical Sunday evening in Kariba and when my companion suggested that we should watch the local news to see what was happening elsewhere, I readily agreed.

Zimbabwe television news was seldom more than a series of sycophantic reports as to what the president had been doing and what a wonderful human being he was, but this one was to be different. The first item on the news headlines told of the arrest of five white people in Nyanga. Hurriedly grabbing my phone, I started to dial Mary Jane for information, only to pause half way through when a picture of the five whites came on to the television screen. It was grainy and blurred, but there on the end of the line, looking old, frail and bewildered was my small friend herself. Sitting slowly down in the nearest chair, I listened to the report.

According to the newsreader, the five whites had been arrested for operating illegal radio equipment in support of the MDC and I could not believe what I was hearing. I knew that Mary Jane hoped for an MDC victory, but so did most of Zimbabwe and I could not imagine her acting as some sort of spy as the report suggested. Besides, who would she have been spying for? She was British born, but despite all the insults thrown at them by the Zimbabwe government, I could not imagine that the Brits would be so interested in the election result that they would employ a little old lady as a clandestine operator.

The news report went on to say that the five had been held in police custody and I shuddered for my friend. Not only was she a chronic asthmatic in need of constant medication, she was acutely claustrophobic and I wondered how she would cope with the confines of a crowded Zimbabwean police cell. It was an awful thought and I slept very little that night.

I was on the road early but it was not a pleasant drive. I had visions of Mary Jane, manacled and helpless in a dank cell and even another meeting with Jack Moyo near Chinhoyi did little to lighten my spirits. The bolt still hadn't arrived and Jack was on the verge of giving up and heading home, crippled wheelchair or no crippled wheelchair. I took the three of them back into Chinhoyi, shared a few cokes and left them with another five thousand dollar note to see them on their way.

It was the last time I was to see that unholy trio on the road and I just hope the little fellow made it as a chicken farmer or whatever it was he had in mind. On subsequent visits I made every effort to find him, but Jack Moyo seemed to have disappeared so I will never know whether he completed his little wheelchair odyssey – a feat of strength and endurance that deserves to be written about in the annals of modern adventure.

I arrived in Harare well before midday but there was no way of getting through to Mary Jane. Her mobile phone wasn't working and there was no answer from her home, so I could only assume she was still in custody. I rang the police station at Nyanga, but Inspector Majoni blithely assured me that he had no idea what I was talking about. There had been no election trouble in his district. Fretting and irritable, I kept trying but it was not until late on Tuesday that I managed to get through to my small friend. She cried and I cried, but I wrote while she spoke and little by little, I learned what had happened.

Mary Jane had been asked to do a four hour telephone stint for the local MDC over the election weekend and on the Sunday, had turned up at the Far and Wide offices, which in happier times – when there were tourists – had been used as a radio headquarters for the local mountain rescue teams. There were four others working with her and their job was to take details of MDC votes and make notes of any procedural infringements that were phoned in.

"There was nothing sinister about it and I knew that these places were operating countrywide," she said tearfully. "I wasn't actually working for the MDC."

The room the volunteers were using was basically furnished, but there was a radio set installed for the rescue teams and the three men working with Mary Jane had walkie talkie handsets which they used for their everyday work on the vast wattle estates of Nyanga.

"There was a stack of bread against one wall," my friend went on. "I was told that it was for the election observers at the remote polling stations. Their delivery truck had apparently broken down and everything had been unloaded in our building so I thought nothing of it."

That bread was to assume awful significance later.

At twenty-five past three that afternoon, Mary Jane was in the office with her friend, Joyce and three men, when there was a flurry of noise outside. She heard weapons being cocked and boots scraping on the step then three armed policemen burst in.

"They were led by Inspector Majoni, the officer in charge at Nyanga," she told me and I felt my hackles rise. That man had told me that he knew nothing about Mary Jane being arrested, but he had been lying. "He immediately asked about the walkie talkie radios on the table and both Joyce and I told him that they were nothing to do with us.

'Joyce runs a small soap-making company," she went on. "She only uses oils and herbs and because she thought we would probably be bored during our stint, had brought samples with her to be wrapped and labelled. Majoni accused her of using 'special soap' to wash ink off voters' hands so that they could vote again and this made us laugh. He would not listen to our explanation for the bread and insisted that we were using it to persuade people to vote for the MDC. Other cops had walked in and there were eight of them altogether so the room was very crowded. One constable produced a rough piece of paper on which he wrote our names and ID numbers, but we weren't unduly alarmed because it all seemed so ridiculous.

'It was when one of the police picked up three apples from the table and Joyce objected because they were hers that the atmosphere changed. Majoni angrily told us that we had no rights and were under arrest."

All five of them were bundled into a police truck, but before they could be driven away, another vehicle arrived with an obviously senior officer on board. He was very aggressive and when one of the men asked what they were supposed to have done, the senior man harangued them all in Chishona for a couple of minutes. They were later told that he came from Harare.

When they arrived at Nyanga police station, they were pushed into the charge office at around five thirty in the evening.

"At that stage, we all thought we would be making statements, then going home, but we were led into a very small room with three policemen who told us that we were being charged and would be detained in the cells. Each of us had to remove our shoes and the men had to take off their belts and socks as well. Joyce and I were made to remove our bras and were also checked to see how many pairs of pants we were wearing. It was all horribly intrusive and degrading."

Even though she told the police about her asthma, Mary Jane was not allowed to keep her medication, but when Joyce's husband arrived at the police station that evening, he managed to slip her a couple of inhalers, borrowed from a friend. They brought her some relief but as soon as she had used them, they were seen and taken away by the police.

"For Joyce, the worst moment was being told to remove her bra," she went on; "but for me it was when we were pushed into a pitch black cell. Two blankets were thrown in after us and we were told that the 'squat' was in the corner. The door clanged shut, two bolts were drawn across it and a padlock was put in place. It really was a desperate moment and one I will never forget."

The cell was bitterly cold and to begin with, the two women huddled together for warmth. It was also dark, desperately uncomfortable and frightening. My small friend had never been so afraid in her life.

"I felt that this could not be happening to me. After all, I have no particular political leanings so how could it be? Prior to being put into the cells we had asked for water to drink, but this was refused. Three or four hours later, I needed to wee but finding the squat in that darkness was a mission in itself. I had to crawl around on my hands and knees, feeling my way and by the time I was in position, Joyce and I were in fits of somewhat hysterical laughter."

In their efforts to keep warm, they lay on one blanket and covered themselves with the other, but it made little difference and their teeth chattered with the cold. When two black women were put into the cell, they asked for more blankets but were told that they would have to share what was there. They had not been allowed to wear jackets or sweaters, so sleep in those conditions was impossible.

"Every time we saw car headlights sweep the top of the cell, we thought we would be let out and told it was all a mistake, but the night wore on and we remained wallowing in our bewildered misery. It was so cold that my bones actually ached."

The two other women were in on similar charges – assisting the MDC – but had been told that they would be shut up for the elections and then released. Mary Jane and her companions had received no such assurances and remained totally bewildered as to what was going on.

"I felt completely abandoned and it was a terrible time for all of us," she said.

Next morning they were taken to a room where a lawyer was waiting. She told them that she had arrived the previous evening but had not been allowed to see any of the prisoners. Mary Jane's daughter arrived with the medication at noon, but a doctor who had been called to see her was refused permission to do so by the officer in charge. The medication did make her feel better, but it was taken away immediately after use.

After a long morning, they were taken outside to find a film crew waiting for them. One of the men gave a short statement and the clip was shown on the ZTV news that evening. It was the piece I had seen and even then it had seemed somewhat remarkable that the reporters and cameramen had known exactly when the alleged miscreants were being arrested or brought out of their cells. I had to agree with Mary Jane that it had obviously all been set up by the authorities.

Late that afternoon they were taken through to Mutare with two policemen as escorts. All seven of them were crammed into the rear of a police vehicle and when they arrived, were led to a CID room where there must have been sixty other prisoners, all held on various charges relating to the election. Another bleak night of incarceration followed with both women coming ever closer to despair.

The whole of Tuesday was spent giving more statements and denying charges which were repeatedly changed, presumably because the police knew how flimsy they were. One policewoman told them that she was sorry for the plight they were in and had done her best for them, but then asked them not to tell anyone else what she had said.

Those little moments of kindness did a lot to keep the pair of them sane but they were few and far between. The lawyer had arranged for them to have drinking water, but they were loath to use the toilet facilities which were primitive in the extreme and shared by a lot of people.

"When we did ask to use the loo," she said, "there was always a reason why it was not convenient for them to provide the necessary escort."

The reasons included the recording of particulars and that was when the absurdity of the situation made itself evident.

"When I was asked what colour my hair was, I said grey but he wrote brown on the form and my blue eyes were recorded as colourless. I don't suppose it mattered though.

'The worst of it was that we were hurried into everything with the threat of the magistrate finishing at five and another night in the cells if we missed him. We were interviewed by Immigration officials as well as the police, but at last we were taken over to the Court. Would you believe that there was another cameraman filming us and his clip was apparently shown on British television that evening.

'What a publicity stunt it all was, but we were the victims and no thought was given to our feelings by anyone involved."

At the Courthouse, they were taken to a small yard with one holding cell and forty odd men in prison garb, handcuffed and manacled in pairs. Their belongings were taken off them again and after requesting the toilet, they were taken one at a time to what Mary Jane described as 'the filthiest bog ever.' It was inches deep in sewage and didn't flush, but worse was to come when she and Joyce were handcuffed together like common criminals and made to sit on a stone step.

"Once again I wondered why this was happening to me," she was crying again but there was little I could say. This was Zimbabwe and such incidents were not out of the ordinary.

In Court, bail was set at sixty thousand Zim dollars – an outrageous sum for an offence carrying a maximum fine of five hundred dollars. They were also required to surrender their travel documents and report thrice weekly to their nearest police station. When Mary Jane queried the severity of bail conditions with her lawyer, she merely advised my friend to count her blessings.

"Apparently the police had asked for us to be remanded in custody for fourteen days."

That might well have finished Mary Jane off but I was pleased to note that she had kept her impish sense of humour despite her traumatic experience.

"Do you know," she giggled, "that the Manica Post when reporting the case, gave my age as forty-eight. With a son turning forty-nine in July, I have at least made medical history."

It just shows that one should never believe what one reads in newspapers.

Our conversation lasted nearly an hour and when I hung up, I was weak with reaction. As a former policeman, I knew only too well what those cells had been like, and the thought of my friend being incarcerated in conditions that would horrify the human rights lobbies of the Western world was not a pleasant one. I couldn't see the case getting very far, but in Zimbabwe the majority of Courts belong to the ruling party and anything could happen.

*　　*　　*

In Norton, two British journalists had also been arrested while carrying out interviews and taking photographs at polling stations. Looking drawn and dressed in prison clothing, Toby Harden and Julian Simmonds of the Sunday Telegraph were pictured in the media as they walked, manacled together into the dusty magistrates' court.

They were charged with illegal immigration and violating the newly promulgated Access to Information and Protection of Privacy Act. Their crime was doing their job without getting official accreditation from the Media and Information Commission – which would not have been granted anyway as Zimbabwe does not encourage foreign journalists.

Both men denied the charges, stating that they were merely visitors to the country. They had not been carrying press cards when arrested and had only been interested in observing how the election process worked in Zimbabwe. It was not a likely story, but I supposed it was all they could think of in the circumstances.

Harden and Simmonds had been held in the Harare Remand prison for some weeks before their Court appearance. There they shared a holding cell with one hundred and seven other prisoners and were fed once a day on vegetable gruel. Although neither man was physically harmed, they were able to hear the screams of prisoners being routinely beaten in nearby cells. An application for bail by their attorney, Beatrice Mtetwa was turned down flat.

Ms Mtetwa, a doughty little lady, hugely experienced at fighting lost causes said that the case was a travesty of justice and pointed out that all the State witnesses had been supporters of Zanu PF. Election monitors who might have given more unbiased evidence had not been called. This argument struck no chord with the Bench.

"My hands are tied in terms of the Act." Magistrate Diza told her severely. "The accused must remain in custody."

If convicted, Harden and Simmonds faced a mandatory prison sentence of two years with hard labour. It was not a pleasant prospect for either man but after a series of Court appearance, charges were quietly dropped and the pair were whisked out of the country. I had no doubt that the power of the British Establishment had been brought to bear and deals made to secure their release, but to me the incident came as a grim warning.

I felt that they had been foolish in working so openly, but I determined to be even more circumspect in my own operations. Harden and Simmonds had the political clout of the Sunday Telegraph behind them, but they were staff reporters and properly employed. I was a freelance and if I ended up in a similar predicament, I would be on my own. Neither my editor or the Sunday Express would admit to knowing me and nor would the British High Commission.

It was a sobering thought.

Chapter Fifteen

(Election Results)

The initial results started coming through late on Tuesday evening. I was staying with friends in Harare and the whole family were busy writing them down as they were announced. It was interesting at first, but soon palled as entertainment, so I took myself off to bed with a book.

All through that night, the family scribbled furiously while I tossed and turned, tormented by visions of my friend Mary Jane being left in a dark, dank cell without recourse to help or any of the normal comforts that most of us take for granted. At five I was up and the gloom on everyone's face as I walked into the lounge was pretty eloquent.

"Comrade Bob is going to walk it." I was told angrily. "None of it makes sense and I reckon they must have cooked the books."

As the world now knows – but won't readily admit - Mugabe and his tame Registrar Tobaiwa Mudede did indeed cook the books, but the overwhelming victory of Zanu PF was a dreadful shock to most Zimbabweans at the time.

On Wednesday morning, there was an air of stunned disbelief among most Harare residents. The resounding nature of Robert Mugabe's victory in the parliamentary election was surely the death knell for many of their dreams and hopes for a prosperous future.

"Now we all die." Gozo Machingura's normally cheerful face was sombre. "If everyone had been allowed to vote according to their wishes, this would not have happened Now there will surely be *hondo*."

It was certainly true that a number of voters around the country had been prevented from casting their votes, but their numbers were not large enough to account for Morgan Tsvangirai's fourteen point two percent deficit. Others were quick to point out glaring anomalies in the official figures.

"Chitungwiza is the largest urban conurbation in the country," Harare businessman Rod Kendall was indignant, "yet only twenty-three thousand votes were counted there, while there were thirty-two thousand from a little place like Kariba. What sort of nonsense is that?

It was a rhetorical question, but on a good day and including the children and resident baboons, Kariba would be fortunate to muster a population of fifteen thousand so the published figures were patently ridiculous.

In the city centre of Harare, an eerie sense of foreboding hung over the populace. Businesses closed down for a few days, new vehicles were moved out of showrooms in case of mass violence and Barbours department store kept heavy metal grilles firmly in place across their windows throughout the day. Police road blocks cordoned off the centre of town, but it was only when I tried to drive into the high-density township of Mbare that I was turned back.

"I want to buy curios," I lied to the armed policeman who stopped me but he was adamant. I was not to enter the township and so I returned to the city centre. I heard later that two white men had been killed in Mbare but was not able to confirm the story and eventually put it down to the Harare rumour machine.

In the City Bowling Club there was a general air of gloom and despondency, lifted only briefly when the overhead television showed Zimbabwe cricketer, Craig Wishart lofting a mighty six to beat India in a one day international. Normally sport-mad Zimbabweans cheered up momentarily then went back to discussing whether there was to be a future for this troubled little country. Someone mentioned widespread arrests of MDC supporters and I was reminded of Mary Jane's ordeal the previous weekend. In her own way, she had been helping the opposition party and had paid a horrible price for her assistance. Others would doubtless find themselves plagued and persecuted by government officials for doing their bit as a matter of principle.

It seemed anomalous that as Zimbabweans, we all prided ourselves on being fair minded and civilised, yet our officials preyed so much on the vulnerable and the innocent, just to keep one old despot in power. The men arrested with Mary Jane and Joyce were innocent of any crime other than supporting a political party, but because that party did not agree with government feelings, they were held in a dank police cell with forty other local election observers. Forty-three people in a room measuring twelve by twelve metres could not have been pleasant and rumour had it that countrywide, the number of local – as opposed to international - observers arrested amounted to close to twelve hundred. If this figure was correct and my sources were excellent, it merely confirmed that no matter what South African and Nigerian observers might have said, the election had not been free and fair. The entire electoral process had been fraudulent and the long-suffering people of Zimbabwe faced another period of corrupt government by an incompetent and tyrannical ruler.

The food shortage could only get worse and as more and more farmers were forced off their property or not allowed to work the land that was theirs, food and export crops alike would wither and die.

"We haven't a hope now," this was Rod Kendall again. "The observers say it was all above board, so the West will wash its collective hands of our problems and what was once a prosperous country will disappear into the general poverty that is Africa. Black and white Zimbos are all in the same boat now."

"The West will surely step in now," David Bradshaw held the opposite view. "They won't allow Mugabe to get away with this."

My own feelings agreed more with Kendall's gloom than the cheery optimism of Bradshaw. The West had done nothing to assist Zimbabwe in the past and although Tony Blair might burble on about Africa being 'a scar on the conscience of the world,' it didn't seem as though his own conscience was particularly scarred by Britain's abandonment of her responsibilities to her last African colony. George W Bush thundered platitudes about preventing terrorism in Africa, but he had American interests at heart and would leave Zimbabweans to face government sponsored terrorism without a qualm.

To my mind, the only way Zimbabweans could help themselves was through mass violence and like Gozo Machingura, many of them seemed to accept that this was the answer.

"We will go back to the bush," the speaker was a tiny flower seller in a print dress. "We fought the white colonials, now we will fight the black Mugabe. It doesn't matter if we all die."

The passion behind her words was frightening, but to me they summed up the feelings of Zimbabweans during those dreadful days after the election. The people felt cheated by the announced result and cheated by those black observers who were supposed to be on the side of freedom and truth. They knew that they were on their own and if that meant fighting and dying for their principles, they were prepared to do whatever was necessary.

It might have come to that too, but Zimbabweans are among the most peaceful and gentle-natured people in the world. Without a fiery leader to inspire them, their warlike rhetoric soon faded away and within weeks, the general population were back to waiting for some miracle to take place.

*   *   *

The Thursday after the election was not a day to be a white man on foot in down town Harare. Twenty-four hours after the announcement of Robert Mugabe's presidential victory, the town was outwardly quiet and almost back to normal, so I set out to speak with people, no inkling of trouble in mind.

I should have known better. On the way into town I passed a number of open-backed lorries, filled to the danger point with cheering, singing people, obviously in the mood for a party. The warnings I had been given before coming out niggled in the back of my mind, but I ignored them and parked on the edge of town. Armed with well-hidden camera and tape recorder, I walked toward Africa Unity Square in the centre of the city. After all, I reassured myself, Zanu PF supporters were entitled to celebrate their victory, no matter how it had been obtained.

I was showing more confidence than common sense. Walking along a pavement, I heard singing ahead and guessed that it was another group of Mugabe supporters. Perhaps some of them might tell me how it felt to be on the winning side. As they emerged around one side of the Ambassador Hotel and came chanting and toyi toying toward me, I moved in against a building to give them room to pass. They appeared exuberantly cheerful and their singing was infectious. I wondered if any of them would stop to talk.

The group was composed almost entirely of women and young men, all clad in Zanu PF colours, whether they were in the form of Mugabe-embossed sweatshirts, colourful skirts or even Zanu PF 'beanies' on their heads. As they danced past me, eyes swivelled in my direction and a couple of the leaders moved sideways, banging me hard against the wall.

"Hey, mind where you are going," I called out a protest, but it was a mistake. I should have kept my mouth shut. A large woman leading the procession turned on me, her mouth working and her eyes flashing hatred.

"Go back to Britain," she hissed, spittle spraying in my face. "We do not want you racist colonials in Zimbabwe. Go back to Bliar and your own country."

Her tirade ended in a scream of pure venom and I forbore from pointing out that Zimbabwe was my country as well. The woman and her companions were obviously anti British and my white face – even though the sun had burned me as dark as many of the marchers over preceding weeks – singled me out for special treatment. Unflatteringly outlining my presumed ancestry in Chishona to those behind her, the woman gave one last aggressive shake of her fist in my face and danced on down the pavement, leaving me jammed between my wall and the rest of the mob. I did not have time to be frightened, but my shoulders were hurting from repeated and fairly violent contact with the stonework behind me. I am not a small man and I was not going to be intimidated by this motley lot, so pushed myself away from the wall and found myself face to face with a young man wearing a brand new Zanu PF T-shirt and carrying a short stick in one hand. His face was contorted with venom.

"Go back to Britain," the rhetoric was unoriginal. "We do not want racist whites in our country. Take all the *mabhunu* with you. Zimbabweans do not want you here."

Prodding me forcefully in the chest with his stick, the youth was screaming into my face while all around him I could see a mass of chanting, laughing women, all eager to see their champion sort out the white intruder in their midst. It was not a nice moment. Even though I towered over my tormentor, such was his rage that I could feel the trembling start in my knees. I was alone in an angry mob and did not enjoy the sensation. To be honest, it was terrifying.

Fortunately perhaps, the youth tired of his tantrum and moments later, the group had danced their way past, leaving me shaking with reaction. I could understand their joy at Mugabe's victory, but Zimbabweans had never been overtly racist and the venomous hatred of my skin colour as expressed by the large lady and the youth was unpleasant to see. It had also been very frightening and I knew that I had been lucky to escape without injury, except perhaps to my pride.

Trying to recover my dignity, I walked on and met the ironic gaze of a big, well-dressed man who had watched the episode from a doorway.

"Don't worry about those people," he smiled gently. "They have been hired by Mugabe to make trouble for you whites. All of them are women or unemployed *tsotsis* from the townships who normally hang around the streets. Now they have a few dollars and free food for the day so they work themselves up into a frenzy. It is the curse of the black man that people like Mugabe can do this so easily. No wonder the world will not take Africa seriously."

My new friend walked on down the street with me and as we went, he expounded further.

"You would not have been badly hurt," the adjective robbed the words of comfort. "All around were MDC supporters and we would have rescued you. We do not want to see white people driven out of our country. We have lived peacefully together for many years and there is no reason for that to finish now. Mugabe will be ousted soon or perhaps he will die and we can get back to rebuilding the mess he has left for all Zimbabweans."

Gravely shaking my hand, the well dressed gentleman disappeared into an office building, leaving me to ponder on the many differing facets of my fellow countrymen. They are kind, gentle, peaceful and generous folk at heart, but work them up with a little rhetoric, give them a few cheap handouts and they become dangerously volatile. In spite of my companion's assurances, I was not at all sure that the revellers would not have torn me limb from limb had I reacted in any way and the encounter left me fearing for the future of my countrymen.

If one man can engender so much hate for a small and powerless minority, what hope do white Zimbabweans really have in the land that belongs as much to them as their black counterparts?

I wasn't sure and it worried me.

*   *   *

As the Boeing lifted off from Harare's bleak international airport, I felt both despondent and afraid. I was leaving my country as it teetered on the brink of disaster.

Below me the landscape looked broad and peaceful, but after travelling extensively through that landscape over preceding weeks, I knew that the air of peace was an illusion. Farms and ranches that had supported the economy for decades, now lay overgrown and unused, or had been divided into small, uneconomic patches of ground where peasant farmers battled to produce enough food for their families. Grand hotels and luxury lodges stood empty and virtually unmanned because visitors to that beautiful country had been scared away by the situation. Even as I flew to safety, brave men and women were being beaten up, tortured, imprisoned or murdered below me, just because they were willing to make a stand against the tyranny of Robert Mugabe's brutal regime. Families from all sectors of society were being forced from their homes, often with only the clothes they were wearing.

To make matters infinitely worse, many Zimbabweans were starving and their hunger would become ever more acute as the drought worsened and the government resettlement policy forced yet more productive farms to be abandoned. Fear stalked the land and no matter what the Good Book said, evil was triumphing over good.

In twelve weeks, I had covered nearly twenty thousand kilometres in four out of five provinces and I had spoken with hundreds of my countrymen. I had interviewed Terry Ford who had since been brutally murdered. I had spent time with Mary Jane who was later arrested and imprisoned on spurious charges. I had spoken with many who had not suffered and others who had, some of them terribly badly. I had spent time in luxury hotels, beautiful farmhouses, suburban cottages and squalid shacks in high-density townships. I had been manhandled by a chanting mob, frightened out of my wits by aggressive youths on a farm road and been treated with friendly courtesy by military men and police officers at roadblocks. This courtesy was more in keeping with the nature of most Zimbabweans and always left me with a feeling of pride in what my countrymen had achieved.

But not all Zimbabweans had proved themselves courteous or gentle. I had seen the horrifying results of government violence at first hand. I had spoken with the lovely Chikafas and Callistus Shumba and my soul had cringed at the sheer inhumanity of those who had so brutally tortured them.

I had listened to many stories in those twelve weeks. Some of them were heartening, such as that of the Ashmores, who gave up successful careers to live 'the good life' in the foothills of Nyanga. Others had been desperately sad and I cried with people like Jack and Trish Marshall – octogenarians who had been forced from their homes by a heartless government.

"Where can we go at our age?" Trish had asked me and I could find no satisfactory answer. They had nowhere to go. Both of them had been born in Zimbabwe and their smallholding had fed local people for many years. Now they were being forced out and their plight was desperate as they pondered the ruin of everything they had lived for.

For all his political naiveté, Morgan Tsvangirai had offered hope to Zimbabweans and the majority of people had been angrily disbelieving when the election results were announced. Every thinking Zimbabwean knew that the voting was rigged, yet the Commonwealth troika of South Africa, Nigeria and Australia had declared the election legitimate and most major western nations accepted their verdict. How could my countrymen believe this nonsense? How could they keep any faith in politicians from the developed world?

Zimbabweans needed help, not betrayal, yet betrayal was what they got. Many bellies in that vast land below me were empty and even the wealthy were struggling to survive. Quite apart from maize meal, basics like cooking oil, bread, sugar and milk were becoming ever more difficult to find. Meat was in desperately short supply and as the aircraft climbed far above their heads, long queues of ordinary people waited outside supermarkets and bush stores, hoping to buy tiny quantities of food that should be theirs by right.

So what did the future hold for Zimbabwe and her people I asked myself as the hostess came around with the drinks trolley. How long could the country last? I didn't know the answer to either question but over succeeding weeks, I listened to sleek and powerful politicians such as Tony Blair, George W Bush and Kofi Annan and when I listened, my heart filled with bitterness. For all their fancy words and phrases about a 'flawed election,' they had accepted the result and thus condemned my countrymen to more misery and more pain. It would be the same at the next election and the one after that, but these people didn't care. If Zimbabweans were to survive, they had to get rid of Mugabe and his heartless government, but nobody would help them do that.

I wondered if in time there would be an uprising of the people. A man named Alec Mataera had expressed the hopes and fears of many when we spoke over a beer in Kariba.

"We must demonstrate our opposition. We have taken too much now and we must unite to get this man and his cronies out of power."

But if that were to happen, many good people would die. Alec shrugged this off as irrelevant.

"Many good people have died already," he said simply. "Others are dying while you and I argue over beer. We must all be prepared to die in order that our children and their children will have a future. I am willing to die for my country and so are my friends."

They were strong words and quite unlike the usual smiling platitudes with which Zimbabweans face up to the vicissitudes of daily life. The ordinary man in the street is a peaceful soul, but so many of them were now feeling abandoned by the world and I wondered if the time for revolution really had come. For the sake of all my compatriots, including the future generations that Alec Mataera mentioned, I really hoped so, but revolution was easy for me to advocate from comfortable exile. I knew in my heart that if the people did make a concerted stand against the government, the carnage would be awful.

I certainly did not want that.

PART FOUR

(Danger, Discomfort and the Bennets)

Chapter Sixteen

(Changes Everywhere)

It seemed that my brief and undistinguished career as an impromptu journalist was not going to be a long one. Following an editorial reshuffle at the Sunday Express, Phil McNeill had moved sideways and his replacement had a more jaundiced view of the situation in Zimbabwe and the reporting of David Lemon – or Bryan Graham as the case may be. The paper had paid for my previous trip, making me feel like a real correspondent, but suddenly, my stories were no longer wanted.

Yet the situation in Zimbabwe was deteriorating to an incredible extent. The value of the local currency was dropping by the day, food was becoming ever more unattainable and the inflation rate was climbing to unheard of levels in a country not at war. I received daily emails and reports from contacts in all sectors of society and although I fashioned these into what I thought were excellent and interesting articles, they were routinely spiked and my queries and calls went unanswered.

The situation went on this way for many months and I became very dispirited and unsure about my own ability to write. I missed my travels and missed the incredible variety of life in Zimbabwe. I missed the excitement too. I was back to being an English gardener and the only minor interest in my daily life occurred when I was up a ladder or ham-fistedly wielding a chainsaw.

My cup of woe was filled when I was cutting creeper from the eaves of a tall house one morning and a neighbour called out, 'old men and ladders are not a good combination.' I was shattered and wondered whether the newspaper for whom I had risked so much, now regarded me as too old for the job. But all was not lost. I hadn't been entirely forgotten and was still on the books of the Sunday Express. One morning I was phoned by a reporter, who shall remain nameless. He asked what I knew about Chikurubi Prison and whether it would be possible to get a prisoner out by force. I told him that nobody had ever managed to escape from Chikurubi, with or without assistance and that it would cost a huge amount in both money and lives to even attempt such a rescue. I pointed out that it had been considered by the South Africans in the early years of Zimbabwe, but even they had backed off, feeling that the risks involved were too extreme. The following Sunday, I read with some disgust that the French government were going to 'spring' Simon Mann, the English mercenary leader from Chikurubi, using helicopters. Even allowing for the terrain and the distance such aircraft would need to travel, the story was quite obviously a load of codswallop, but I stifled my resentment at such slap happy journalism and tried to ignore the piece.

Simon Mann was eventually deported under protest to Equatorial Guinea, the oil rich country in which he had been intent on staging a military coup. After a couple of years in the notorious Black Beach prison, he was then repatriated back to Britain and hasn't really been heard of since. I could only wonder what underhand deals were made to secure his release.

Truly modern politics is an evil business and despite his aristocratic upbringing – or perhaps because of it – and the millions in his bank account, Mann had become just another political pawn by which governments could demonstrate their superiority over each other.

For me though, it was a case of forgetting about journalism and going back to being a 'garden boy' in rural England. Life resumed its boring routine and week followed week in digging, mowing, hacking and pruning the manicured gardens of paying clients. It was all very humdrum and old age seemed to be rushing up on me with indecent haste. Then, after a very short tenure as News Editor, the man who had obviously consigned me to the waste bin lost his job in some sort of scandal and not long afterwards, I was contacted by the new incumbent, James (Jim) Murray.

"Have you any trips to Zimbabwe planned in the near future?" He asked and my spirits lifted. They needed me after all.

"I was intending to go back in a month or two." I lied. Winter was upon us, there was little gardening money coming in and I could hardly afford a bus trip to Gloucester, let alone an aeroplane to Harare.

"How about coming down to London for a chat?" He invited. "We will pay your expenses."

It was too good an opportunity to miss and so for the first time, I found myself in the hideously square, glass-fronted building in Lower Thames Street that houses Express Newspapers. Jim Murray was a softly spoken man who introduced himself with a firm handshake.

"Do you know Roy Bennet?" He asked over lunch at a nearby pub. I didn't, but knew of him. The firebrand MDC politician had recently been sentenced to fifteen months in prison for assaulting the Minister of Justice, Patrick Chinamasa. The assault had been sorely provoked and the severity of the sentence had sent shivers of shock throughout Zimbabwe. Bennet was incarcerated in Mutoko prison, a notoriously inhuman establishment in the harsh North Eastern corner of the country.

Murray must have sensed my indecision.

"It is his wife, Heather I am interested in," he told me. "She is apparently standing for her husband's seat in Parliament and I would like you to get me an interview with her."

"No problem," I wondered if I sounded any more confident than I felt. "I know where she lives so it shouldn't be difficult."

"Do you think you can get me pictures of Mugabe's new mansion while you are there?"

Despite the rapidly escalating poverty and hunger in the country, Comrade Bob and his young wife Grace, who already owned a number of mansions in various Zimbabwean centres, were building a massively ostentatious edifice in the exclusive Borrowdale Brooke suburb of Harare. I didn't think I would be allowed anywhere near it, but the opportunity was too good to miss.

"That shouldn't be too difficult," I lied valiantly once again. "I have a couple of contacts who can probably get me in there."

So it was agreed. The newspaper would send me out again and Bryan Graham was back in business. With my heart singing and a feeling of euphoria pervading my system, I went home to Gloucestershire and made arrangements to fly home as soon as possible. I knew that I would face enormous problems in tackling either of the tasks he had given me, but hoped that Lemon's Luck, in which I have always been a firm believer, would help me out once again.

* * *

With their country economically ruined and their people on the verge of starvation, Robert and Grace Mugabe seemed determined to flaunt their own wealth for the ordinary people to see. Despite the personal sanctions applied to them and their closest cohorts by America and the European Union, they were frequently abroad and Grace was famed for her lavish ideas on personal shopping. She also owned spectacular homes that stood out like blisters on a pale skin in places like Chivhu and Chitungwiza. Who lived in these magnificent buildings, nobody knew but they were both visible from afar, providing stark contrast with the clustered shacks among which they had been built.

The latest Mugabe extravaganza was a supposedly palatial residence nearing completion in Borrowdale Brooke. A number of home owners had been moved out and their houses demolished to make space for the new building, but it seemed that they had all been adequately compensated. Everybody knew of the place and stories abounded about the size, number of rooms and degrees of elegance involved, but my problem was how to approach it. The house would be heavily guarded even though the president wasn't yet in residence and I didn't see how I could possibly get close to the building during the day. The alternative would be to approach it at night, but that was probably suicidal. The guards would be armed and wouldn't hesitate to shoot on sight.

I spent a couple of days pondering the problem and finding out all I could about the Mugabes' new home. Following a tip from an acquaintance who worked in the Customs department, I hurried out to Harare airport one morning, only to be turned away from the baggage terminal where three Army lorries had been deployed to carry away tons of carefully covered 'household equipment' that Grace had brought back from a trip to Malaysia and the Far East. Armed soldiery were much in evidence to oversee the loading and dispersal of this equipment and another Customs official told me that it consisted of luxury furniture, fittings and household linen.

"It is for Grace's new mansion," he said somewhat wistfully. "It will surely be a beautiful house and she has three others already. That does not seem right."

It wasn't right – of that there could be no doubt, but nor was it my problem. That lay in actually getting photographs of the mansion itself and I didn't know where to start. I had driven up the road above Borrowdale Brooke on a couple of occasions, but armed guards in military uniform eyed me with acute suspicion and I didn't want to push my luck too far before I'd had a chance to enjoy being home again.

I needed help but didn't know where to look for it. I have always tried to be alone when attempting anything silly or remotely dangerous, as that way I have only myself to worry about. For this job though, I needed someone to get me into the building and that meant someone who knew the possible pitfalls and how to get around them.

In mild desperation, I approached Henry Ndhlovu – he who had finagled documents for the Ganja Bus and offered me a Zimbabwe passport. If anyone knew somebody who could get me in to Comrade Bob's house, it would surely be my tame Mr Fixit.

A little to my surprise, Henry didn't turn a hair when I told him what I wanted.

"I think it is impossible," he told me seriously. "You will be arrested or even killed but I do know a man who works for the MDC and if anyone knows a way, he is the one. I will contact him for you and see what he says."

Two days later, my telephone – I had inherited a mobile job from my son – rang and a guarded voice asked if I was Bryan Graham. Having admitted that I was, I was directed to a particular road in Mabvuku Township and advised that if I was there at a specified time on the following Saturday, a solution to my problem could possibly be found.

It was all very melodramatic and I smiled inwardly at the secrecy, but this was Zimbabwe and the locals knew far more about the situation than I did. I would need to humour them.

Mabvuku is one of the more basic high-density townships in Harare and having been dropped off by disapproving friends, I felt very conspicuous as I waited in the road at the requisite time. I wasn't there long however, as one of the ubiquitous, Kombi minibuses swooped down on me and a young man urgently gestured for me to get in to the back. I did as I was told and moments later, we were heading east at high speed along the Mutare road. The young man chattered away beside me, but the driver said not a word and didn't answer my questions as to where we were going.

"Just wait," the young man told me gleefully (He was obviously in his element). "We will soon be there."

'There' was the Marondera Hotel on the main road, a place that I had often visited in the past, both as a police officer and an ordinary imbiber. Stopping outside the main entrance, the ever silent driver jerked his head at the veranda and as soon as I was out, sped off along the road. I wondered how I was going to get back to Harare.

Curious, I looked around me. The only person in sight was a very tall black man, thin to the point of emaciation, wearing a woollen hat and sipping from a bottle of fruit juice. He studied me warily as I approached.

"I am Tonderai Ndira," he said quietly as I sat down at his table. "You need my help?"

He seemed very young and I wondered whether I could trust him. If this went wrong, it was my head on the block and the consequences would be awful, but I had to do something. This man had been recommended to me, so I had to go with that recommendation.

When I told him what I wanted to do, Tonderai Ndira looked vaguely incredulous and I couldn't really blame him. Even to me it sounded daft and eminently suicidal.

After a long pause to consider the matter, he smiled thinly and took out a mobile phone. It seemed that no matter how poor Zimbabweans seemed to be, all of them carried very smart phones. Looking at me throughout the conversation, Ndira spoke rapidly into the instrument and listened briefly to whatever was said in reply. Folding the phone away, he replaced it in his pocket and assayed a smile. It lit up his gaunt face, but I wasn't sure that it contained much amusement.

"That was a man who can help," he told me simply. "But it will cost you a great deal of money."

I waved that aside as being of no consequence but wondered where I could lay my hands on the money if I didn't have enough. Feeling sure that I could borrow it from friends or family, I just hoped I wasn't biting off more than I could chew.

However, having now told two virtual strangers of my plan, it was too late to pull out and besides, if I did get the photographs of Mugabe's house, they would surely be worth a lot of money, even without the newspaper. There had to be a profit in this somewhere, provided I survived.

Ndira smiled at my agreement and spoke once more into the phone while I ordered a beer from a passing waiter.

* * *

Two days later, we met again in an outdoor coffee shop in Central Harare. Still wearing his woollen hat, but with dreadlocks showing from beneath it, Tonderai was accompanied by a thick set man, who turned out to be a colonel in the Zimbabwe National Army. We shook hands in the double gripped African way and his clasp was firm. He was dressed in a neat brown suit without a tie, but the colonel had the hard, compact frame of a soldier and his eyes told of a man who was accustomed to command. As far as I could make out, he was part of the presidential guard, but I didn't like to question him too closely.

"You are going to plant a bomb?" He queried roughly and when I held my hands up and vehemently denied any homicidal intention, he did not seem overly convinced. Mind you, I had the distinct impression that he wouldn't have cared if assassination was involved. He was in it for the money.

"It can be done," he told me and I felt a surge of relief. "I am in charge of checking alarm procedures and we are close to the date of a routine test. I can arrange for the systems to be shut down for a while, but you know it will be very dangerous? If we are caught…"

He didn't finish the sentence, merely shaking his head at the thought.

I had thought hard on possible consequences and told him so. For a long moment, he studied me in silence and I knew what he was thinking. This sort of escapade was for young, fit, military men, not visibly crumpled geriatrics like me.

"You will be contacted in the next three days," he told me. "Just make sure you are ready to go at any time."

"Who will contact me?" I was getting tired of the cloak and dagger stuff. I don't think I would have made much of a spy.

"Me," he grunted irritably. "Without me, you do not have any chance of success. Have the money ready."

We had agreed on a sum that would more than just decimate my travelling budget, but I had already arranged a fairly substantial loan with a friend.

"How do I know I can trust you?"

It was a bit late for that and his smile showed that he knew it.

"You already have, my friend – you already have."

He was right. Three people now knew of my intentions and in paranoid Zimbabwe that meant that all three had my life in their hands.

I glanced at Tonderai Ndira who had been silent through the brief conversation.

"And what do you get out of this?"

I was genuinely interested as he had not asked for anything. Perhaps he would take a commission out of what I was paying the colonel.

The tall man smiled again, but this time his face remained set in bleak lines.

"I am a man of the Party, Sir," He said simply. "I do what I do in order to help my fellow Zimbabweans."

I was not overly convinced, but decided that Ndira was a little like Chris Sheppard in Karoi and enjoyed the excitement involved in behaving like a spy or secret agent. I was way off beam and events were to prove me so in time, but I was heartily fed up with feeling helpless.

For two days I waited for the promised phone call and two very long days, they were. For obvious reasons, I couldn't discuss the matter with anyone. My family would have been horrified and I would have been putting others into danger if I did tell them of my plans. I knew that my disappearance was a distinct possibility if anything went wrong and so, feeling somewhat melodramatic myself, I wrote letters to Sandra and my children, outlining my plans and apologising for not telling them what I had in mind. In the letters to Brian, Graeme and Deborah, I told them how proud I was to be their father and inwardly prayed that the maudlin epistles would not be read for a few years yet. I left them all in my unlocked briefcase, just in case things went wrong.

When he did call, the colonel was brief and to the point.

"Seven o'clock this evening at the toilets behind Sam Levy's village," Was all he said and the rest of the day passed in anxious self examination. I really was putting my head into the lion's mouth and nervousness built up into a physical pain in my stomach as the afternoon crawled along.

However, I had burned too many bridges by then and so it was that at ten past seven that evening, I found myself dressed in dark clothing and huddled in the back of an obviously government- issue van, on my way to I knew not what.

*   *   *

Suddenly I was alone in what was undoubtedly the most magnificent residence I had ever seen. The rest of that great house was as awesome as the entrance hall. It was like a modern version of a baronial hall in rural England I suppose, but there were obviously Eastern elements to the decor that seemed to clash with the more traditional. Moving as quietly as I could, I slipped through high-ceilinged bedrooms, lounges and what appeared to be dressing rooms. This edifice in one of the poorest countries in Africa must surely have matched Buckingham Palace or the White House for opulence. No expense had been spared and wherever I looked, the splendour of the place took my breath away.

Fitted out in various shades and grades of marble and darkly glowing wood, the house was like a self contained town in its own right. I don't know how many *en suite* bedrooms there were – I lost count after the sixth - but they were all decorated in different designs and colour schemes and all lavishly furnished, most of them with four-poster beds, some curtained but others with the drapery not yet attached.

Much of the furniture was covered in dust sheets, but a few of the beds had been made up and unable to help myself, I ran my hand gently over one vividly coloured counterpane. I am no connoisseur of household linen, but it had to be satin or something closely akin to it. An ornate headboard towered above my head and the general theme of that particular room was crimson and gold – a little garish for my taste, but splendid in its own right.

Catching a glimpse of my reflection in a gold-framed wall mirror, I paused a moment and despite the circumstances felt myself smiling inwardly. Black clothing and a pulled down balaclava probably looks quite good on actors in crime movies or men of the SAS on clandestine operations, but on a venerably rotund sixty year old, they merely looked ridiculous. Pulling that wool off my face with a wry smile at my own pretentiousness, I continued with my exploration. Spotting another vast staircase, I hurried up to the floor above. The house around me seemed almost unnaturally quiet and that added to the occasional flashes of vulnerability, I felt as I wandered through the rooms. Time and again, I paused to listen for I knew not what, then hurried on to get in as much as I possibly could.

There were two luxury flats in the top storey that the colonel later informed me were for the Mugabe offspring and more lounges and reception areas than I could get my numbed mind around. Each and every bathroom was spectacularly fitted out. Bathtubs came in varying designs and were far larger than any other tubs I had ever seen. Many of the fittings appeared to be in gold and there were mirrors, jacuzzis and heated rails in abundance. Most of these rooms even contained bidets, which I couldn't imagine being particularly popular in Africa.

In the corner of a bathroom, one massive elephant tusk was propped incongruously against the wall and on a section of the stairs I almost tripped and fell when my foot caught in a pile of animal skins. I presumed they had all been donated by grateful sycophants and rather sourly wondered why Zimbabwe's precious wild life was being slaughtered for the benefit of one crazy old despot. There was no time to explore the thought though and I hurried on.

Deep carpets oozed luxury from every room while heavy velvet curtains adorned most of the windows. Chandeliers glittered from the ceiling in many of the main rooms although the bedrooms were discreetly lit up from recesses in various walls. Even what appeared to be linen cupboards were more like small rooms in their own right and ornately framed paintings littered the place like so many forgotten children's toys. Most of these seemed to be traditional landscapes and although I know nothing about art, they looked expensive to my untutored eye. Although actual building work appeared to have been completed, all the pictures were either lying flat or propped against walls preparatory to being put into their allotted places. In one room, a six foot statue lay on its side against a wall.

I had heard so many tall stories about the building and its surrounds, but to me it was strangely disappointing. As a writer, I felt a bit piqued that there were no bookshelves in evidence. Robert Mugabe was said to be highly intellectual. Surely he read books?

There were other anomalies too. Many parts of that great mansion seemed more like Hollywood film sets than rooms in a house and even allowing for the fact that it was not yet lived in, I found the internal decor somewhat confusing. European mixed with Eastern, mixed with African just didn't seem to jell somehow and there was no particular theme to any of the rooms or suites. Pushing the conundrums out of my mind, I hurried from room to room. Time seemed to be rushing by and I had to keep checking my watch. The colonel had explained how he had neutralised the various alarm systems between seven and eight o'clock, but I wished I could slow things down. I was still very nervous, but it was overlaid with a feeling of intense pleasure. For the first time in years, I was living life as it ought to be lived and although it probably was not good for my blood pressure, I found myself revelling in the excitement.

Murmuring descriptions into my dictaphone as I crept through the rooms, I sank into a deeply cushioned armchair to get my breath back, only to be yanked back on to my feet by the colonel, who to my *chagrin,* I hadn't even heard approach. Some burglar I would have made!

"We don't have time to rest," he murmured. "If we are discovered, we will die. These people know no mercy and will shoot us without even thinking about it. Also, to be captured and interrogated will be worse than death."

Before I left England, I had read about the security arrangements apparently in force to protect Mugabe from unwanted visitors. According to the report, there was a 'no flying' zone around the fourteen acre property, alarm sensors to warn of impending chemical attack as well as more conventional onslaughts, and an array of armed guards and dogs that should be able to detect an intruder even before he had thought about intruding. When I had queried all this with the colonel, he agreed that the alarm system was extremely complex but pooh-poohed the idea of the chemical sensors.

"How could that possibly work?" He asked and being the technological dodo that I am, I couldn't answer the question. To this day I have no idea how he had managed to switch all the regular alarms off for even a limited time, but I suppose it goes to show that not even the most sophisticated system is truly impregnable.

The colonel was in an obvious hurry to leave, but I was busily taking photographs and pleaded for a little more time. With frowning reluctance, he agreed and walked ahead of me, quickly checking out each room before allowing me to enter. The dining hall – it was too large to be called a mere room – was of particular interest. A table, the size of an aircraft carrier's flight deck was covered in a white linen table cloth that seemed to gleam silver in light, reflected off an immense chandelier above. The mental picture evoked of Bob and Grace shouting to each other from either end of that incredible table almost brought me to semi hysterical giggles.

After what seemed like an age but was probably less than a quarter of an hour, my companion whispered that we were pushing our luck and it was time we got out of there. He shrugged at my unspoken question.

"I don't know how anyone can afford to even maintain a place like this," he whispered. "It will cost billions of dollars in cleaning materials alone."

I suppose we left along the route that had brought us into the mansion, but I had long since lost any sense of orientation.

I had probably only explored one small portion of the building, but my senses were shell-shocked with the opulence on view. Had I not had that incredibly brave man to guide me, I would probably still be wandering around that dreamlike building – if I hadn't been shot out of hand.

At last though, we were out of the house and heading toward the van. I breathed deeply of the cool night air and sweat ran down my face and body in copious streams. My companion looked similarly discomfited but suddenly I wanted to laugh. We had done it. Together, the two of us had penetrated one of the most heavily fortified and sensitively alarmed buildings in the world and I had the pictures to prove it.

Photographing my surroundings had really been a big risk to take, as my camera was an unsophisticated little digital model that required lots of light in which to operate. That meant closing heavy curtains and switching on overhead illuminations, while hoping that no chink of light was escaping to be seen by the guards. In the end, it was a risk that could have killed us both and it proved totally useless. When he looked through the photographs many weeks later, Jim Murray asked me whether the pictures had been taken legally.

"Of course not," I exploded. "We broke in to the place and were very lucky not to be caught."

I presume the legal eagles who advise tabloid newspapers on such matters were then consulted and turned down publication on grounds of spurious legality. Whatever the case, neither the pictures nor the resultant article were ever published and I felt terribly let down by the newspaper hierarchy. I am sure their reasons for the rejection were good, but to me it all smacked of terrible hypocrisy. My brief foray into upper class burglary had been all for nothing, but looking back on the evening many years later, memories of the intense excitement I felt will make me smile well into my dotage.

"It is time for drink," the colonel told me firmly as I climbed back into the dark rear compartment of the van. It still smelled bad, but now it was more a sanctuary than a prison and once we were under way, I hugged myself with glee, even though my whole body was trembling with reaction. This time, we merely slowed at the main gate and I heard the colonel shout something to the man on duty, then we were free and on our way to the Keg and Sable bar in the nearby shopping centre. The pub was crowded and I don't know what the patrons must have thought about two middle-aged gentlemen in dark clothing who stumbled in and sat at one end of the bar. I think we were still in a state of shock and after downing two beers in quick succession, we both burst into somewhat hysterical laughter. Clutching at each other with unfeigned enjoyment of the moment, we talked about what we had seen and periodically guffawed at the way we had cheated the system.

When we left that pub, we were both much the worse for wear, but we had shared a moment that must surely be unique and although we have not seen each other since that strangely exciting night, I will remember one particular officer in Robert Mugabe's presidential guard with considerable affection for the rest of my life. He had told me that the money I paid him would go toward school fees for his children, but whether it was for financial reasons or not, he had proved himself to be a truly brave man. Together he and I had taken an almost insane risk and the fact that we are both still alive says much for his leadership and courage.

It was a pity about the photographs though. The newspaper business seems very strange at times.

In an interesting corollary to that eventful night, a couple of years later my son Brian sent me a long email that was doing the Internet rounds and purported to show parts of Robert Mugabe's mansion. Together with a series of photographs depicting an opulent selection of rooms, a vast white building and an awe-inspiring swimming pool, the question to readers went, '*Imagine who would have such taste and live in such opulence? An American billionaire? A Saudi Prince? Louis X1V of France?*'

And after the photographs, the text went on, '*This mansion is in Harare and belongs to the President of Zimbabwe - Robert Mugabe - while his people starve, and die because of no medical help....and we are asked to help his people over and over again...he and his family live like this.......his GREED kills his people.....'* The message ended with the exhortation to *'send this to everyone you know, they can send it to everyone they know and soon the world will know what this man is doing to his people.'*

I am no fan of Comrade Bob, but the pictures were not mine and unless the design and decoration of his house had changed radically since the time I had wandered so gleefully around a part of it, nor did they depict the mansion of Robert Mugabe.

It just goes to show that one cannot believe everything one reads on the Internet either.

* * *

Mind you, it wasn't only the Mugabes who were guilty of appalling ostentation. A few days after my clandestine visit to their mansion, I was shown around an only slightly less spectacular house by a Harare businessman I will call Obert Nyangondo. We had met quite by chance in the good old Hunters' Bar in Meikles and become fleeting friends over a couple of beers.

Obviously feeling that a party was starting, Nyangondo invited me to his house for a few more drinks. Accompanied by two glowering bodyguards, we headed out to Borrowdale again and Obert proudly showed me around his mansion.

"Nice isn't it," the businessman beamed as he led me through the sort of bedrooms that were reminiscent of the building I had prowled through such a short time previously. His house wasn't as large as the president's but it must have cost almost as much and was sumptuously furnished. I asked him how he felt when he travelled through the rural areas but he was unrepentant.

"I like nice things," Obert Nyangondo told me unapologetically. "It is my money so why should I worry about the povo?"

It sounded like a fitting epitaph for Zimbabwe.

Chapter Seventeen

(Heather Bennet)

That was one of my two major objectives achieved, but I had airily assured Jim Murray that I could get an interview with Heather Bennet. The trouble was that I did not have the slightest idea how to go about it. Everyone knew of her and I managed to get hold of her telephone number but whenever I rang, my call went unanswered.

"She is worried about security," a friend told me gently. "She has announced her intention of standing for Parliament and by doing so, has put her own head on the block. I am sure she won't want to talk with anyone she doesn't know."

It was a reasonable assumption and I was in despair until I was speaking with an MDC friend who immediately made a few phone calls and handed me a name and phone number.

"Try this chap," he said with a grin. "He deals with all Heather's appointments."

'This chap' – I'll call him Andy – was enthusiastic and helpful.

"I'll give you her cell number." He said, but that too remained unanswered. When I rang him back, Andy was apologetic.

"Where are you?" He asked and when I told him, he advised me to stay put and have a coffee.

"I'll see whether she can meet you right now," he said. "She isn't far from there at the moment."

So it was that I sat somewhat nervously in a pavement coffee shop and wondered what I was going to say. Heather Bennet was a celebrity in Zimbabwe and her imprisoned husband enjoyed almost cult status among local people. Known as *Pachedu* (one of us) by the people of Manicaland, he spoke

Chishona like a native and had been asked by the Manyika chiefs to be their representative in parliament. Initially a Zanu PF MP, he had become an independent and then joined the MDC. As an outspoken member of The House he had long been a thorn in the side of Robert Mugabe, but he had paid a high price for speaking his mind.

Bennet had lost his profitable Charleswood Estate in Chimanimani, seen two of his workers shot dead by marauding squatters and dealt with the rapes of seven women who were working for him. He had seen his wife held hostage and made to dance and sing Zanu PF songs while heavily pregnant. As a result of that experience, Heather had miscarried with what would have been the Bennets' third child.

Bennet himself had been arrested, detained and roughly questioned on a number of occasions, but when his temper finally snapped and he pushed Patrick Chinamasa to the floor in Parliament, he was sentenced by a parliamentary committee to fifteen months in hard labour, three of which were conditionally suspended. Although he had publicly apologised to Chinamasa and the Speaker, this terribly harsh sentence was confirmed by a small majority in the predominantly Zanu PF parliament and Bennet had been carted off to serve his sentence. Ironically, the only person who sustained any damage in the attack on Chinamasa was Bennet himself. He was kicked violently in the back by former Speaker, Didymus Mutasa.

In his plea of mitigation to the parliamentary committee, Bennet provided documentary proof of over three hundred attacks on himself, his family, his workers, his colleagues and his property – all committed by supporters of Zanu PF or other branches of State security. These were cordially ignored by the committee.

All this I knew, but I knew nothing about his wife and I had promised Jim Murray an interview so I had to think of something to ask.

I didn't even know what Heather Bennet looked like, so when a petite and pretty woman walked hesitantly into the coffee shop, I merely glanced appreciatively at her to begin with before I realised that she was making her way over to me. We introduced ourselves and sat down to talk over coffee. Heather Bennet was a delight to be with. I had been half expecting a battle-axe with a big chip on her shoulder, but she was every bit as sweet and gentle as she looked. If there was bitterness in that slender frame, she kept it well-hidden and answered my questions with a frank sincerity that had me totally captivated from the start.

She told me that she was allowed to see Roy every fortnight, an effort that entailed four hundred kilometres of hard driving for a ten minute visit. I was aghast but she smiled at my obvious horror.

"It is worth it," she told me simply. "I think Roy just lives for our visits and they are keeping him from cracking up in that place. Easter is a bonus," That initial meeting between us took place on Easter Saturday. "We have an extra visit and that is nice. I took the children with me yesterday, but my daughter Casey cried all the way home, so today it will just be me. All he wants me to bring him is a hot cross bun."

'That place' was Mutoko prison, a hot, uncomfortable hell hole where Bennet lived on half a cup of Dickensian gruel and cabbage stew twice a day.

"He has lost a lot of weight," Heather said matter of factly. "He is just skin and bone, but is still expected to work hard on the prison farm. Like the rest of them, he is dressed in rags and not allowed to wear a hat, so he is suffering from sunburn and an infestation of lice. You know how hot it is in Mutoko."

I did indeed. I had spent time there during my police career and Mutoko is savagely hot country. Daytime temperatures climb well above forty degrees Celsius and I shuddered to think of anyone outside in that without a hat. It would be hard enough with a black skin, but as I remembered from pictures I had seen, Bennet was a fair-skinned, almost blond man.

"He needs medical treatment badly," Heather went on, "but there are no doctors available to treat his obvious decline in health. I think it is all down to malnutrition. When I visit, we have to talk through a wire fence and all I can give him is a tiny tube of toothpaste, a bar of carbolic soap and six pieces of fruit, which he shares out among his fellow inmates. It is so sad to see.

'Mind you," she went on thoughtfully. "His mental health is worrying too. The authorities have really put him through the mincer and it is wearing him down. He isn't bitter though." She smiled and her face lit up. "He gets quite cross with me when I express any anger about the situation. He reckons it is 'just Africa' and if we want to live here, we have to put up with it. I do find it difficult at times though."

I asked her about her own bid to take the Chimanimani seat that Roy had held prior to his incarceration.

"I have never wanted to be a politician; never even thought of myself as being in politics, yet when Roy was locked up, it seemed the natural thing to do," her tone was pensive. "Someone has to stand and speak up for democracy in this country and he wasn't allowed to stand for election from his prison cell. We both love Chimanimani and the people there were so good to us through the really bad times that we couldn't let them down. Besides, Zimbabwe is my home too and I want peace and prosperity for all my countrymen before it is too late. The public speaking and electioneering scare me though. I don't know if I will ever get used to addressing large crowds of people."

She smiled impishly when she told me how she practiced putting vehemence into her voice when uttering the Movement for Democratic Change's mantra of '*Chinja*.' (Change)

"After every meeting, I am told that I still don't have it right, but I'll get it eventually. I even practice in my bath."

Pausing briefly to marshal her thoughts, she went on and for the first time, there was bitterness in her voice..

"Roy and I discussed whether he should go into politics before he did so in 2000. I agreed it was good to serve the country. We knew it would be tough but we had absolutely no idea how bad it would be, that it would be a cesspool and that so many people would suffer for being connected with Roy. If the fight had been just Roy and me it would not have been so bad, but when people around you are being destroyed, raped and murdered, you start thinking, is it worth it? Now the people of Chimanimani send me messages that they feel guilty for having chosen him to represent them.

'His campaign manager wept when he saw Roy in prison but I never do because I don't want him to think I am struggling."

Heather told me that she had been born and brought up in Chivhu – a place I knew well as Enkeldoorn and the place where I had been serving in the Police Support Unit, when Robert Mugabe had been swept into power in 1980. How well I remembered that area, as my beloved Charlie Troop had suffered a number of casualties in the nearby Wiltshire Tribal Trust Land – as it had been known in those days.

"Dad owned a garage and my Mom worked in a bank," Heather was speaking as memories flooded my mind. "Roy also came from a family with little money. He learned Shona because he grew up with the kids on his dad's farm. When I first met him, I thought Roy was an obnoxious guy, very rowdy. He was wearing shorts and needed long trousers, so he just swapped pants with another guy.

'I had my first child Charles, a year after we were married, then Casey in 1987. Roy wanted six kids but I wasn't having that. It was all so hectic, as at the time of Casey's birth we were struggling to pay loans back on the farm in Karoi. Roy visited Chimanimani and fell in love with it, so we sold up in Karoi, but still had to borrow money to buy and run Charleswood. I missed my friends at first and didn't like having to send the kids to boarding school. We only finished paying back the loan on Charleswood six months ago, long after we had been kicked off."

I asked her how she had felt when her husband had been charged with striking Chinamasa and she frowned.

"When Morgan was acquitted on that stupid treason charge, I knew they would send Roy to prison. They had to have something they could brag about. I begged him for weeks to skip the country but he wouldn't. He told me that so many MDC people have been jailed unfairly and they didn't have the option of leaving Zimbabwe. He said that if he left, Zanu PF would turn round and say 'of course we weren't going to send him to prison.'

And what did she feel about world reaction to the case? She smiled but this time there was no humour in her eyes.

"You know how everyone shouts about democracy and when somebody like Roy stands up to try and do something about injustice, they applaud him and say it is the right thing to do. Yet when he was arrested, the international community lost all interest and turned its back on us. I believe that Australia, Canada and the EU have formally protested at Roy's treatment but the rest of them, including Britain and America have been silent. It really isn't fair."

But wasn't she frightened of becoming a government target just as Roy had been? She frowned and sipped from her coffee cup before answering.

"I don't think that will happen, David," I had told her my real name, which in itself was unusual, but she could charm the birds out of the trees, could Heather Bennet. "I am not as confrontational as Roy anyway. If they do get at me, I will cope as best I can. People have been very protective as you have already discovered and anyway I am pretty strong too."

She flexed a trim bicep as she said it and we both laughed, but I had already decided that for all her good looks and gentle manner, Heather Bennet was a very strong character indeed. She had been through so much, endured so much suffering and yet still she was willing to fight what had to be a totally unequal battle against Robert Mugabe and his thuggish party.

"We can still get things right," Heather interrupted my thoughts. "Zimbabweans are a tough people and we have a wonderful country. It is up to each and every one of us to do his or her best and we really can make change for the better."

And would she win? Heather giggled at the question.

"I quite fancy myself as an MP and Lord knows, having lost everything we need the money, but this is Zimbabwe. I have drawn huge crowds at my election rallies but God only knows what will happen on the day."

If she were to get through, Heather Bennet would be representing fifty thousand rural voters from the North Eastern corner of the country, but the future certainly didn't hold any fears for her.

"It will be difficult at first and I won't know what to do, but the more experienced parliamentarians will guide me through the initial problems and after all, most of our government MPs are totally corrupt, so we can only do our best."

And how did she spend her time when she wasn't electioneering? She made a face at the question.

"There just aren't enough hours in the day. My eighty-five year old mother recently fractured her hip, so now I have to add that problem to running a home, visiting Roy when I am allowed to, winding up his businesses and trying to sell my own. I also have two teenage children, so motherhood has to take precedence over most things.

'I try to take one day at a time, so there is one day less to worry about. I have to sell my two little businesses, a pottery shop and decor management firm somehow. I just don't have time to run them. I am so busy sorting stuff out that Roy would normally have handled. I pay wages, spend lots of time with accountants to tie up details of Charleswood and I try hard to keep Roy's panel beating shop going. It is all he has left."

When I pressed her as to how Roy was coping with his incarceration in such horrible conditions, she frowned.

"As I told you, he isn't well physically and I worry about his mental health. Roy is quite a spiritual guy though. He doesn't go to church or talk about religion, but he reads his bible morning and night, so that keeps him going. It's a habit he got into as a child from his mother. I think I may be more affected than Roy. I am not bitter," She shook her head in obvious exasperation and smiled somewhat helplessly. "No of course I am but I have to work on that. Yes, we have lost everything, but so many have others have too and lots of them are even worse off than we are."

Had she been offered any help? I knew it was a silly question but Heather laughed.

"Yes of course. Everyone has been wonderful. Mind you, there was this farmer from Karoi who phoned offering support. He is older than me so I didn't want to be disrespectful, but I told him I didn't want his help because he is doing deals with Zanu PF to stay on his farm, and that I had plenty of support from principled people. We have old friends who will stick by us whatever happens, but we don't have much in common with some friends from before. Roy feels far happier with his MDC mates these days and they are predominately black.

'You know, it was horrible when I had to pay off Roy's workers." There was pain in her eyes as she spoke. "In the circumstances, we knew they would never find other employment and I cried with each and every one of them. They still come to greet me when I am in Chimanimani though and that is nice."

Would she ever leave the country? I asked the question even though I knew in my heart what she would say. The answer was emphatic.

"No; we have come too far to leave now. My children are at the age where they must make their own lives, but Roy and I are here for good. He would love to go farming again, but…" she hesitated before continuing; "it will be difficult for me with the memories."

After she had allowed me to photograph her in the shopping centre car park, Heather Bennet gave me a kiss and a hug, then marched away, leaving me marvelling at her fortitude. What a strong voice she would make in any parliament. With her trim good looks and forthright manner, she would be an asset to any political party in the world and Zimbabwe was lucky to have her.

Heather had invited me to call in whenever I was in town and I resolved to hold her to that. Quite apart from her charm, hers was the sort of character that gave me the feeling that Zimbabwe would eventually find its feet.

*   *   *

I was to meet Heather Bennet on many more occasions and I like to think we became friends. She should have won the election for the Chimanimani seat as after half the votes had been counted, she held a massive lead in the poll. But, this was Zimbabwe. During the night when votes were being recounted, four additional boxes, all crammed with votes for Mugabe's man were suddenly 'discovered' and that was that. The result was duly challenged through the Courts, but four years later, no verdict had been handed down and all will be forgotten in time.

In all, I wrote four articles on the Bennets and was the only overseas journalist present at the gates of Chikurubi prison when Roy was released. It was a momentous morning and an occasion that brought tears to everyone's eyes.

The tension was almost palpable as we gathered outside the gates of Chikurubi well before seven and strain was apparent on Heather's face as we waited.

"I have awful butterflies in my tummy," she said to me as the time scheduled for Roy's release came and went. "I just hope they won't change their minds now and keep him in for the full twelve months."

Their son Charles, who had flown out from Cirencester for the occasion looked equally worried.

"I won't believe it until I see Dad walk through those gates." He said.

Also present was feisty little lawyer Beatrice Mtetwa, a personal friend of the Bennets. Although not Zimbabwean by birth (I think she came from Swaziland) she was the person everyone turned to when they were in trouble. Totally fearless, she had defied the government and its thugs on numerous occasions and had been badly beaten up herself only a year or so previously. Mtetwa was arrested on specious allegations of drunken driving. She was taken to a police station, where she was held for three hours, beaten and choked, then released without charge.

Although she was unable to speak for two days as a result of that assault, she returned to the police station on the third day with medical evidence in hand, to file charges.

She smiled when our eyes met, so I wandered across and introduced myself, again using my own name rather than Bryan Graham. When I tried to explain what I was doing, she laughed and cut me off.

"I know why you are here and what you are up to," she told me quietly. "I think perhaps you ought to take down my telephone number, as you might well need it at some stage."

I did and it is still in my notebook should I ever need the services of this wonderfully inspiring woman.

The tension of the morning increased when CIO agents appeared to record the registration numbers of the assembled cars and a prison official began noting down names and identity card numbers. I wasn't sure what to do as I had no business being there and didn't want to draw undue attention to myself, but when the woman approached me and began asking questions, it was Heather herself who noticed my dilemma and distracted her with a question. This allowed me to get out of the way and I smiled my gratitude.

Under Zimbabwe's draconian security laws, we could all have been arrested for holding an illegal gathering, but fortunately nobody seemed to have thought of that.

Moments after nine fifteen, Roy Bennet appeared, holding two paper bags containing clothes and more than a hundred letters from well-wishers that had not been given to him before. His face was gaunt, but he was smiling broadly, his long white hair and straggly beard giving him the appearance of an Old Testament prophet.

Tears flowed freely as he hugged his loved ones, but Heather managed not to cry.

"I am sure I will later," she giggled to me as we hurried to our cars in order to get Roy safely away. "What a wonderful moment this is for all of us."

At the home of a friend, tea and sandwiches had been laid on and Roy moved across to introduce himself

"Heather has told me about you," he murmured. "It is nice to meet a Brit reporter who tells it as it is."

Later, we had a few moments together and he told me about his ordeal.

"When I arrived at Chikurubi straight from Parliament," his tone was matter of fact. "I had to stand naked in front of the senior staff before being issued with a filthy uniform. The trousers were stained with excreta and torn at the front so that my privates were exposed. They were determined to break me but I was equally determined that I would not be broken."

It was the support of his fellow prisoners that helped Bennet survive an ordeal that would have shattered most men.

"They were incredible," he said quietly. "They shared their blankets with me and would pinch me to keep me quiet when they saw me getting angry with officials. They kept me out of trouble even when it meant risking punishment themselves. When anyone had food, it was shared and for men who had absolutely nothing, they were incredibly generous.

'Conditions in the prison were appalling," other friends had gathered around to listen and the entire room full of people was eerily silent as we shared Roy Bennet's pain. "My cell was designed to hold eight people in bunk beds but the beds had long since disappeared and at times there were twenty of us in there. Fifteen-man cells often contained as many as fifty inmates and condensation would run down the walls in rivers. Dysentery and the like were common so the smell was terrible.

'It was impossible to shower without touching those around you and shower rooms also contained the toilets, all of which were broken and leaking. If animals were treated like that, the whole world would be up in arms."

When I asked what the guards had been like, he smiled grimly.

"Most of them are just caught up in the system, but there were a number of Youth Brigade graduates in there and they were just cruel thugs. They would lie prisoners down on their stomachs and beat the soles of their feet till they were broken and bloody. Even now, a young man is lying helpless in there with broken bones in his lower limbs. His crime was to have one matchstick in his possession."

Was he ever beaten, I asked and he frowned.

"I challenged them to beat me on occasion," he said "When we came in from the fields we were supposed to be strip-searched and I refused. I told them they could strip me themselves and beat me as much as they liked, but I was not going to take my clothes off for them.

'On another occasion I tried to help a boy who had been beaten and couldn't walk. When I stood up to the guard, he threatened to beat me too so I told him to get on with it. He was totally thrown. None of the guards knew how to deal with defiance."

While we spoke, Heather listened quietly, her hand in her husband's. She frowned when I asked him what he was going to do.

"I want to do more for the people of Zimbabwe," he said. "If they will have me, I am quite prepared to go back into politics."

"Not until we have had a damned good holiday," Heather interrupted firmly. "We are going away for at least a month and politics can wait."

It was Roy's religious faith that saw him through his ordeal.

"I used to read from the bible every day," he said. "It sustained my spirit and saw me through the worst of times."

Amazingly and in spite of all he had been through, Roy Bennet did not appear to be at all bitter but it was Heather who had the last word on that momentous morning.

"Why does the Western World allow it?" She asked me angrily. "They have just had that stupid Live Aid concert for the people of Africa but do nothing about a system that treats its own people so brutally. When will they wake up to what is actually happening?"

There was no answer to that and I thought back to my Gloucestershire MP, David Drew and his fatuous pronouncements on the problems of Zimbabwe. How I wished he could have been there to listen to Roy and Heather Bennet.

Chapter Eighteen

(Murambatsvina)

In 2005 amid scenes reminiscent of the apartheid era in South Africa, Robert Mugabe unleashed his military might against the most vulnerable sector of Zimbabwean society – the urban poor.

With unemployment at over eighty percent in the country and an inflation rate that for years had been impossible to calculate, many thousands of Zimbabweans had turned to street trading in order to survive. Their wares ranged from a few home-grown vegetables to wicker baskets, curios and whatever basic commodities they had been able to lay their hands on. They cleaned shoes, repaired radios and watches or found parking spaces for harassed motorists. Some of them advertised themselves as building contractors or experts with a chainsaw, even though they had no official qualifications.

In short it was the informal traders who kept the battered Zimbabwean economy going but that made them obvious targets for the president and his thugs.

Cruelly choosing the onset of winter as the most suitable time for the operation, paramilitary police, backed up by armed soldiers raided street markets and roadside stalls in towns throughout the country. Over thirty thousand vendors were arrested and fined for illegal trading, tens of thousands of stalls were wantonly destroyed and anything valuable was seized, with the result that many people lost their entire life savings in a matter of minutes. The exercise was dubbed *Murambatsvina* by the government and in allied operations, thousands of allegedly illegal houses were demolished by policemen using bulldozers and sledgehammers. This left hundreds of families homeless and struggling to survive sub zero night-time temperatures in the open air. Any householder who could not immediately produce title deeds or planning permission was deemed to own an illegal property and no excuses were accepted. It was estimated at the time that two hundred thousand people were made homeless by *Murambatsvina*, but my own sources confidently told me that the true figure was well over a million.

Murambatsvina was alleged to mean 'restore order,' but the literal translation from Chishona is 'drive out the filth.'

The government explained the evictions by blaming the informal traders for stoking an illegal but thriving black market. Illegal perhaps but it worked and was the source of nearly every basic commodity in the country, from food to foreign currency and even birth control pills.

President Mugabe publicly supported the raids and told Zimbabweans that they were intended to 'restore our towns and cities to their former beauty,' but even as he spoke, armoured cars and heavily armed soldiers were being deployed in Harare suburbs to counter resistance by newly dispossessed citizens. Tear gas mingled with smoke from burning houses in Mbare Township and intelligence sources said that both army and police had been put on a state of full alert to quell any possible uprising by a restless population.

Harare Metropolitan Governor, David Karimanzira laughed off suggestions that the exercise was designed as retribution against city dwellers who had voted for the opposition Movement for Democratic Change in recent elections.

"There is no retribution. We are simply cleaning up the city." He said but added that the crackdown would be extended to farms outside Harare to 'eliminate illegal houses' on those farms.

The MDC urged Zimbabweans to take action against President Mugabe's government as the clean-up campaign spread across the country.

"A government that destroys the property of people who are trying to make an honest living is evil," said MDC spokesman, Paul Themba-Nyathi. "We call on all Zimbabweans to mobilize against this assault on their dignity, livelihoods and well being."

However, another opposition MP, Trudi Stevenson put the mobilisation call into perspective.

"The police come in with this massive force of three thousand armed officers and if you are only three to five hundred people without weapons, you cannot resist. Seven thousand of my own constituents are now homeless and will struggle to survive the winter."

Resistance grew in many places however. The Glen View suburb of Harare was almost destroyed after angry citizens and displaced vendors engaged in pitched battles with the police. Cars were burnt by angry mobs while council offices and shops were looted. In Mbare, worried residents blockaded roads with boulders in futile efforts to prevent the authorities from reaching their homes, while in the Eastern city of Mutare, residents pleaded with their MP for weapons to wage war against the people who were destroying everything they possessed.

At an open meeting attended by thousands of disgruntled townsfolk, Innocent Gonese of the MDC was openly asked to provide guns for his constituents. Even the presence of police at the meeting did not prevent one middle-aged man from declaring war on the government.

"We want you to provide us with guns," he shouted and with the crowd urging him on, continued. "This government has no respect for the people. Our houses have been destroyed, our businesses have gone. We have nothing to live for so we are prepared to die removing Mugabe."

Gonese had difficulty calming his audience who wanted him to say whether his party was prepared to lead an armed resistance against the government.

"That is not the answer," he tried to explain. "Of course we have a wicked government but we should seek legal recourse."

It was a refrain that Zimbabweans had heard so often in the past, but most had lost faith in the legal system and for many, the only answer was an uprising. In the event, cooler heads prevailed. There was no firm leadership for an armed insurrection and had it taken place, the carnage would have been awful. Mugabe's army was one of the best equipped in Africa and they were prepared to deal with whatever was thrown at them.

The fact that most of the insurrectionists would have been innocent civilians would not have deterred the government from mowing them down.

* * *

For me, *Murambatsvina* offered another opportunity to go home at the expense of the Sunday Express. Jim Murray was on leave, but I had a meeting with his deputy, Stuart Winter who was enthusiastic about my plans. He even offered to supply me with a decent cell phone to replace my ancient model.

"It will be a safer way to take pictures." He offered and I fully agreed. "Check flights out for me and I will speak with the Editor."

Two days later, he was back on the phone.

"It seems there are difficulties with insurance," he told me bleakly. "Our accountants don't want to send you out under our auspices, in case you are arrested or hurt in any way."

I was cross but it wasn't Stuart's fault. The newspaper had paid for previous trips and I had put my life on the line for them on many occasions. God only knew why they were baulking now. None of it made sense but I would have to pay my own fare if I wanted to see things for myself. I would even have to make do with my old telephone.

* * *

One of the things Jim Murray wanted me to do was work on a story about Joice Mujuru, the newly elected vice president of

Zimbabwe, who was said to be a war hero in her own right. She had come to power in a surprise move by Mugabe and her success had led to bitter infighting among the Zanu PF hierarchy. Emmerson Mnangagwa, long seen as the president's protégé and widely expected to succeed Mugabe when he does go was regarded as the natural heir, but he had fallen by the wayside, together with a number of other notables. One of these was Jonathan Moyo, who promptly resigned from the party, won a seat as independent MP for Tjolotjo and proceeded to rant in print against Robert Mugabe and all his policies. As Moyo had been the most sycophantic and willing praise singer for Mugabe until his star fell, his somewhat hypocritical rantings merely made Zimbabweans smile.

But getting an article on Joice was not going to be easy. The woman was reputed to be an out and out racist and during the start of the farm invasions she had urged Mugabe supporters to go out and return with the blood-soaked T-shirts of not only whites, but any blacks who wanted them to stay on the land. Her husband Solomon had been known as Rex Nhongo during the war years and although I knew a friend of his very well, asking for an interview with Joice would blow my cover and see me living in Chikurubi prison for at least two years.

However it was not difficult to find out quite a bit about Africa's first female vice president and she certainly proved to be a colourful character.

Barely five foot tall, she had a formidable record as a guerrilla fighter and at forty-nine, was set to become the most powerful woman in Africa if and when Robert Mugabe were to finally hang up his crown.

So how had this diminutive mother of five climbed to power so quickly in the male dominated world of African politics? Although she was appointed a government minister in her mid twenties and had been in Mugabe's cabinet for twenty-five years, her sudden appointment surprised most Zimbabweans and horrified many. At the start of her political career, she had been illiterate and even though she had taught herself to read and write, her English was laboured and difficult to understand.

After talking with a number of people on the subject, I decided that the answer to Joice's considerable achievements lay with the sheer force of her ambition. Born Runaida Mugari in Dotito, North Eastern Zimbabwe, the teenage Joice announced to her startled parents that she was leaving home to join the liberation struggle against the Rhodesian forces of Ian Smith.

"I want to be known as Teurai Ropa (Spill Blood)" she told them, "because I want to spill as much white blood as possible."

Once in the field, she proved herself a natural leader. Her crowning glory as a fighting soldier was said to be the single-handed shooting down of a Rhodesian helicopter with the loss of its crew. As a very young woman, she was not allowed to carry a weapon, but allegedly took the rifle off a dying comrade.

"A helicopter saw me," she recalled almost wistfully. "I lay on my back, aimed and fired. Bullets hit the machine and it fell out of the sky. There was black smoke everywhere as it hit the ground."

I was not able to verify that story but it was commonly believed by Zimbabweans, although most of those I spoke to who had served in the Rhodesian security forces scoffed at it.

"The woman is a murdering liar," a former Rhodesian officer exploded. "Women in ZANLA (Mugabe's military wing) were used as sex objects and not allowed anywhere near the fighting."

Be that as it may, Teurai Ropa went on to command a number of ZANLA camps outside the country. At Chimoio in Mozambique, she met and married Rex Nhongo, then an up and coming guerrilla who went on to become the first commander of the Zimbabwean Army.

"My war experiences changed my entire life," Mujuru said. "I became very strong and learned to make decisions and not to wait for men to decide everything."

It was as Teurai Ropa Nhongo that Mujuru entered the first Zimbabwean Parliament in 1980. She held a number of cabinet posts over the years and on 4th December 2004 was appointed vice president after much squabbling among her senior colleagues. Joice had told friends in Harare that she was determined to serve her country to the best of her ability but few of those friends doubted her hunger for supreme power.

A senior Zimbabwean journalist told me that with the vice-presidency secured, it was almost certain that Mujuru would become Mugabe's number two. The other vice president was eighty-one year old, Joseph Msika who had already announced his intention of leaving politics when Mugabe retired, thereby clearing Mujuru's route to the presidency. This should have been a great blow for women all over the world, yet the women of Zimbabwe didn't seem entirely convinced.

"We have to ask why Mujuru is being elevated now?" Leading feminist journalist Everjoyce J Win commented. "What is it that Robert Mugabe and his men have suddenly seen in her that they failed to see in twenty-four years? Once again we could see a woman being brought in when things are so bad that she ends up getting the blame when nothing changes for the better."

I couldn't help smiling at this cynical interpretation of male motives, but there was no doubt that Mujuru enjoyed the trappings of power and was an extremely strong woman. She owned several farms, travelled in the back of a chauffeur-driven Mercedes Benz and took her holidays in Cape Town. Her children were educated in England and before the European Union imposed selected sanctions on Mugabe and his cronies, her favourite place to shop was Harrods or the boulevards of Paris.

But Mujuru also posed as a champion of the poor.

"She likes to see herself as Zimbabwe's answer to Winnie Mandela," Sikota Chiume of the Movement for Democratic Change told me. "She is kind when she wants to be, but she has ultimate power in mind."

In spite of her loyalty to President Mugabe, Mujuru seemed well aware that international money was needed if Zimbabwe was to survive and to this end, she had already held secret talks with the International Monetary Fund to arrange financial support programmes when she became president.

A senior official of Innscor – one of Zimbabwe's leading financial institutions - told me that this was the time to buy property in Zimbabwe. "Mugabe will be out by the end of the year," he predicted confidently. "Msika will go with him and Mujuru will be left holding the reins. Then we will see the country develop."

He was wrong, as everyone who has predicted Robert Mugabe's demise or overthrow over the years has been wrong. Mujuru remained as vice president and will probably stay in the post until the Old Man does go, but she did not appear to hold any influence in the party or the cabinet.

She remained very much in the background but I have no doubt at all that should Joice Spillblood Mujuru ever become president of my ruined country, she is young enough and strong enough to oversee ruthless reforms in the way Zimbabwe is governed. She had already been vice president for two years at the time of my visit and achieved nothing notable, but with her background and the support of her ever-more-powerful husband, she was still very much a woman of the future.

* * *

My article on the new vice president was responsible for yet another moment of acute panic on my part before it finally appeared in the newspaper. There had been widely circulating rumours around Zimbabwe that the CIO had been given sophisticated new monitoring equipment by the Chinese. This was supposed to be able to intercept emails, phone calls and text messages, concentrating on certain key words that would betray seditious material. That put me in a quandary. My laptop computer was of the vintage variety and incapable of sending emails from Zimbabwe, so I relied on the brave generosity of friends to file my reports. In view of my comments on Joice Mujuru, I did not want to put anyone else in danger, so the only answer I could see was to use an internet café.

That was all very well but I had never been in that sort of establishment and didn't know the procedure. With my floppy disk at the ready, I wandered into a shop in Railway Avenue that advertised itself as an internet café. The place was packed and I glanced anxiously around for burly gentlemen wearing impenetrably dark glasses – the badge of office espoused by the secret police. I couldn't see any and when I brandished my disk and asked the proprietor what to do, he smilingly showed me to a computer, set in one corner of the shop.

It all seemed horribly exposed, particularly as people were wandering around and often looking over the shoulders of those working at other machines. Feeling distinctly nervous, I set to work.

It wasn't easy. Ever increasing nervousness made me somewhat ham-fisted and I struggled to set the system up. My heart nearly stopped when the proprietor came up behind me and asked me to stop what I was doing.

"May I just borrow your disk," he asked and when I handed it over, he wandered away. There was nothing aggressive or menacing about the man but I sat and waited with my mind in a whirl. I was in trouble. I was going to be arrested. That would mean being carted away in handcuffs, probably tortured and then inevitably, imprisoned in Chikurubi. I knew that I would surely die if I was locked up and although it was a hot day, I felt distinctly chilled.

A few minutes later, the proprietor returned. My disk was in his hand and he was smiling but I could feel my muscles trembling with apprehension.

"I will take you to another machine," he told me. "This one is giving too much trouble."

At a different computer, I made myself work with grim efficiency, concentrating on every movement and trying to ignore the people around me. The email flashed off into the ether and I removed my disk as soon as I could. Half expecting trouble, I had labelled the disk 'Baby J with pictures' and wondered whether that had convinced the proprietor of my bona fides or whether he had actually been genuine in his concern to get me a different machine.

Hurrying out of the shop, I took a deep breath of the smelly, smoky air in Railway Avenue and sent a brief prayer of thanks to Whoever was looking after me.

After that experience, I telephoned my reports in to the girls on the copy desk whenever I possibly could. That also proved nerve-wracking at times but I didn't feel quite so vulnerable and helpless. I could always hang up.

Chapter Nineteen

(A Night in the Cold)

Operation *Murambatsvina* was probably the greatest single human rights violation of the twenty-first century, yet the world allowed it to pass almost unnoticed

When it was all over, the United Nations special envoy on human settlement issues, Mrs Anna Kajumulo Tibaijuka did visit the country to see for herself and her report was scathingly vitriolic. I don't know where the good lady went but I admired her courage in standing up against the status quo in Africa. Her boss Kofi Annan then announced that he would involve himself in mediation talks between the government and MDC, in hopes of bringing about a peaceful solution and eventual good governance to the country. Ordinary Zimbabweans felt a sudden surge of hope that at long last somebody in a position of power was going to do something, but perhaps true to form, Annan pulled out of the proposed talks and they were abandoned.

According to the Zimbabwean government, less than two hundred thousand people were made homeless by Operation *Murambatsvina,* but Mrs Tibaijuka's report gave that figure as well in excess of seven hundred and fifty thousand. I had no intention of counting, but my sources told me that there were a million or more. In every town I visited, there were piles of rubble everywhere and the normal cheerful chatter of street vendors had given way to a quiet that was oddly depressing. How often had I shooed away importunate youths trying to sell me something or look after my car, yet how I missed them once they had disappeared.

The occasional brave vendor could be seen on the more secluded street corners with a few vegetables or eggs for sale and their eyes swivelling to catch sight of approaching policemen. One of them, Betty Makurove pulled me behind a hedge when I stopped to talk with her.

"I mustn't be seen," she told me urgently. "If the ZRP catch me, they will take all my stock and my children will starve. If I am talking to you, I cannot keep my eyes open for them.

'Besides," she examined me critically, "if I am seen talking to you, we will both be arrested. White people do not speak with street vendors, so you are obviously a journalist."

Betty was the mother of five children and my heart hurt when she told me how they struggled for bare survival.

"We eat when we can," she started to cry and I didn't know what to do, "but it is not often, so my kids are very hungry. My eldest daughter has become a sex worker so we have a little money but it is not enough to feed and clothe everyone."

How old was the eldest daughter, I asked and her face was sad.

"She is about to be thirteen years. Already she is a woman and she looks older than me."

My gift of a few thousand lousy Zimbabwean dollars was accepted with the innate dignity of the Zimbabwean people. Betty gently clapped her palms together, curtseyed with bowed head and took the offering in two hands to signify that it was a greater gift than she could hold.

"It will buy us some food," She said. "Thank you Sir."

Five minutes later she was back on the corner with her pitiful box of tomatoes and her eyes scanning the surroundings for any sign of approaching policemen.

* * *

If Hatfield Extension had been in Britain, it would have been termed an overflow town. On the opposite side of Harare from the suburb of Hatfield, I wasn't sure how it had come to be named, but it had grown over the years and contained all the usual amenities, such as churches, mosques, trading stores, bars and barber shops. It was home to a flourishing community of people who came from all corners of the country and lived settled, satisfied lives in their little dormitory town. Most of them worked in Harare or the suburbs and there was a regular bus service to and from Hatfield Extension.

It was also a bastion of the opposition MDC and the Member of Parliament for the area was Trudi Stephenson. Perhaps that was why Robert Mugabe chose to make an example of the place. When the troops and bulldozers moved in, they showed no mercy.

"It was truly terrible," John Kadzvayi was a smartly dressed office worker, staring numbly at the ruins of his home. The building had been totally flattened and John did not know what he was going to do.

"Everything I owned was in the house," he told me. "They would not give me time to get anything out."

But surely he had received ample warning from other areas? After all, Hatfield Extension was not the first township to be bulldozed. He shrugged at my question.

"I have lived here with my family for nearly ten years. We bought the house and paid good money for it. We had electricity and running water. We paid taxes to the Harare Municipality. We did not imagine we could possibly be looked on as living here illegally."

Nor was John the only one in that predicament. When I first visited Hatfield Extension, I was truly appalled. Not a building remained standing. The entire area had been reduced to rubble. I had seen and photographed buildings destroyed by rockets and mortar bombs during the bush war, but that was random damage and did not seem as obscene and horrifying as the carnage I was now witnessing. Piles of crushed bricks lay everywhere, with the occasional piece of building still surviving to make the scenario seem infinitely worse.

One such was a ZRP suggestion box, which implored the public to report matters and gave a telephone number.

I wondered if that had survived by pure accident or whether the policemen involved had hesitated to destroy their own creation.

A mosque lay in absolute dissolution, apart from what might once have been a small altar at one end. A large bottle store had three walls still standing, two of them adorned with signs for Coca cola and other household necessities. The interior had been gutted. What had once been a public toilet still displayed the '*varume*' sign for gentlemen but the '*vakadzi*' half was another pile of rubble.

Not far from the bottle store, a large tractor and an elegant old Mercedez Benz had been burnt out and I felt sad at such deliberate destruction of objects that had to have been very precious to someone.

Official MDC election posters could still be seen and some pieces of wall that remained vaguely upright were adorned with the usual political graffiti, urging people to vote for MDC and Morgan Tsvangirai. This must surely have inflamed the thugs who had arrived to carry out that cruel destruction of lives and I wondered who the people would vote for next time.

On the other hand, they were now homeless and probably would not be able to vote. Many residents of Hatfield Extension had been removed to a makeshift refugee camp on a nearby farm and if they were still there when the time came to vote again, they would have to walk a long way to put their crosses on a ballot paper.

As I watched and surreptitiously photographed the scene, I saw a few people wandering listlessly among the wrecked buildings. They were obviously scavenging for what scraps they could find and half a kilometre away, I found about two hundred of them camping in truly awful conditions beside a foully oozing stream. The water was almost black with effluent and other detritus while the entire camp had a deeply miasmic stink of its own. Men, women and children sat listlessly in the shade of stunted trees and I couldn't help contrasting that scene of desolation with the elegant comforts of the Borrowdale suburb less than three kilometres away. I didn't think the residents of Borrowdale even knew that this sort of place existed.

Back in the open area, I found three young men sitting beside a small fire made from beams and other discarded building timber. They greeted me warily.

"You must be careful Sir," the eldest was Boniface and they were the sons of the Maunganidze family. "With a white face you are in danger here and your camera makes you too obvious."

It was true enough, but I was too horrified to be overly worried. I squatted on some stones and we began to talk. They told me of their fears, not only at the time when the bulldozers had arrived, but also for the future.

"We do not have jobs," Boniface said sadly. "I have just standard two education, so am only fit to be a labourer. These, my brothers Ignatio and King have no learning at all. Our mother is still trying to sell vegetables in town, so if she is caught we will have nothing. Our sister is a sex worker now because there is nothing else for her to do. Our father was drowned while working for a white man."

When I asked where they slept at night, Boniface indicated a wide slab of cement that had once been the floor of a building.

"We are lucky because that tap still works," he indicated a spot where small stone slabs had been put together to cover something up. "We have to hide it because if the police come back and see that it works, they will rip out the pipe. There is too much disease in the river water and those who drink it will surely die."

I found myself numbed by the enormity of their plight. Looking around I could see no sign of clothing or blankets and the only household items apparent were two tin mugs, a blackened pot and a couple of empty jars that obviously did duty as cups.

"If we are lucky, we have a little bit of sadza," Boniface answered my question. "We sleep on the floor and stay together to keep warm. Our blankets and all our other possessions were burned by the police and soldiers.

"Do you have a job for me, Sir?" He asked as I prepared to leave. "Telling him quite truthfully that I wished I had, I gave the three of them a little bit of money and moved away.

"I might see you later," I told them, wondering whether I dared to come back.

* * *

Never in my life have I felt as cold as I did during that mid winter night in 2005. I have walked in wintry Scotland, camped out in Chimanimani, Nyanga and the Kinangop hills of Kenya, but for acutely chilly discomfort, my night among the homeless of Hatfield Extension ranks as one of the most horrible experiences of my life.

"You must take a flask and some blankets," big sister Sandra admonished before I set out. "It is mid winter and you will freeze."

She was right but I couldn't take extra comforts, however much I would have appreciated them. I wanted to write about the conditions being suffered by the victims of *Murambatsvina*. To do that, I had to experience those conditions for myself.

I was dropped off a kilometre from the ruined town and walked carefully in through swiftly gathering darkness. A million glittering stars guided me and as I approached the massed piles of rubble, I could see the pin-point flickers of a dozen small fires. They had to be small so that they did not attract the attention of wandering policemen, although I didn't think there would be too many of those worthies abroad on such a cold night.

My heart jolted in my ribs as a dark figure suddenly loomed out of the shadows and a hand gripped my elbow. A wanly faded torch beam was directed at my face.

"Ah it is you Sir," there was a note of relief in Boniface Maunganidze's tone. "We could hear somebody creeping up and although King recognised your steps, I wasn't sure."

Boniface wasn't sure of my motives either when I told him what I was doing and I couldn't really blame him. Even to me, it sounded a ridiculous idea. There was a hot meal, a gentle whisky or two and a warm, comfortable bed waiting for me in Highlands, yet here I was feeling desperately uncomfortable among people who must have felt that I had lost my marbles. Boniface guided me across to meet the rest of his family.

Stella Maunganidze was a tiny, bird-like woman but she held my hand and looked deep into my eyes when her son presented me.

"Will you help us Sir? Will you tell people how thousands of good Zimbabweans are forced to live?"

I promised her that I would try but could see from her reaction that she didn't really believe me. In general, the ordinary folk of Zimbabwe felt that they had been abandoned by the international community and they no longer expected anything from the Press.

Two younger women were introduced as family friends and although neither of them spoke, like Stella Maunganidze, they looked searchingly into my face.

There followed one of the longest and most uncomfortable nights of my life. We huddled around that tiny fire, each of us trying to extract as much warmth from the flickering flame as we could. We sat with bodies touching to give each other extra comfort but within half an hour of my arrival, all feeling had gone from my limbs and my bones ached abominably.

It was all very well wanting to share the agony of ordinary people in order to get myself a story, but yet again I had been foolishly thoughtless. My presence in the family meant that Stella Maunganidze had another mouth to feed and I cursed myself for a selfish fool.

She coped though and as a visitor, I was served first. The meal consisted of a small handful of sadza and what looked like some sort of soup, served in a dish made from the cracked plastic top of what might have been a jar or container. The soup was hot and had tiny flecks of meat floating in it. The taste was fairly bland but it did at least warm me up slightly and I asked Stella how she had made it. Her eyes flickered and she gave me a tiny smile.

"We make it from the leaves of the *mahobohobo* tree," she told me and I marvelled. I had often enjoyed *mahobohobo* fruit as a boy and they were delicious on a hot day, but the leaves were another matter. I didn't think they would do me any harm though.

And where did they get the meat? At the question, Stella giggled and put her hand across her mouth.

"Since the police moved in and tore our homes down, we have been infested with *gundwane*," she told me, smiling broadly at my obvious horror. "They are not easy to catch, but my sons have laid down traps all over the place and so we have meat."

I have eaten all sorts of strange meals during my wanderings through Africa and had eaten field mouse before, but a soup made from leaves and shredded rat was surely unique. I wondered what my friends in Highlands were having for dinner that night.

Supper was washed down with tea made from one teabag, shared among seven of us so that it was not a lot like the cups of tea I was accustomed to. Nevertheless it was warm and that helped.

By eight thirty, we were laid out like a row of sardines on the hard stone floor of what had once been their house. The Maunganidze's owned but two blankets and these were carefully spread over us all so that nobody was left entirely out in the cold. Nevertheless it was an uncomfortable experience. Quite apart from the icy night air, a deep chill rose from the concrete and permeated right through my body. At first it was merely uncomfortable, but after a while it became acutely painful and I shifted in my discomfort, drawing an annoyed grunt from the men on either side of me. This surely wasn't living, yet these people and thousands like them slept like this every night. I have always abhorred the word 'hate,' but as that interminably long night wore on, I actively hated Robert Mugabe and the cruel thugs who so mindlessly carried out his orders.

Even the vivid panoply of stars overhead did nothing to alleviate my unhappiness and when the new day began its gentle spread across the heavens, I still hadn't slept.

My companions obviously had and everyone was incredibly cheerful as they climbed achingly to their feet and staggered across to the solitary tap. The water was so cold that it made my teeth ache, but I could look forward to a hot bath and a big breakfast. The Maunganidze family had another day to endure and another three months of icily similar nights to get through before winter waned and the weather warmed up.

When I said my farewells, Stella gripped my hands again.

"You will tell people how we are living?"

I promised that I would, but the piece I wrote on that dreadfully uncomfortable night was 'spiked' by unsympathetic editors. They wanted death and violence with lots of blood and perhaps the odd little household pet thrown in. Comfortable in their warm homes and relative prosperity, the people of Britain were not interested in the plight of a family living in the most inhuman conditions I had ever encountered.

Later that day, I delivered a large hamper of food and cigarettes to Boniface Maunganidze and his gratitude brought tears to my eyes.

"We thank you, Sir," he said simply, "but please try and find me a job."

It was something I could not do, but how I wished I could. No matter what happens to me during the rest of my life, I will never forget one icily painful night amid the ruins of Hatfield Extension or the wonderfully brave and pitiful family I shared it with.

*   *   *

Arnold Chikoro was employed as a cook for a white family living in the affluent Northern suburbs. I was visiting the family when Arnold somehow managed to spill a full pot of boiling water over his arms and upper legs, causing horrible blisters and a great deal of pain. The household first aid kit was not comprehensive enough to deal with his injuries so I volunteered to drive him through to the casualty department of Parirenyatwa hospital. It would give me a chance to see how the Zimbabwe health system was coping with the current crisis and I seized the opportunity. It was to prove another shock to my system.

Leaving the Ganja Bus in the almost empty hospital car park, I helped Arnold into the casualty department, explained to a bored looking nurse what had happened and left him to her ministrations while I explored.

I was lucky enough to encounter the hospital superintendent Dr Chris Tapfumaneyi on the first floor landing. Looking tired and drawn, he asked me my business and for some strange reason, I immediately told him that I was a reporter. It was something I had avoided till then – after all, I wasn't even a real journalist – but for some reason, I instinctively trusted Tapfumaneyi. He didn't ask for my accreditation, but peered searchingly into my face, then invited me into a sparsely furnished office.

"Five of our lifts have broken down," he told me over a cup of luke-warm coffee. "Toilets and sinks are blocked all through the hospital and in many wards, the ceilings are falling down.

'Our lab has virtually ground to a standstill, many anaesthetic machines are no longer functioning, incubators run at reduced capacity and three out of our five kidney dialysis machines have broken down. Is that enough for you to be getting on with?"

I listened in thunderstruck horror. How could this be happening in what was once one of the finest hospitals in Africa?

"Most of our machines are obsolete and cannot be repaired even if we had the money to repair them. Some of them have been like this for ten years or more. Without lifts, we have been reduced to nurses carrying patients up the stairs, while bodies being removed from wards to mortuaries are placed in body bags and just dragged over the floor. It is easier than finding usable trolleys."

Leaving Dr Tapfumaneyi to his worries, I continued my exploration.

"Be careful," he called out as I left his office. "There are spies everywhere in this place. You had better come back here before you go, so that I know you are safe."

On his recommendation, I spoke to Sister Nyabareka in the Maternity Wing.

"Look at all this," she snorted contemptuously and gestured at a badly leaking ceiling.

"Nothing gets repaired because we don't have the money."

In some places, electrical cables dangled precariously from the ceilings and I shuddered to think of the risk they posed in that damp atmosphere.

"We have more than sixty deliveries every day in here," Sister Nyabareka went on. "At the moment, we have thirty-six sick and premature babies being cared for in the nursery, but the central heating system broke down last year and still hasn't been fixed."

Many of the babies lay in cracked wicker cradles and sometimes even in large dishes while the only heating in the nursery came from three-bar heaters.

"The heaters aren't controlled in any way," Sister Nyabareka's eyes glinted in her anger. "The staff have to switch them off when the place gets too warm. What chance do these little people have with this sort of start in life?"

Maternity Matron, Sister Mukunyadze was even more scathing.

"We have so many children dying from infections that come from the hostile conditions," she said bitterly. "Their mothers are not supposed to give birth in their own clothes, but we no longer have clothing to loan them and that leads to further infections. Our steriliser is no longer working and that leads to more problems. The whole place needs major refurbishment, but there is no chance of that.

'Not while this government is in power anyway." Chris Tapfumaneyi smiled mirthlessly when I asked him about the lack of funds for refurbishment.

"Foreign currency is the problem," he told me. "There isn't any or at any rate, none available to us. I have over two billion Zim dollars lying in the bank in order to purchase laboratory equipment, dialysis machines and other things we need, but they have to be bought from abroad and nobody wants payment in our useless currency."

He told me that conditions in Parirenyatwa had started deteriorating in 2002 when foreign currency began to dry up in the banking sector.

"No major institution can function properly without the injection of forex," He used the colloquial Zimbabwean term for more reputable currencies. "Now we are desperate, I suppose you saw some of the blocked drains and sinks?" I hadn't but listened intently. "Many of them are full of blood and God knows what else, while the water temperature is rarely above luke warm. Dirty linen is flung into corridors and washed only occasionally. If a patient has clean bedding when he or she comes in, then they are very lucky.

'I have personally begged Dr Parirenyatwa (the minister for Health and Child Welfare) to intervene and get us some forex, but he just shrugs it all away. This hospital that bears his name has nearly fifteen hundred beds and was once the pride of all Zimbabweans but now it ought to be shut down and perhaps burned to the ground to be safe.

'I just don't know what is to become of any of us now."

Nor did I and after talking with Dr Tapfumaneyi, I hurried back to casualty and rescued poor old Arnold who was still waiting for medical attention, in spite of being in considerable pain.

"There are others," he said mildly as I started to protest. "We could be waiting here for a long time."

It was true enough. The entire accident and emergency wing was filled with listless, dull-eyed people awaiting attention from the two nurses who were all that I could see on duty. Neither lady seemed in any hurry and when I expostulated on behalf of my friend Arnold, one of them shrugged her shoulders and smiled without humour.

"What can we do? I don't have drugs, bandages or burn salve. All I can do is give him a few aspirin and send him on his way. You would do better to take him to a chemist. They might have a few bits and pieces.

At Chisipite chemist, I managed to purchase the necessary medicines to ease Arnold's pain, but after my visit to the place, I remembered as a truly magnificent hospital, I vowed not to get sick while I was in Zimbabwe. The medical care and expertise that Zimbabweans had always taken for granted had gone and would probably never be replaced. Chris Tapfumaneyi had been right. The old hospital should be burned down and replaced with a new one. This was surely a cause for concern in the International Community or the United Nations. Where were all the NGOs and Aid Agencies when they were so badly needed.

In truth, most of them had been driven away by Robert Mugabe and yet again, it was the little people of Zimbabwe who were suffering. A few I spoke to on the subject were surprisingly supportive of government efforts to keep the hospital going.

"Some people are responsible for this collapse and they should be made accountable," a newspaper vendor told me in curiously classy English. "It cannot all be down to the government. The hospital administrators must explain to the people, because anyone would conclude that the Government was ignoring these institutions, yet some people tasked with managing these operations sit on these things."

It sounded a bit complicated, but I knew what he meant. His words brought Chris Tapfumaneyi's anxious face to mind and I had to wonder if any of the blame could be attached to him.

I didn't know but he had seemed a likeable man and was genuinely worried.

Rachel Nyabunda was a nurse at The Avenues clinic and she too felt that the crisis at Parirenyatwa was not entirely down to government policies.

"It is hard on the patients," She told me. "Their rights must be recognised and protected. At the moment, the government is injecting trillions of dollars into the health sector but those funds are being channelled elsewhere instead of being used in the maintenance and development of hospitals."

I suppose I should have approached the Minister of Health for comment, but I would have had to tell him who I was and that could have caused problems for me, so I left him in peace. My own feeling was that until Zimbabwe received some form of official recognition and donor money was poured in, the situation at Parirenyatwa could only deteriorate further. Nobody was really interested and the only way Zimbabweans – particularly poor Zimbabweans – could avoid the very real dangers of attending the main hospital in Harare, was to remain healthy. With very little food to eat and no home to live in, that was a tall order.

As Stella Maungandidze had said to me, life was becoming one big vicious circle.

PART FIVE

(What Now for Zimbabwe.)

CHAPTER TWENTY

(A Fateful Year)

The year 2006 was a particularly bad one for Zimbabwe and her people and the first half of the year was a pretty bleak time for wandering scribbler, Bryan Graham.

In February, the Movement of Democratic Change managed to split itself down the middle, thereby losing all credibility as an effective opposition. The problems had begun during the previous October when the party's decision-making national council met to decide whether MDC should participate in forthcoming senatorial elections.

Although argument was intense, the eventual vote in favour of participation came in at thirty-three votes to thirty-one. This was overruled by Tsvangirai himself who argued that it was no use contesting an election where 'the electoral field breeds illegitimate outcomes and provides for predetermined results.' He announced publicly that the council had been split down the middle and to prove this, ruled that Sekai Holland and Grace Kwinjeh, both members of the national council, but neither present when the final vote was taken, should be allowed proxy votes. They both supported his view and their votes brought the 'for' and 'against' tallies level.

Tsvangirai's casting vote decided the issue, but most of those who had voted for participation went on to contest the election anyway. To my mind, it had not been a golden moment for the MDC or democracy and the party lost heavily, gaining only five of the sixty seats on offer. Amid increasing acrimony, a breakaway faction led by Tsvangirai's former deputy, Gibson Sibanda announced that it would also be known as the

Movement of Democratic Change. Sibanda was joined by many members of the party executive, all apparently fed up with Tsvangirai's increasingly autocratic rule. Among these were Welshman Ncube, Gift Chimanikire and Paul Themba Nyathi, although Chimanikire and some of the others later defected yet again to rejoin the Tsvangirai faction. David Coltart was another of Tsvangirai's senior colleagues who defected.

The ruling party seized on the MDC in-fighting with relish and CIO agents were deployed to add fuel to the flames. Cracks also emerged along ethnic lines with the age old animosity between Shona and Matabele coming to the fore. Watching from a distance, I wondered why on earth there should be such problems in the twenty-first century, then realised that the same thing went on in Britain between the English, Welsh and Scots. It seemed to me that mankind still has a great deal of growing up to do.

The Zimbabwean public were confused and angry, particularly when a young academic was brought in from South Africa to lead the breakaway faction. Arthur Mutambara was undoubtedly intellectually brilliant, but his only political experience was as a student leader and he had been out of the country for a very long time. Nevertheless, he was a polished orator and suddenly Zimbabweans were faced with two opposition parties bearing the same name and allegedly following the same agenda. It did little to bolster public confidence in the MDC.

This was reflected in the Budiriro by election, held soon after the split had taken place. The seat was won by Emmanuel Chisvuure of the Tsvangirai faction but the combined votes won by himself and the Mutambara man, Gabriel Chaibva amounted to less than half of the MDC vote in previous elections.

It all gave me the ideal excuse for another trip home, but it was when Roy Bennet was forced to flee the country that I felt I really had to be there.

Having lost his farm and everything he owned, endured eight months of inhuman prison conditions and done everything but give his life for his country, poor old Roy surely didn't deserve any more persecution, but it seemed that the government were out to lock him up again

A somewhat far-fetched plot to assassinate Mugabe by pouring oil on the upper slopes of Christmas Pass outside Mutare, just before his motorcade came through was announced by police. This followed the alleged find of an arms cache in the Mutare home of a former Rhodesian soldier and licensed firearms dealer, Peter Hitschmann. The cache was reported to consist of guns, ammunition and radio equipment, so Hitschmann was arrested, routinely tortured and placed in solitary confinement.

In Harare, the government-controlled media reported that it was Hitschmann who told the police of Bennett's involvement and I immediately rang a contact in the CIO who had been helpful in the past.

"The Old Man (Mugabe) flew into a rage when he was told about the alleged assassination plot," he told me cheerfully. "You have never seen such activity. There are teams of police and security agents scouring the country for Bennet, even though anyone can see that such a plot would be patently ridiculous. It could never work in practice, even if they knew exactly when the motorcade was coming through."

For Roy Bennet, it was the last straw.

"The battle is here. I will stay and fight it out in Zimbabwe," he had told me on his release from Chikurubi. "We have to fight this regime."

They were brave words but when the Hitschmann nonsense erupted, Roy told close friends that he could not bear the thought of going back to prison, even on trumped up charges. I couldn't blame him for that and when the news came that he had made a dramatic dash for safety through the mountainous Manicaland countryside that he knew so well, I cheered inwardly and wished him luck. When I spoke to him many months later in Johannesburg, he merely smiled when I asked him how he had managed his escape.

"I still have many friends and am well loved among the people of Zimbabwe," Was all he would tell me.

The arms found in Peter Hitschmann's house led to the arrest of six other men, including opposition MP Giles Mutseyekwa, three senior members of the MDC and two policemen. State prosecutors alleged in Court that the group plotted to kill President Mugabe when he travelled to Mutare for his eighty-second birthday celebrations on February 25th. The accused men said that they had been tortured by officers of the Central Intelligence Organisation. It was through torture that the name of Roy Bennett was first mentioned in connection with the case. I had absolutely no doubt that it had been suggested by the torturers themselves and I was right.

Knowledge Nyamhoka, the MDC's Manicaland provincial youth chairperson told Mutare magistrate Hosea Mujava that he was subjected to beatings and other forms of abuse, including having a firearm pressed against his temple.

"They promised to release me on bail," he told me later, "but only if I signed an affidavit implicating Mutseyekwa and Roy Bennett in activities connected with an armed insurrection. I was told that if I signed the document, I would be treated as a state witness in the case."

To make the entire scenario even more ridiculous, a police spokesman announced that the arrested men were members of the Zimbabwe Freedom Movement, a shadowy group who were introduced to the world in November 2003 by the British gay rights campaigner, Peter Tatchell. Tatchell, a brave man who had twice attempted citizen's arrests of Mugabe and tried through the courts to have him picked up and extradited to Britain on torture charges, described the claims as 'Mugabe fairy tales' and 'downright laughable.'

So they were and everyone knew it, but that was cold comfort for Roy Bennet. In South Africa, he applied for asylum and his application was backed up by Amnesty International.

Nevertheless, asylum was refused on the grounds that 'he would not be in any danger should he return to Zimbabwe.' The letter he received from the refugee Reception Office in Pretoria contained the immortal sentence, 'you were born and bread in Zimbabwe.' In view of the nationwide shortage of that particular commodity, it made me smile and even Bennet grinned as I read the letter.

The MDC denied all knowledge of Peter Hitschmann and were probably justified in claiming that the alleged plot was an attempt by the State to derail the party's forthcoming annual congress.

"We wish to place it on record that the MDC does not have any links with Mr Hitschmann or any group that seeks to effect regime change through unconstitutional means," Party spokesman Nelson Chamisa said. "Roy Bennet is a very important person in the MDC and highly respected countrywide. He will be attending the MDC conference this weekend."

He did not, but in his absence, was elected Treasurer General of the party and carried out his duties as such from exile in Johannesburg.

While all this was going on, Security Minister Didymus Mutasa warned anyone planning violence: "If it comes to a position where we have to eliminate them physically because of what they are doing, then it is their fault and we will not hesitate to do that."

In due course, Mutare Magistrate, Mujava ordered the release of all the accused men except Hitschmann and instructed that the State should proceed against them by summons. The charges were then dropped, but Peter Hitschmann still languished in prison two years later, his health deteriorating and his plight forgotten by the world.

Heather Bennet joined her husband in Johannesburg and although I hadn't spoken to her in ages, I understood from mutual friends that she was feeling understandably stressed, but she was getting on with life. I would have expected no less from a very strong lady.

To me, it all seemed an excellent story and a great follow up on previous pieces I had written on the Bennets, but after initial enthusiasm from Jim Murray, my article was 'spiked,' thereby adding to my disillusionment with tabloid newspaper reporting and my own newspaper in particular.

Nevertheless, Harare is a wonderful place to be in April and I set out to find stories that would help pay for my trip.

* * *

April 18th was the twenty-sixth anniversary of Zimbabwe's independence and as usual, the president was delivering his Independence Day address from Rufaro Stadium. Slightly against my better judgement and very much against vehement warnings from my family, I decided to attend the gathering and drove down into Mbare in the Ganja Bus.

Approaching the stadium, I found that all roads were packed with walking people. They were obviously heading for the celebrations but there was none of the usual laughter and joking that characterises such occasions in Africa. People looked wary and worried, many of them glancing sideways at my garishly exotic vehicle then looking quickly away when they saw my white face.

It didn't take me long to realise that I had made a bad mistake and should have watched Mugabe's speech on television. Mine was the only white face in the whole of Mbare and I would be even more conspicuous once I was in the stadium. That would make me an obvious target for security agents and hecklers. I might even be singled out by Mugabe himself and for one, supposedly intent on keeping a low profile, I was being extremely stupid.

Had I been able to, I would have turned around and gone home, but on the narrow, rutted road to the stadium, there was no chance of that. Despite the throng of pedestrians, buses kept roaring past me and turning my cumbersome truck around in that melee was not going to be easy.

My indecision was brought to an end by a diminutive soldier who stepped into my path, one hand bidding me to stop and the other grasping an AK47 rifle that looked enormous in his grasp. Walking around to my side of the vehicle, he motioned for me to wind my window down.

"Where are you going?" He demanded and I saw a gaunt looking policeman move up behind him.

"I am on my way to hear the President speak."

It was definitely an occasion to be very polite and respectful.

"You cannot go there. It is forbidden."

The soldier could not have been more than eighteen years old, but he was confident in the power of his uniform. For me, it should have been the ideal excuse to get out of there, but some foolish imp of mischief was at work in my brain.

"How can it be forbidden?" I demanded. "I am a Zimbabwean and Robert Mugabe is my president. I want to hear his address."

"It is forbidden." He said woodenly and the policeman nodded his head. "You must turn around."

"Why?" I was getting cross and angry men say silly things. "Is it just because I am white? I am as Zimbabwean as you are."

"Let me see your identification." He held out his hand and I cursed myself for an impetuous fool. The only official Zimbabwean identification I carried was my son Brian's ID card. We were both short of hair and wore glasses, but there were twenty-one years between us and the card had caused raised eyebrows in the past. Fumbling in my wallet, I handed it over and as I did so, an American ten dollar note fluttered to the ground. The soldier bent down to retrieve it and examined it closely.

"What is this?"

"It is ten dollars in American money," I explained hesitantly. Now I was in trouble. Zimbabweans were not allowed to possess foreign currency at that time and I noticed the policeman looking over the little soldier's shoulder.

"Why have you got this?" The soldier looked at me with supreme suspicion.

"Because I have just come back home from a visit to Britain and haven't had time to change it at the bank."

One thing I had learned in my brief career as a journalist was how to lie with aplomb. The soldier was not impressed.

"Where is your driving licence?"

Back into the wallet I went, praying that neither the soldier nor his silent companion would notice the thick wad of foreign currency tucked into one side of the folder. I had been stupidly careless to carry it with me and the prospect of an indefinite stay in Chikurubi once again seemed very real. Hauling out my driving licence, I handed it over and the soldier passed his rifle to the policeman so that he could examine both my documents.

If it hadn't been so serious, it had all the makings of a Whitehall farce. In one hand, the soldier held a Zimbabwean identity card in the name of Brian Lemon. In the other, he held a British driving licence in the name of David Lemon. He hadn't asked my name but I wondered which one I should use if he did.

Frowning myopically, the little man examined both documents in turn, then solemnly handed them back to me and retrieved his rifle.

"You cannot go any further," He announced firmly. "You must turn around."

Relief hit me like a towering wall of water and I could feel my legs trembling with reaction. It seemed that the soldier couldn't read and had merely been going through the motions, but I had been incredibly lucky yet again. Policemen were required to have a basic standard of education and had the silent officer checked the documents himself, I would not have escaped so lightly. Taking full advantage of the unexpected reprieve, I hauled the Ganja Bus around and manoeuvred my way through the mob of pedestrians. When I saw the policeman stopping an oncoming vehicle so that I could get around, I had to stifle a giggle. The entire situation was like a particularly bad dream but I wasted no time at all in getting away from there.

I never did hear the President's speech but it was reported as being the usual vituperative attack on colonialism, Tony Blair and George W Bush.

Back in Harare and relatively safe, I realised that the soldier had kept my ten dollar note. In the circumstances, I felt he deserved it.

* * *

One of the problems with being a visitor to Zimbabwe was carrying cash. With sterling in my pocket, I could live like a king on the black market exchange rate, but it is amazing how much space a few million Zimbabwe dollars took up. The poor old Ganja Bus was filled with bricks of banknotes, stowed haphazardly in every conceivable nook and cranny. I had more cash in plastic supermarket bags, slung carelessly over the seat and on the floor.

Jerry cans of fuel added to my strange cargo and there were times when I wondered where to stow my meagre luggage. It was forbidden to carry fuel without a permit and forbidden to carry more than a certain sum of money, but even the police tended to disregard the regulations. Provided one drew up to road blocks with a smile and a cheery word, most policemen I encountered were friendly and helpful. Like all Zimbabweans, they were struggling to make ends meet on the money they were paid, and their general demeanour contrasted vividly with the image painted of them in the overseas press by other journalists. Policing had changed since my days, but those members of the force I encountered were invariably young men and women merely trying to get on with their jobs in difficult times.

On one occasion, I was giving a very pretty friend a lift to Kariba when we were pulled to a halt in Chinhoyi.

"Where are you going?" A young policewoman stuck her head in through the window.

"Kariba," I told her and she looked wistful.

"I was stationed there for two years," she smiled at us both. "It is a lovely place to be."

That imp of mischief which gets me into trouble far too often was at work again.

"We are going up on honeymoon," I told the policewoman and my companion glanced fiercely at me. "We intend to enjoy ourselves."

"Ah, I hope you will be very happy," the policewoman waved us on and we were both in fits of laughter as we pulled away.

"That is one way to avoid questioning at a roadblock," my companion agreed. "I am glad my husband didn't hear you though."

A year later, I was stopped again while driving through Chinhoyi. With my mind on other matters, I pulled the Ganja Bus to a halt.

"How is your wife?" Was the first question and somewhat nonplussed, I informed the lady cop that she was 'very well, thank you very much.' I wondered why anyone in Zimbabwe would be interested in the well-being of my wife over there in Britain.

"Ah, she was a very nice lady." I was told. "I recognised your car so I stopped you so that you can send her my love."

Suddenly I realised that my questioner was the young woman who I had lied to so blatantly and I felt really guilty about having done so. Assuring her that I would pass her message on, I drove away, laughing inside but as so often, truly impressed by the sheer 'niceness' of the average Zimbabwean – even their sadly maligned police officers.

* * *

Despite the ever escalating poverty and sense of crisis in Zimbabwe, I enjoyed my first trip home in 2006, although from the journalistic point of view it was a waste of time. None of my stories were used and although I did a couple of features for the paper, urging the relevant powers-that-be not to encourage Mugabe by playing cricket with Zimbabwe, I felt flat, deflated and let down by the newspaper hierarchy.

"It is a sort of compassion fatigue," Jim Murray told me when I complained at the lack of media interest in what was happening to my fellow countrymen. "There is so much disaster in the world and with our soldiers dying in both Iraq and Afghanistan, I'm afraid Zimbabwe is well down on any scale of importance."

So I went back to gardening but my heart was sore.

Chapter Twenty One

(Elephants and Adventure)

On my return from one of my trips to Zimbabwe, I had been approached by a friend, living in Stroud – a town near my home.

"How would you like to come and talk to us about the problems of Zimbabwe?" He offered. 'Us' was a Probus club for retired professional men and although the only audiences I had ever addressed before were policemen during my service in the BSAP, I readily agreed.

It was amazing. My talk was scheduled to last an hour and half way through, I realised that all these serious looking gentlemen were hanging on my every word. I enjoyed the experience and soon found myself in demand with other Probus and Rotary groups. I expanded my repertoire to include talks on elephants, the building of Kariba Dam and even modern policing in Britain. I travelled all around Gloucestershire with occasional forays further afield and discovered that I had a definite talent for public speaking.

There were occasional setbacks, such as the time when I hammered on the table with my fist to emphasise a point and almost caused two octogenarians in the front row to fall off their chairs. They had been fast asleep and I suppose I was lucky not to give them heart attacks.

On another occasion, one gentleman stood up half way through my talk on modern policing to call me a 'fascist' and walked out. The Chairman asked me to continue the talk and when it was over, I was approached by three former policemen in the audience to compliment me on being brave enough to say what I did.

All in all, it was and is great fun and although I don't get my views home to as large an audience as I used to with the Sunday Express, it does at least give me a chance to have my say and be heard.

I only wish I had discovered the talent somewhat earlier in life. Who knows, with the way I had learned to lie so convincingly on my journalistic forays, I might even have become a politician.

* * *

At the end of 2006 I was back in Zimbabwe but this time the visit was for me and not to publicise the things going wrong in my country.

Although I was sixty-one and far too old to embark on any new adventures, I had determined to walk around the southern shoreline of Lake Kariba, using Kariba Town and Binga as my start and finish points. It had never been attempted before, but in spite of my advanced age, I felt sure I could do it.

"What about lions," they said. "What about elephants, buffalo, crocodiles and puff adders. You will die out there and we will never find your body."

I was brought up among elephants, lions, buffalo *et al* so wasn't too worried about them, although the sheer physical challenge of walking over a thousand kilometres through some very wild countryside was a little daunting. However, I duly set out on the twentieth of October in searing heat and arrived in Binga ten and a half weeks later.

I had many adventures on the way and the walk provided memories that will keep me going through my dotage. In addition to a number of close encounters with wild life, I was arrested once, suffered extremes of heat and thirst, was forced to stitch up a gash in my own leg and lost nearly a third of my body weight.

It was fun to look back on though. I enjoyed spectacular sunsets, unmatchable scenery and that special sense of peace that comes from being totally alone in the wild places of Africa.

* * *

My Binga walk provided me with material for another book, but it also added to my growing disillusionment with the international media.

While wandering around the Sengwa Basin, I had come across two baby elephants. One of them was alive and she led me to the other one which had been killed by a spear and then butchered. At first it seemed like just another bushveld tragedy, but I could not understand how two babies – neither of them old enough to be away from their mothers – could have been abandoned in the same place.

A few days later, I discovered a possible answer. Talking with a man named Moses in Mukuyu fishing camp, he told me that he worked for a professional hunter, I know very well. I will just call him Adam.

When I asked after Adam's whereabouts, I was told that he was out with a client, looking for a bull elephant to shoot.

"They shot two cows earlier in the week," Moses told me cheerfully and a horrible penny dropped in my brain. I had always thought of Adam as a fine bushman and an ethical hunter, but shooting two cows with infants at heel was a heinous offence among conservationists and hunters alike. I resolved to write about it on my return to civilisation but when I did, I met up with a wall of editorial indifference.

I approached editors in South Africa and Britain. I offered them photographs and names. I approached conservation agencies with requests for help, but even those that bothered to reply were not particularly interested.

Shortly after completing my walk, I approached Derek Watts of the South African TV 'Carte Blanche' programme. At first he was enthusiastic, but when I phoned him as arranged a week later, that enthusiasm had been replaced by a hesitant assertion that it was 'dangerous to work in Zimbabwe.' Of course it was. I knew that only too well but I wasn't asking him to go there with cameras at the ready. All I wanted was publicity for the plight of the Zimbabwe elephants that were being ravaged by callous mankind.

"Don't be naïve," my brother in law who is a Johannesburg businessman told me. "The hunting lobby is huge in this country. They bring in an enormous amount of money and won't allow you to have your say."

Hunting was a dirty word in Britain but it seemed that even there, I would not be allowed to air my disgust at the treatment meted out to those two elephants. The national newspapers were more intent on publicising the goings on that were taking place on various 'reality' television programmes and eventually, I rather wearily put my pictures away and tried to drive the visions of two sad little elephants out of my mind.

My already jaundiced opinion of my fellow man had taken another large knock.

* * *

While I was in Johannesburg, I received a message through my publisher, Peter Stiff that the Deputy Secretary General of the MDC, Tapiwa Mashakada had read my book Never Quite a Soldier and wanted to meet me. We duly exchanged emails and although I had doubts as to his motives, I agreed to phone him on my return to Harare.

"Be careful," I was warned by a senior member of the MDC in Johannesburg. "He is a very clever man but we are not sure where his loyalties really lie."

It seemed too good a story opportunity to miss though, so I duly made the telephone call and Mashakada sounded pleased to hear from me.

"I enjoyed your book," Every writer loves to hear that and I duly preened. "It was so true to life, even though I was only a boy during the war years. I often wish I had been old enough to experience what you blokes did."

It sounded odd coming from a senior African politician and I wondered which side he would have fought for, but he seemed genuinely interested and invited me to his house in Hatfield, the area for which he was the serving Member of Parliament.

I was due to fly home shortly afterwards and he had commitments, so the only time we could arrange for the visit was a Wednesday evening, which made me worry a little. Hatfield after dark might not be the best place for a white undercover journalist to be picked up by the police and I promised the folk I was staying with that I would be very careful. As I drove out for the proposed meeting, I was nervous and wished I had brought someone along with me for company. Apart from Roy Bennet, I had avoided contact with public figures during my journalistic forays into Zimbabwe. I had concentrated on stories about the common people, but this man had actually gone out of his way to contact me. I couldn't help wondering why.

Hatfield is a vast sprawling suburb of Harare. The streets are wide and the houses are generally well built, but it is by no means an affluent area. When I arrived there, it was already dark and without working street lamps, I struggled to find the address Tapiwa had given me. When I did, the fact that the house was surrounded by a very high wall did nothing to ease my growing nervousness. It would be quite easy for me to disappear in a place like this, but steeling myself, I got out of the truck and approached wide iron gates with as much confidence as I could muster. My call was answered by a man wearing a muffler around his face and carrying a large baton. When I explained why I was there, he wordlessly pushed the gate open and indicated that I should drive in.

With the gates shut behind me, I was well and truly trapped, but my knock on the front door was answered by an attractive, well-dressed woman who introduced herself as Tapiwa Mashakada's wife, Nyarisai.

"He called to say that he will be a bit delayed," she told me. "Please come in and I will get you some tea."

At that stage, I would have preferred something stronger, but I sat down and made desultory small talk with Nyarisai until the tea arrived, together with a plate of sandwiches. Shortly afterwards, my host exploded into the room.

I use that word advisedly, because everything about Tapiwa Mashakada was big. Not a particularly tall man, he was running to fat, but there was an impression of latent power in his bulky frame. His voice was big and booming as he greeted me with a firm handshake. Although I was theoretically the larger man, I felt completely dominated by the politician's energetic personality.

Tucking into the sandwiches with enthusiasm, he told me a little about himself and the work he was doing for his constituents.

"Hatfield is the largest urban constituency in the country," he said with obvious enthusiasm. "The people have a variety of problems and I am kept very busy trying to sort them out. In Parliament, I am the shadow Minister of Finance so that keeps me on my toes as well. As you know, the economy is a complete mess at the moment."

Would it ever get back on an even keel, I asked mildly and he rolled his eyes heavenward.

"Who knows? Who in God's name really knows? Mugabe seems intent on driving us all into starvation, which actually is quite a good ploy on his part."

How so I wondered.

"Starvation and worry about merely surviving tend to leech the spirit out of people," he explained. "While they do not have enough to eat, they are unlikely to revolt and every time elections are on hand, he distributes largesse in the rural areas and they vote for him. Simple African politics I'm afraid."

Eventually I managed to get him on to what really interested me. What was happening in the MDC? Surely the factional split had hurt them badly?

"Indeed it has, David." With the book connection, I couldn't very well call myself Bryan Graham and perhaps it was better that he didn't know what I was doing in any case. "The people don't know what is happening or who to vote for. It is all playing right into Mugabe's hands."

But how had it come about? He smiled tightly.

"I don't think there is any doubt that it was all engineered by Mugabe and the CIO. Welshman (Ncube) is an obvious plant and has been given a fine farm for his political assistance. Whether Mutambara is also 'one of them' is not clear, but he is certainly being used and hasn't the political experience to see it."

I found it all very confusing. In Johannesburg, this man had been named as a CIO plant. Here he was naming others and seeming quite genuine about it. My journalistic cap was spinning around on my head, but the evening passed very pleasantly. As befits any senior politician, Tapiwa was an excellent conversationalist and we discussed many aspects of life in modern Zimbabwe, without finding any solution to the main problems affecting our ravaged country.

Still a little nervous, I stood up to leave and Tapiwa put his hand on my arm.

"So early?" I shrugged to say that I had no choice, but he insisted on showing me around his house.

"It was small when I bought it," he enthused, "but I have made a number of extensions and it is comfortable now. But first you must meet the kids."

Having been introduced to the little Mashakadas by a smiling Nyarisai, I followed my host around the house. Furnished throughout in the modern style, it was certainly big. Room went into room and there were bedrooms for everyone. I noticed a copy of my book on a bedside table and Tapiwa saw where I was looking.

"You must sign it for me," he said, so I inscribed something about 'my friend Tapiwa' and he seemed happy. Feeling more than a little bit cynical, I wondered if the book had been deliberately placed where I could see it, but perhaps that was unworthy of me. Tapiwa Mashakada seemed genuinely interested and I found myself warming to him by the moment.

Outside, I was introduced to the sinister looking fellow who had let me through the gate earlier.

"My bodyguard," Tapiwa explained. "He goes everywhere with me and would willingly die in defence of my safety. Mind you," he added. "I usually carry a pistol with me when I go out of town. I won't allow myself to be ambushed by Mugabe's thugs."

But he had a sense of humour, did Tapiwa Mashakada. Having been shown around the house, offices and outbuildings, I was preparing to get into my car when he indicated a wide, ornately-railed patio jutting out from the top storey wall of the house.

"I had that built," he told me with a wry smile, "so that I could sit with my coffee in the mornings and look out over my entire constituency. It was a lovely idea and it was only when the patio was complete and the scaffolding withdrawn that anyone realised, we had forgotten to add a staircase so I couldn't get up there anyway. By then I had run out of money for building, so my morning coffee is still taken inside the house."

Roaring with laughter at his own stupidity, Tapiwa Mashakada shook my hand again and opened the gate himself.

"See you on your next visit," his voice boomed after me and I wondered whether it was a signal to waiting footpads or CIO officers. "If you need anything like accommodation or transport, let me know."

Nothing happened on my return journey and I have seen Tapiwa in Britain since that initial visit. I didn't ask what he was doing in this country, but he had put on even more weight and looked extremely prosperous. When we met in the centre of Coventry, he was still bubbling with enthusiasm for life. This time I felt safer and we talked for hours. As I left him in the cold, winter darkness of England, he enveloped me in a huge bear hug.

"You are a true Zimbabwean, David Lemon," he announced. "When we of the MDC are in power, you will always be welcome to live once again in your own country."

With his strength, his acute intellect and his enthusiasm for life, Tapiwa Mashakada could yet go a long way in African politics. The people of Zimbabwe are in need of a real leader to counter Mugabe and driving back to Gloucestershire, I couldn't help wondering whether or not, I had been hugged by a future African president.

It is still too early to tell but wherever his allegiances lie, I liked Tapiwa Mashakada and enjoyed the time I spent with him.

CHAPTER TWENTY TWO

(Tabloid Values)

I have written in the past that I was never quite a soldier, despite having fought through a particularly brutal civil war. Suddenly it seemed that I was never quite to be a journalist either.

Another reshuffle had taken place in the hierarchy of the Sunday Express and Jim Murray's role as News Editor had been taken over by Stephen Rigley, who had radically different ideas as to what might be termed news emanating from my troubled country.

It seemed obvious to me that the 2008 elections – both parliamentary and presidential – were going to be hugely interesting. Despite an unprecedented (except perhaps in 1985 when Joshua Nkomo's Zapu were the opposition) outbreak of violence throughout Zimbabwe in the run up to polling day, the spirit of the people was high and for the first time ever, there seemed a genuine chance that Mugabe might be unseated.

It was to prevent that eventuality that the violence was unleashed and it was horrific in its scope. All over the country, rapes, murders and extreme acts of intimidation were taking place and some of the details sent to me by concerned friends were stomach churning.

It seemed that the military men from Joint Operational Command were coordinating official Zanu PF electioneering and they cared nothing for the lives and feelings of the people. Many young men were shot out of hand merely for attending MDC meetings and others disappeared after being picked up by uniformed police or soldiers. Fear swept through the countryside, but once again Zimbabweans were prepared to show their resilience and vote to get Mugabe's government out.

"You need me there to report on it," I told Mr Rigley and for a moment or two he seemed interested.

"We could send you," he mused, 'but rather than concentrating on the election, I would like you to get me some stories on Chelsy Davy and her family."

Miss Davy was a very rich Zimbabwean girl, romantically involved with Britain's Prince Harry at the time. Her father, Charles Davy ran a huge hunting and safari conglomerate, (HHK Safaris) with camps and concessions all over the country. I had little doubt that to be as successful as he was, he had to be in cahoots with senior government officials, but I was more interested in finding stories about the ordinary people who were showing such spirit despite being tortured, raped and murdered.

Having told Mr Rigley that I was not 'that sort' of reporter, I went home in a huff, but the end result was that I wasn't sent out by the newspaper and had to watch and listen to events in my own country from an attic office in England.

It was initially wonderful though. Despite all the intimidation, votes for the MDC in the parliamentary elections flooded in and the end result was that they won ninety-nine seats to Zanu PF's ninety-seven. Mutambara's faction took ten and there was one Independent winner, so in theory the MDC had finally gained control of the Zimbabwe parliament. Lovemore Moyo became the first MDC Speaker and my friend Tapiwa Mashakada had increased his Hatfield majority to well over eight thousand. I was especially pleased about that.

Of course there were many complaints about the results from Mugabe's people and I wondered how long it would be before opposition MPs began meeting up with fatal accidents. Three of them had died in the run up to the election and I was sure there would be more, if only to even the respective representation in Parliament.

The presidential election was to prove even more interesting.

In fact, the election for president had been complicated by the entry into the fray of Mugabe's former finance minister, Simba Makoni. His Mavambo/Kusili/Dawn party had not shone in the general election, but he was expected to take quite a few votes from both Tsvangirai and Mugabe in the fight to be president.

Despite what had to be seen as a defeat for Zanu PF in the parliamentary polls, the results were only delayed a day or two, but that was not the case with the election for the top job. Days, then weeks went by before it was finally announced that while Mugabe had only polled forty-three percent of the votes, Tsvangirai with just under forty-eight percent did not have enough votes to win the election outright. The winning candidate needed to poll at least fifty percent to avoid a run off and I wondered how many hours had been spent rigging the polling boxes to ensure that the MDC leader did not get the requisite amount.

In fact, after the first round but before the counting was completed, Jose Marcos Barrica, the head of the Southern African Development Community observers, described the election as 'a peaceful and credible expression of the will of the people of Zimbabwe.'

I could only wonder whether the worthy Mr Barrica had been allowed to see anything. He certainly could not have been watching the election I had been reading and hearing about for days.

Mugabe immediately announced that a rerun would be held in June and the violence then increased to an unprecedented extent. In the weeks following polling day, a campaign of intimidation was unfurled that ought to have shamed the world. As usual though, it seemed to have little effect, apart from the usual hand wringing from a few major political figures. Huts, houses and entire villages were burned down and diplomats in Harare collected many eye witness accounts of the horrors being unleashed in the countryside by people variously described as war veterans, militias or soldiers.

It was truly horrific and it hit home personally when I learned that Tonderai Ndira was one of the many victims. It seemed that following the elections, Ndira had embarked on his own electioneering duties. He would disappear for days at a time to rally the masses and give them the benefit of his own enthusiasm and on Tuesday 13th May, he came home to Mabvuku and slept the sleep of the truly exhausted.

Early the following morning, a pickup truck, packed with ten men who were armed with revolvers and AK assault rifles arrived at Ndira's house. They took the tall man away in front of his children, beating him with rifle butts to get him into the truck. From there he just disappeared. For a week his family and friends tried to find out where he had been taken, but it was only when MDC officials went to claim two other bodies from the mortuary at Parirenyatwa, that they were told there was another one that had not been claimed.

Tonderai Ndira had been battered to death and a pair of bloody shorts was plastered to a face clearly broken and shattered. The crowning horror was the fact that his tongue had been cut out.

Some months later, I spoke to Jimmy Chidakwa, another MDC activist who told me that they had only known that the body belonged to Ndira by his ring, his bangles and his unmistakable height.

"His jaw was shattered, his knuckles broken, there was a bullet hole below his heart, many, many stab wounds and a large hole at the back of his head which seemed to have been caused by a hammer." Chidakwa said bitterly. "They are cowards, all of them. Ten men to take down one unarmed man.

'And where were our leaders? Out of the country as usual."

It was true. For reasons best known to himself, Morgan Tsvangirai had embarked on a six week tour of other African states, seeking to drum up support for himself and his party. He did not return to Zimbabwe until the end of May and in the meantime, many more horrors had taken place.

In a Harare suburb, five month pregnant Pamela Patsvani was burnt alive in her house because her husband was an MDC activist. Her son died with her and in an even more horrific event, Didiro Chipiro, a forty-five year old mother had her hands hacked off and was pushed into her house in Mhondoro before it was set alight by chanting soldiers.

For me, it was all too much. All these horrors were taking place in my country, the world was ignoring them and my News Editor wanted scandal stories on Chelsy Davey. Feeling very upset with life in general, I flew out to Zimbabwe again, hoping to be in time for the presidential re run.

I need not have worried. There was not going to be a story. As the violence increased throughout the country, Morgan Tsvangirai announced that he was pulling out of the race in order to protect his own followers. My own feeling was that those followers had suffered so much already that he was letting them down by not going ahead, but I am sure Tsvangirai's advisers knew what they were doing.

Smiling with grim satisfaction, Mugabe went on with what was a charade of a polling day. Nobody really cared and when he was eventually sworn in for a sixth term as president, the only people present at what was usually a lavish ceremony were his wife, a few of his cronies and those army generals, who according to rumour were the people actually running the country.

It was a very sad day for all Zimbabweans and a frustrating one for me because I wanted to write about it, but was damned if I would approach Stephen Rigley again.

Chapter Twenty Three

(Global Political Agreement)

In theory Zimbabwe was finished. There was no change in the regime at the top, no food in the shops and nobody in the outside world seemed to give a damn.

The recently found diamond fields in the Eastern part of the country were making fortunes for many people, but unlike a similar find many years previously in Botswana, this did nothing for the ordinary Zimbabwean. The Botswana authorities had used their diamond income to boost a faltering economy and in the process, made themselves one of the most prosperous little nations in Africa.

In Zimbabwe, the finding of diamonds led to many more violent deaths and made a group of individual politicians and military men into some of the most prosperous people in the entire world.

But Mugabe had to do something. If he hadn't known it before, the election would have told him only too clearly that he could not hang on much longer and it seemed that other African leaders were also urging him to join up with Morgan Tsvangirai.

Tsvangirai's reaction was that he would never join up with Mugabe and this was echoed by two of his senior men, Roy Bennet and Tendai Biti, but on 15th September 2008, the Global Political Agreement (quite where they got the 'global' from, I don't know) was signed. Mugabe stayed on as President, Tsvangirai became Prime Minister, Mutambara, the Deputy PM and Biti the Minister of Finance. Bennet was appointed as Deputy Minister of Agriculture but was promptly put back into gaol on spurious treason charges when he returned to Zimbabwe. These were thrown out by the Courts and he was bailed on lesser charges, but two years after his appointment, he was still waiting to be sworn in by the president.

The entire exercise was all too reminiscent of the Unity Agreement signed between Mugabe and Joshua Nkomo, way back in December 1986. In that case, Nkomo's acquiescence to Mugabe – no matter how coerced he might have been – led to the end of his political career, his banishment from his own country and eventually to a lonely death.

Morgan Tsvangirai has already received at least one tangible reminder of Nkomo's fate. A few weeks after the agreement was signed, Tsvangirai was involved in a road accident in which his wife was killed. He immediately declared publicly that it had been a genuine accident, but Zimbabweans have grown accustomed to their more effective politicians dying in unexplained traffic accidents. His announcement was greeted by almost universal national cynicism.

There have been so many of them over the years. From Josiah Tongogara, the hope of so many Zimbabweans in 1980 to Border Gezi who was speaking out against Mugabe's policies, to a couple of recalcitrant army generals in the late nineties, inexplicable car crashes have accounted for many a worthwhile life. It seemed that whenever President Mugabe felt himself in any way challenged, the challenger was likely to find himself involved in a fatal road accident – with himself as the fatality.

Morgan Tsvangirai was lucky in this instance, but the death of his wife cast a pall on the celebrations for yet another 'New Zimbabwe.'

* * *

Early in 2009, I was trying to get together enough money for another trip home. I wasn't interested in writing for the Sunday Express – I hadn't heard from Stephen Rigley since I had told him that I was NOT a scandal seeking reporter – and only wanted to see for myself exactly what was happening.

I had enough money for my fare and on checking my Zimbabwean Post Office savings book, into which my book royalties were automatically paid, was gratified to see that there was a long string of noughts behind the total indicated. It probably wasn't worth much – at that stage few people could keep up with the amazing decline of the Zimbabwe dollar – but I decided that it would keep me going while I was home.

I should have known better. In April, the Zimbabwe dollar was scrapped in favour of United States currency or the South African rand. Overnight, my hard earned capital was worth absolutely nothing and I knew that many people would have suffered far greater losses than mine.

Yet in a way it was an inspired move on the part of Tendai Biti. When I did get home, the shops were full again for the first time in years. I could buy whatever I wanted, as long as I paid in US dollars or South African rands and there were far more smiles in evidence among the people than there had been on my previous visit.

The cost of living had rocketed though and I couldn't help wondering how rural people could get access to what was virtually foreign currency. Trying to find out what village life was really like, I travelled extensively among the Tonga in the northern part of the country, but even they seemed happy with the situation. Mind you, the Tonga have never had much in the way of money or possessions, but their enthusiasm for the new regime made me wonder if the GPA could actually work.

A couple of years later, it is in serious danger of falling apart. Morgan Tsvangirai seems to have adapted very well to the trappings of power and while I don't hold that against him, his rantings around the world, sometimes in defence of Robert Mugabe and then railing against the difficulties of working with the man do tend to make me feel somewhat cynical. He is proving himself just another politician and I have never liked the breed.

Another round of elections is due to be held in Zimbabwe in 2011 and I sincerely hope to be there again – perhaps not writing for the Sunday Express but at least seeing for myself what goes on.

Mind you, although not yet back on track, my career as an unofficial scribbler might not quite be over. In the latter months of 2010, Stephen Rigley phoned to ask what I knew about Gamuchera (Gamu) Nhengu and the fact that she could be deported back to Zimbabwe. I told him that I had never heard of the girl, but it turned out that she was a contestant in the television reality show, The X Factor.

I had never watched the show, but at Rigley's request, I researched what I could – through the miracles of modern technology, I even heard Gamu sing – and submitted a piece in which I said that if her deportation order was rescinded, Simon Cowell should be appointed Prime Minister of Britain, as he obviously carries far more clout than the current incumbent.

My article was duly printed under the by line of Bryan Graham, so although Mr Rigley's preferences are obviously still with the gratification of the Great British Public's baser instincts, I just hope I can persuade him that those wonderfully cheerful and resilient people in Zimbabwe deserve a little more coverage of their plight.

Having quite blown my cover with this book, I might even get to see my own name in the Sunday Express, but I really did enjoy being Bryan Graham. I was never quite a soldier and never quite a journalist, but I will always be a Zimbabwean and whatever name I write under, I can only hope that my scribblings will somehow make a difference. The people of Zimbabwe are desperate for the outside world to take notice of what they are going through and if nothing is done to bring their suffering to an end, can western politicians really look at themselves with any vestige of self respect?

I honestly do not think so.

EPILOGUE

So many people helped me during my trips around Zimbabwe and all of them will remain in my mind for one reason or another, but the man who made the deepest impression on me was Tonderai Ndira. Immensely tall and thin, he spoke softly at all times although his deep brown eyes displayed a look of rare intelligence and purpose. He had accepted my preposterous plan to break into the Mugabe mansion with complete equanimity and had shown no surprise at my wanting to do so. Nor was he out to make money out of it and once he had decided that my writing was for the general good of Zimbabweans, he had assisted in every way he could.

On my last visit in 2010, I went back to Mabvuku Township to find out exactly who he had been and why there had been such a huge outpouring of grief at his death.

Nixon Nyikadzino, who was another activist, but with the Crisis in Zimbabwe Coalition described Ndira as, 'a quiet comrade who could only speak through action.'

"Most of our mobilisation in Mabvuku and Harare," he told me quietly, "was done through Ndira. He was so connected to the people that we could not do without him. His ability to stand against police brutality, his skill in rising above the rest and his ability to stand up when all chips were down lit our revolutionary hope."

Thirty-two year old Tonderai was a veteran of police arrests, clocking up an incredible thirty-five during the last five years of his life. Curious to know more, I had looked up the dictionary definition of 'activist' and it read 'a person who is passionate about what they believe in and helps educate other people about the subject at hand.'

That was definitely Tonderai Ndira. Not only did he organize meetings among young people everywhere to teach them about their rights and the state of government, but he was passionate in his beliefs and prepared to take on a prominent role that made him an inevitable target for the thuggish killers of Mugabe's Zanu PF.

Tonderai may not have had the international renown of Steve Biko, the founder of the Black Consciousness Movement in South Africa, but throughout Zimbabwe he was recognized and admired as one of Mugabe's most implacable and fearless opponents. It says much for the man that he worked tirelessly for others right up to his brutal death.

Ndira's official role was as the MDC Security Secretary for Harare province and in that capacity, he always managed to keep one step ahead of the authorities. When the police or CIO got too close in the area he was working, he moved on. He would be gone from his home for weeks at a time and twice he escaped custody by jumping out of a moving truck.

Student leader, Beloved Chiweshe described Tonderai as a 'popular comrade' who braved the harsh political climate in Mashonaland and when I asked why Ndira had not received more assistance from the Party, Chiweshe lamented how Zimbabweans had failed the man in his moment of greatest need.

"I never thought we could turn on each other with such brutality after the bitter struggle that our people went through to be free. It pains me, but his blood will water the revolutionary tree and keep the revolutionary garrison going."

Brave words but Tonderai's brother Cosmos was more forthright.

"We in Zimbabwe are like chickens waiting for the knife to reach our throats," He told me bitterly. "Given his position in the party, my brother should have had more protection."

It seemed that Ndira had fully expected that the day would come when his luck ran out. In 2002, he spoke to reporters from the BBC Panorama programme and said,

"We are prepared to die. It is just the same, we are still dying in Zimbabwe. We are dying by hunger, by diseases, everything, so there is nothing to fear, nothing to be scared of."

My heart churned with emotion when I visited the Ndira household and met his children Rafael and Linette, both wide eyed and bewildered at what had happened to their father. His widow Plaxedes said simply,

"I do not know what those people did to my husband, but he died for the people of Zimbabwe. I do not know the pain and suffering he went through and I do not know what his last thoughts and words were, but I want whoever murdered my husband to face justice. His killers should be arrested and sentenced to life imprisonment. You cannot take life and live your life as if nothing happened. As long as it is protecting these people, the inclusive government cannot bring healing to me."

Nor do I think it will bring healing to the country at large. There is a great deal of trouble ahead for the people of Zimbabwe and I fear that it is only the rest of the world that can finally sort out the problems of my troubled country. Yet senior politicians everywhere seem to have lost all desire to help the little people of the world.

It is not so long ago that Lord Renton told the British House of Lords that Robert Gabriel Mugabe should be allowed a comfortable retirement in Britain. As Timothy Renton, he was a junior official during the Lancaster House talks that led to Zimbabwe's independence, so I suppose he is regarded as an expert on the place, but this was surely fatuous nonsense.

When I read Renton's words, my soul cringed and I thought immediately of all the people like Tonderai Ndira who had done what they could to help me in my travels and thereby ensure that people like Renton had some idea as to what was actually going on in Zimbabwe..

It seemed that we had all been wasting our time and taking huge risks for nothing. What a terrible betrayal Renton's suggestion was of ordinary Zimbabweans. Mugabe should be brought before the International Court in The Hague, but I know in my heart that won't happen. The African block would scream 'racism' and in the twisted morality of this modern world, no national leader is prepared to risk that.

He was cruelly killed to keep him quiet, but I can only hope and pray that Tonderai Ndira's dreams of a free and fair Zimbabwe will one day come to pass.

The End

GLOSSARY

Chefs	:	Leaders; important individuals – from the Portuguese word *'chefe'* – chief.
Chimurenga	:	Wars for freedom.
Chinja	:	Change and the mantra of the MDC.
Chishona	:	Language of the majority Shona people in Zimbabwe. Sometimes referred to as Shona.
Dagga	:	Cannabis or marijuana. Also known as Ganja.
Entumbane	:	A high-density suburb of Bulawayo.
Gukuruhundi	:	Operational name for 1980s massacres in Matabeleland. Can be translated as 'The Storm that washes away the chaff before Spring rain.'
Gundwane	:	Chishona word for rat.
Hondo	:	Chishona word for war.
Kraal	:	Tribal village.
Lobolo	:	Bride price – traditionally paid in cattle to father of the bride.
MDC	:	Opposition political party, the Movement for Democratic Change.
MKD	:	A very small opposition party, Muvambo/Kushile/Dawn, led by former Zanu PF stalwart, Simba Makoni.
Mabunhu	:	Derogatory term for white farmer.
Manyika	:	Minority tribe of Eastern Zimbabwe.
Marungu	:	Chishona for white person – plural 'warungu.'
Makhiwa	:	Sindebele for white person.

Mahobohobo	:	*Uapaca kirkiana* -Small evergreen tree with large, brittle, ovate leaves and orange-yellow fruits
Mealies	:	Maize.
Mealie meal	:	Also known as sadza – a stodgy porridge, made from maize and used as a staple food throughout Southern Africa.
Mombe	:	Chishona word for cow – plural 'mombies.'
Mopani	:	*Colophospermum mopane* - tree that grows in hot, dry, low-lying areas, in the northern parts of Southern Africa.
Msasa	:	*Brachystegia spiciformi* - a medium sized African tree, having compound leaves and racemes of small green flowers. Usually found in high veld.
Murambatsvina	:	Loosely translated from the Shona, means 'driving out the filth.'
Muti	:	Medicine or tonic.
Nyama	:	Colloquial word for meat.
Povo	:	The peasants or poor people.
Protea	:	Spectacular Southern African flower, sometimes known as sugarbush.
Pungwe	:	Political indoctrination meeting, usually held at night.
Rondavel	:	Round, thatched house or chalet.
Sekuru	:	Grandfather.
Shamwari	:	Close friend.
Sindebele	:	Language of the Matabele people.
Toyi toyi	:	A ritual dance.
Tsotsi	:	Petty criminal or thug.
Vakadzi	:	Chishona for 'Ladies' as seen on public toilets.
Varume	:	Chishona for 'Gentleman' as seen on public toilets.

Veld	:	Undeveloped countryside – the bush.
Veldskoens	:	Traditionally made, loose-fitting canvas shoes.
Warungu	:	See Marungu.
Zanu PF	:	Zimbabwe African National Union (Patriotic Front) – governing party of Zimbabwe.
ZANLA	:	Zimbabwe African National Liberation Army – predominately Shona, military wing of Zanu PF.
ZAPU	:	Zimbabwe African Peoples Union.
ZIPRA	:	Zimbabwe Peoples Revolutionary Army – Matabele-based military wing of ZAPU.
ZRP	:	Zimbabwe Republic Police.

Note

If you have enjoyed this book, why not visit David Lemon's website at www.elephantlemon.com to find out more about the author, his life and his writing.

Lightning Source UK Ltd.
Milton Keynes UK
UKHW041805010319
338245UK00001BA/24/P